The Illusion *of* Net Neutrality

• •

"You will rue the day when you called in the government"
—MILTON FRIEDMAN

The Illusion of Net Neutrality

· ·

Political Alarmism,
Regulatory Creep, *and the*
Real Threat to Internet Freedom

Bob Zelnick & Eva Zelnick

HOOVER INSTITUTION PRESS
STANFORD UNIVERSITY
STANFORD, CALIFORNIA

www.hoover.org

Hoover Institution Press Publication No. 633

Hoover Institution at Leland Stanford Junior University, Stanford, California, 94305-6010

First printing, 2013
19 18 17 16 15 14 13   9 8 7 6 5 4 3 2 1

Manufactured in the United States of America

The paper used in this publication meets the minimum Requirements of the American National Standard for Information Sciences—Permanence of Paper for Printed Library Materials, ANSI/NISO Z39.48-1992. ⊗

Library of Congress Cataloging-in-Publication Data
Zelnick, Robert, 1940– author.
The illusion of net neutrality : political alarmism, regulatory creep, and the real threat to Internet freedom / Bob Zelnick and Eva Zelnick.
    pages   cm. — (Hoover Institution Press publication ; no. 633)
ISBN 978-0-8179-1594-0 (cloth : alk. paper) –
ISBN 978-0-8179-1596-4 (e-book)
1. Network neutrality—United States. 2. Internet—Government policy—United States. 3. Internet service providers—Government policy—United States. 4. United States. Federal Communications Commission. I. Eva, Zelnick, author. II. Title. III. Series: Hoover Institution Press publication ; 633.
HE7583.U6Z45 2013
384.3'3—dc23   2012045816

CONTENTS

PREFACE

THE INTERNET IS ARGUABLY the most important technological development of all time. It has grown from a small, government-funded project to an international network of networks and a mainstay in our social, political, economic, and academic lives. And we are only beginning to recognize its potential. It is perhaps not surprising, then, that there is a battle being waged for control of the Net. Under the rubric of "network neutrality," a cacophony of purportedly likeminded interest groups, individuals, scholars, and government officials have fought to bring Internet governance under the regulatory auspices of the Federal Communications Commission (FCC). As enthusiastically as we look to the future of the Internet, we are disheartened about the way that many in the field ignore the lessons of history; instead, they appear willing to turn the Net into a political grab bag on behalf of those with scant confidence in the sort of free enterprise that has gotten the Internet off to its unprecedented start. The Internet has proven it needs no government ownership or control, no special bureaucratic vigilance, and no policy that would replicate the suffocating FCC attention directed toward radio, television, phone, and cable operations. Instead the industry has thrived, and will continue to thrive, when left to the free play of market forces and subject only to antitrust enforcement—the body of law well-suited to preventing anticompetitive behavior without the stultifying oversight that brought us the Fairness Doctrine, equal-time requirements, and Rube Goldberg bureaucratic concoctions.

We hope that this book contributes to the formation of sound and enduring policies that assist the Internet in living up to its full potential. We recognize that the opposition, which includes some smart and well-motivated people, has come forward with a master plan for government control. We only wish they devoted their skills more toward helping this new technology achieve everything it appears capable of, rather than squeezing it to the point of suffocation, like a rock star whose fans love him to death.

ACKNOWLEDGMENTS

TRYING TO UNDERSTAND THE INTERNET, to appreciate its potential, and to draw the line against those who would deprive it of the competitive oxygen needed to perform at its best has been a daunting but rewarding task. I was delighted to receive the generous backing of John Raisian, director of the Hoover Institution at Stanford University. This project would not have been possible without his generous support. My gratitude also goes to Richard Sousa, Hoover's deputy director. I have worked with Richard on several previous projects and have found his judgment sound, his enthusiasm genuine, and his confidence in my work reinforcing. Richard is truly a scholar's scholar, and I look forward to our continued professional association.

It is with particular pleasure that I recognize and applaud the efforts of my eldest daughter, Eva Michal Zelnick, who chose this moment to work professionally with her dad. Eva is a *cum laude* graduate of both the University of Virginia and Boston University School of Law, who has specialized in public policy issues linked to the Internet. This book could not have been written without her participation, and I look forward to working closely with her again.

I also take this opportunity to acknowledge the strong and constant across-the-board editorial assistance provided by Kimberly Wexler. Kimberly served as our primary research assistant since we began this project, and her work was impeccable. Kimberly was a fine student of mine at Boston University, and has since matriculated to the University of Pennsylvania Law School, where she has developed an interest and expertise in communications law. I predict great things for Kimberly in the future, and only hope she will allow me to continue to work with her.

I also thank James Wellington Wiley III, likewise at the University of Pennsylvania Law School, who lent us his expertise on telecommunications and spectrum reform in the United States.

Additionally, Alexander Shoulson, at the University of Pennsylvania Law School, provided the important diagrams in Chapter 3, and assisted with technical edits for the book.

And a thank you goes to Erin Blake, a student at Georgetown Law School, for her research assistance as we began this project, and to Robert Michael Engel, a student at Suffolk University Law School, for his research and editorial help.

And none of this would have been possible, of course, without the love and support of our family: Pamela Zelnick, my wife of forty-three years, was always there when needed, which was often. My youngest daughter, Marni, who has worked with me on other projects, offered as much help as she could spare, given that she was working during this period on her first feature film. And Dara, my middle daughter, was in the process of making partner at her Boston law firm, but still had time to offer sound editorial guidance.

Eva would especially like to thank her husband of ten years, Daniel Connelly, for his love, support, and assumption of extra childcare duties during the lengthy writing process. Eva also thanks her two wonderful sons, David Isadore Connelly and Nathan Gies Connelly, for their patience and understanding as their mom spent many nights and weekends writing instead of playing superheroes and trains.

To the faculty and administration of Boston University
for their many acts of kindness and support.

Chapter One
THE NETWORK-NEUTRALITY DEBATE

ON DECEMBER 17, 2010, a Tunisian street vendor named Mohamed Bouazizi set himself on fire outside the governor's office in the rural Tunisian town of Sidi Bouzid. He was protesting the harassment and humiliation inflicted upon him by a municipal official and her aides. Within months, anti-establishment uprisings had swept through much of the Arab Middle East and North Africa. Fueled by resentment of widespread corruption among autocratic regimes, human rights violations, poverty, and unemployment, protestors took to the streets demanding change. Before this so-called "Arab Spring" had turned to summer, long-reigning governments in Tunisia and Egypt had toppled, a full-blown civil war had erupted in Libya, and demonstrations in Saudi Arabia, Yemen, Bahrain, Morocco, Jordan, and Iraq had resulted in bloodshed and varying degrees of government concessions. In Syria, massive protests triggered violent suppression by the government, which has repeatedly failed to deal with its people's grievances using democratic tactics.

While it may be years before the history books lay claim to the conclusive narrative of the "Arab Spring," one thing is already certain: the Internet played a central role for both demonstrators and regimes as a powerful weapon, and an essential political tool.[1] As one Egyptian

---

1. Commentator Anthony E. Varona claims the Internet has similarly "served as a powerful check on governments and elected representatives, both by exposing government

organizer put it, "We use Facebook to schedule the protests, Twitter to coordinate, and YouTube to tell the world."[2]

The Internet has fundamentally and irrevocably changed the way we conduct our daily lives, do business, communicate, engage in political debate, educate our children, deliver health care, manage energy, and ensure public safety. Broadband, or high-speed Internet in particular, is understood in the United States and around the world as the foundation for future economic growth, job creation, and global competitiveness. Broadband services fulfill a national economic role, best described by President Barack Obama in his State of the Union Address: "Incomplete high-speed broadband network [sic] prevents a small business owner in rural America from selling her products all over the world."[3] Equally understood is that the Internet's tremendous success is due in large part, if not entirely, to its having been allowed to flourish in the absence of government intrusion or meddling. It is a "sort of libertarian heaven," current Federal Communications Commissioner Robert McDowell (Republican) remarked in a February 21, 2012, op-ed in the *Wall Street Journal*. The absence of regulation, he insists, has made the Internet "the greatest deregulatory success story of all time." But keeping the Internet free of government regulation has been the goal of "free market" conservatives alone: a

---

abuses . . . and by providing citizens of speech-repressing regimes a vehicle for dissenting, information sharing, and organizing." He writes, "The Internet and the political blogosphere have become especially good sources for in-depth analysis and discussion of political candidates and their campaigns." By demonstrating the Internet's subversive effect on "'insider' versus 'outsider' distinctions in political campaigning," Varona seemingly advances a broader definition of political speech in which the Internet is the platform. Varona claims the Internet is a "democratic mechanism." Anthony E. Varona, "Toward a Broadband Public Interest Standard," *Administrative Law Review* (2009): 39, American University Washington College of Law.

2. Philip N. Howard, "The Arab Spring's Cascading Effects," Milton-McCune, *Pacific Standard*, February 23, 2011, http://www.miller-mccune.com/politics/the-cascading-effects-of-the-arab-spring-28575/.

3. President Barack Obama, State of the Union Address, January 25, 2010, http://www.nytimes.com/2012/01/25/us/politics/state-of-the-union-2012-transcript.html?pagewanted=all.

massive overhaul and deregulation of the entire telecommunications industry (codified in the Telecommunications Act of 1996) was the deliberately and aggressively pursued policy of the Bill Clinton administration. We will analyze the successes and failures of the construction and implementation of the act with respect to the individual telecommunications industries later in this book, but for now we stress only that deregulation was the goal.[4]

On July 20, 1999, at a speech before the Federal Communications Bar in San Francisco, then-FCC Chairman William Kennard (Democrat) first proposed what he called a "high-tech Hippocratic Oath" for Internet regulation: "First, do no harm." As he explained, "The fertile fields of innovation across the communications sector and around the country are blooming because from the get-go we have taken a deregulatory, competitive approach to our communications structure—especially the Internet." "Broadband is the future of the Internet," he proclaimed, and promised that under his watch, regulators would exercise intentional regulatory restraint since no one in the government or industry could predict how the Internet would develop.[5] Maintaining an environment in which the Internet can flourish is a bipartisan objective. Moreover, as evidenced by the Clinton administration's deregulatory overhaul of the communications industry in 1996, and the comments by Chairman Kennard and Commissioner McDowell, it is agreed that unnecessary regulations generally hinder the growth and

---

4. *See generally* Filippo Belloc, Antonio Nicita, and Pier Luigi Parcu, "Deregulating Telecommunications in Europe: Timing, Path Dependency and Institutional Complementarities," European University Institute, Working Paper 47, 2011, http://cadmus.eui.eu/bitstream/handle/1814/18359/RSCAS_2011_47.pdf. Academic research on the "liberalization" of the telecommunications sector in Europe stresses the importance of reducing distortive regulatory structures. The research demonstrates that market-driven competition is cost-effective and better suited to the task of determining the correct prices for balancing innovation and spurring a robust and consumer-friendly economy.

5. William E. Kennard, FCC Chairman, "The Unregulation of the Internet: Laying a Competitive Course for the Future," July 20, 1999, http://transition.fcc.gov/Speeches/Kennard/spwek924.html.

progress of the Internet and surrounding industries.[6] Consequently, any means by which regulators propose governing cyberspace should be scrupulously scrutinized, and heavy-handed regulations must be regarded with the utmost suspicion.

The FCC's 2002 ruling (under Republican Chairman Michael Powell) classifying cable Internet access as an "information service" under Title I of the Communications Act, rather than a "telecommunications service" subject to Title II common carrier obligations, complements Kennard's approach.[7] Title I common carrier obligations are a series of regulatory requirements imposed on plain-old telephone service (POTS) providers. By excluding the Internet (and cable) from telecommunications requirements, Congress apparently determined that the regulatory regimes would be a hindrance to the growth and progress of these new, less entrenched technologies.

The impact was undeniable. Internet access exploded through the 1990s and into the 2000s. By 2000 more than 44 million, or 42 percent, of Americans could connect to the Internet from their homes. This was up from 26 percent in 1998, and more than double the 18 percent of households with Internet in 1997, the first year the U.S. Census Bureau began collecting data on Internet use.[8] By 2004 nearly three out of four houses with a phone line had Internet connectivity, translating into roughly 75 percent of the population or 204.3 million people.[9] By 2011 that number was up to almost 350 million.

---

6. The universal truth that overregulation of an industry necessarily predicts its demise is certainly not one limited to the Internet. Recall, for example, the perilous condition of an overregulated trucking industry in the 1970s. That industry was brought back to life, not simply with the eradication of the regulatory scheme that governed it, but with the dismantling of the regulatory agency—the Interstate Commerce Commission—responsible for its demise.

7. See *infra* Chapter 4; *see also* Federal Communications Commission, "FCC Classifies Cable Modem Service as 'Information Service,'" Press Release, March 14, 2002, http://transition.fcc.gov/Bureaus/Cable/News_Releases/2002/nrcb0201.html.

8. U.S. Department of Commerce, Census Report P23-207, "Home Computers and Internet Use in the United States," 2001, http://www.census.gov/hhes/computer/publications/.

9. Nielson, Nielson/Net Ratings, 2004, www.nielsen-online.com/pr/pr_040318.pdf.

Broadband access also spread like wildfire, up from 3 percent of U.S. homes in 2000 to 66 percent in 2010.[10]

Yet, network-neutrality proponents have heightened calls for federal regulation in the name of Internet "freedom," and the Obama administration has capitulated. In fact, it seems determined to do what every single administration for the last sixteen years has resisted: submit the Internet to federal control. Under the leadership of the president's old friend Julius Genachowski, in December 2010 the FCC circumvented Congress, blatantly disregarded a recent court ruling, ignored public sentiment and the vehement dissent of two of its five commissioners, and passed rules that purport to give the government authority to sink its talons deep into the inner workings of the Net. Genachowski's "Open Internet Order" turns on its head the phenomenally successful "bottom-up" approach to the Internet, in favor of "top-down" regulation that threatens to politicize Internet governance, stifle innovation, and discourage investment.[11] At the same time, by signaling to the rest of the world that the United States is abandoning its policy of leaving the Internet free from government meddling, it invites other countries to do the same, setting the stage for a global regulatory pandemic. Already, a fierce international debate is being waged over a flourish of new regulatory proposals backed by Russia, China, Brazil, and India, which would give the United Nations unprecedented regulatory power over the Net. If successful, the proposals would upend the terms of a 1988 International Telecommunications Regulations (ITRs) treaty in which delegates from 114 countries agreed to a "multi-stakeholder" bottom-up governance model that helped to facilitate the international growth of the Net and insulated it from top-down economic and technological regulation.[12] Under the new proposals, the United Nations

---

10. Federal Communications Commission, "Connecting America: The National Broadband Plan," 2010, 20, http://download.broadband.gov/plan/national-broadband -plan.pdf.

11. See generally Howard A. Shelanski, "Adjusting Regulation to Competition: Toward a New Model for U.S. Telecommunications Policy," Yale Journal on Regulation 24 (2007): 55.

12. See "Dubai Conference Could Change How Internet Operates," CSPAN 2012, http:// www.c-span.org/Events/Dubai-Conference-Could-Change-How-Internet-Operates

would have wide regulatory latitude over cybersecurity, data privacy, technical standards, and the Internet Protocol (IP) addressing system.[13] The future looks bleak: gone will be the days where the Internet ecosystem evolved at a mind-shattering pace, fueled by billions of dollars of private investment and American innovation and bridled only by the pace of technological development and business-model creativity. Now, the government will determine both the players and the rules of the game. Innovation will wilt and die in a wasteland of bureaucratic red tape and political deal-making along the cracked banks of an empty riverbed through which a white water of investment once gushed.

How could this happen? The story has all the elements of a page-turner: a confluence of political agendas, ideologies, and even personal vendettas have brought society to crossroads between abandoning unwieldy regulations or submitting to yet another regime that has the potential to fundamentally alter the future of the Internet.

The December 2011 action by the FCC is the latest move in a long campaign, masterly crafted to mandate "network neutrality" on the Internet. In large part, the radical left-wing "media-reform" group known as Free Press, and the more temperate group Public Knowledge, spearheaded the campaign. Founded in 2002 by Josh Silver, John Nichols, and Robert McChesney, Free Press's anti-corporate vision of government-controlled media is not surprising considering its founders' pedigrees. Silver previously ran a successful ballot initiative in Arizona to implement publicly funded elections. Nichols is the Washington correspondent of *The Nation*. McChesney, a leftist media theorist and University of Illinois communications professor, is also the former editor of the *Marxist Monthly Review*.[14] Lest there be any confusion regarding his personal ideology, McChesney once told John Fund of the *Wall Street Journal* that he is a socialist and "hesitant to

---

/10737431086/; *see also* Robert M. McDowell, "The U.N. Threat to Internet Freedom," *Wall Street Journal*, February 21, 2012, http://online.wsj.com/article/SB1000142405297 020479240457722907402319322.html.

13. *See* United Nations, World Conference on International Telecommunications, forthcoming (December 2012), http://www.itu.int/en/wcit-12/Pages/default.aspx.

14. John Fund, "The Network Neutrality Coup," *Wall Street Journal*, December 21, 2010.

say I'm not a Marxist." When asked, in 2009, to explain his network-neutrality agenda to the website SocialistProject.ca, he explained, "At the moment, the battle over network neutrality is not to completely eliminate the telephone and cable companies. But the ultimate goal is to get rid of the media capitalists in the phone and cable companies and to divest them from control."[15]

Throughout the course of their network-neutrality campaign, the groups have controlled both the trenches and the war room, drawing their intellectual might from the leftist prose of ivory-tower heavy-weights like Harvard University's Lawrence Lessig, and Jonathan Zittrain, Columbia University's Tim Wu, Seton Hall's Frank Pasquale, and Stanford's Barbara van Schewick. They have dealt a one-two punch by leading the battle for the hearts and minds of anyone who will listen under the seemingly innocuous and sympathetic banners of "open Internet," "neutrality," and "Internet freedom," while simultaneously targeting and capturing the most bumbling, inept, if not corruptible of all the federal agencies: the FCC. The apparent leftist strategy: cede control over the Internet to the FCC, then seize control of the FCC.

They have also, and unsurprisingly, garnered industry support from the Democratic-leaning Internet content and application developers in Silicon Valley. These so-called "edge" companies like Google, Netflix, Yahoo, and Amazon share distinct but related reasons for helping to steer the network-neutrality bandwagon. First, as already suggested, while most of the edge companies claim to be politically neutral, many of their top executives are outward and ardent supporters of the Democrats, and particularly Barack Obama. Google CEO Eric Schmidt, for example, spent a week stumping for then-candidate Obama in the run-up to the 2008 elections, and served as an adviser on technology issues to Obama's campaign.

But the network-neutrality debate should not be dismissed as a merely partisan one. It is not. Its roots are not political; they are both

---

15. Tanner Meerless, "Media Capitalism, the State, and 21st Century Media Democracy Struggles," *The Bullet*, August 9, 2009, http://www.socialistproject.ca/bullet/246.php; *see also* John Fund, *supra* note 14.

ideological and economically based. And the companies involved—those at the "edge" of the networks and those at its "core" see themselves as having diametrically opposed interests. As one congressional committee insider put it, "That tension [between the edge and the core] is always going to exist. The edge guys are always going to try to commoditize the networks, and the networks are going to try to maintain their high revenues." While edge companies' support for network neutrality has been steadfast, its raison d'être has evolved somewhat. In the beginning, the great concern among edge companies was that the network providers, who not only own the physical networks but control the so-called "last mile" where individual users connect to the networks, would become a bottleneck to their own access to the Net. In those days Google, eBay, and Amazon were just small start-up companies—each, the proverbial "guy in a garage" who comes up with a really great idea for an Internet company, but whose access to its lifeline would be at the mercy of corporate fat cats controlling the networks. Imposing regulations on these network providers would level the playing field and potentially eliminate the so-called "first-mover advantage" enjoyed by Internet service providers (ISPs) like Comcast and Verizon and digital subscriber line (DSL) providers. But yesterday's Internet start-ups are today's Internet behemoths, with millions of customers in this country alone, a nationwide system of servers, and built-in infrastructure to support their businesses. The wealth and dominance of the mega-edge corporations like Google and Amazon are as much potential barriers to market entry for the little guy as the corporations at the Internet's core. In fact, Google is experimenting with becoming a broadband provider itself.[16]

Now, these same companies clearly have a great interest in leveraging the status quo for as long as possible. After all, it is hard to stay on

---

16. *See* Milo Medin, "Ultra High-speed Broadband Is Coming to Kansas City, Kansas," Google Blog, March 30, 2011, http://googleblog.blogspot.com/2011/03/ultra-high-speed -broadband-is-coming-to.html; *see also* Minnie Ingersoll and James Kelley, "Think Big with Our Gig: Our Experimental Fiber Network," Google Blog, February 10, 2012, http://googleblog.blogspot.com/2010/02/think-big-with-gig-our-experimental.html.

top in an industry evolving as rapidly as the Internet. Remember when AOL and Netscape ruled cyberspace? While a law mandating network neutrality cannot completely stop this evolution, it necessarily picks winners and losers, and here the edge companies come out on top.

So what exactly is network neutrality? Pinning down a precise definition has been almost as elusive as the logical foundations for the arguments that purportedly support its existence. While some definitions seem in concert when discussed in general terms, proponents advocate a widely varying range of applications of the principles. We will briefly explore the breadth of these definitions and the various mechanisms individual proponents advance for achieving his or her ideal later, and note that the concept of a neutral network dates back to "common carrier" regulation of the phone networks. But ultimately we will rely on definitions forwarded by two of the movement's foremost thinkers: Tim Wu and Lawrence Lessig.

Columbia law professor Tim Wu is generally credited with coining the term "network neutrality" with respect to the Internet in a 2003 paper. As he put it, "Network neutrality is best defined as a network design principle. The idea is that a maximally useful public information network aspires to treat all content, sites, and platforms equally."[17] In Lawrence Lessig's words, "Net neutrality means simply that all like Internet content must be treated alike and move at the same speed over the network."[18]

As we will explain in Chapter 2, all data that travels over the Internet is broken into manageable chunks or "packets." At its most fundamental level, network neutrality is the belief that all of these packets traversing the Internet should be treated equally. Technically this means that routers—which are the traffic-management devices that send packets of information from one computer or server to the

---

17. Tim Wu, "Network Neutrality FAQ," TimWu.org, http://timwu.org/network_neu trality.html.

18. *See, for example,* Lawrence Lessig and Robert W. McChesney, "No Tolls on the Internet," *Washington Post,* June 8, 2006, http://www.washingtonpost.com/wp-dyn /content/article/2006/06/07/AR2006060702108.html.

next—should treat each data packet the same irrespective of what kind of data the packet is carrying. So e-mail would be treated the same as video, and music would be treated the same as an instant message.[19]

The idea is largely based on the principles of "end-to-end" and "first-in-first-out" data transmission at the heart of the Internet protocol (which will also be explained in Chapter 2), and to a certain extent is historically the way most data travels over the Net.[20] Still, network-neutrality proponents argue that new technologies give network providers, particularly last-mile providers (like Comcast, Verizon, and RCN) at the so called "on ramps" of the Internet, the ability to discriminate between different pieces of information traveling over their networks. They maintain that without government regulation to preserve nondiscrimination, providers will use their ability to block or prioritize network traffic to exert coercive power over consumers and content and application providers.[21]

---

19. To the extent possible, packets can vary wildly in size. For example, packets for file transfers are much larger than those for chat programs. So, irrespective of content, some packets place more of a demand on the network than others. And the FCC's Open Internet Order does allow for networks to exercise "reasonable network management practices"; however, the term is not defined and we will argue that network management alone will not maximize the utility of the networks, especially as the ecosystem continues to grow.

20. Note that this is true for Transmission Control Protocol (TCP), but User Datagram Protocol (UDP) is a bit different. TCP "guarantees" that once a stream is established, packets sent through will arrive successfully on the other end, in the correct order. This is accomplished through a "SYNACK," composed of a "SYN,"which is a sign from the source that content is forthcoming, and an "ACK," which is an acknowledgement from the receiver that it is ready to receive. This SYNACK is an initial handshake that readies two nodes for communication. After the SYNACK, TCP sends packets at an accelerating rate until the message is complete or a packet is dropped. In the latter case, TCP resends the dropped packet, and cuts its throughput rate before beginning to accelerate again. This principle of additive increase and multiplicative decrease is the efficiency maximizing Internet protocol for data that must be received with complete integrity. UDP just sends packets out without any stopgap in the case of a dropped packet. UDP is faster and largely used for games, video, and voice, where consistent throughput speed is more important than accuracy.

21. The concern is often explained as follows. Network access providers would "block or degrade" network traffic. The term "degrade" implies that some data would receive lower

Specifically, network-neutrality proponents list six major concerns: 1) network operators will block, degrade, or prioritize content and applications on their networks; 2) vertical integration by ISPs and other network operators into content and applications will result in limited consumer choice; 3) discrimination or pricing arrangements between network providers and certain content and applications will have the effect of stifling innovation on the "edges" of the network (that is, by content and application providers); 4) consumers who are unhappy with their broadband provider will be forced to stay with it because of lack of competition in "last mile" broadband Internet access markets; 5) legal and regulatory uncertainty in the area of Internet access will stifle innovation; and 6) there will be a diminution of political and other expression on the Internet.

On its surface, network neutrality sounds reasonable and even desirable. After all, why should mega-corporations like Comcast, RCN, and Verizon be allowed to block or degrade one's access to content on the Net? Who wants deals between greedy network operators and pet application or service providers to dictate whether or not one can access CNN's website or Netflix, for example? Even the terms used interchangeably to define the position—"network neutrality," "open Internet," "Internet freedom"—make taking the other side unappealing: if you oppose network *neutrality*, do you advocate network *discrimination*? And who wants to be on the side that opposes Internet *freedom*? Plus, hating your cable provider (usually also your broadband provider) is as American as apple pie. However, while the slogans are seductive, if one takes the time to fully understand how the Internet works, from its architecture to the way data travels over its vast networks, to the business relationships that characterize it, it becomes apparent that network neutrality is the nuclear option. Sure, it will take out the big network operators, but it will wipe out the entire ecosystem, too.

---

priority than other data. Thus, the same data arrives at its destination, but some people's data will get there faster than others'. (A person who downloaded a competitor's media content or did not pay extra for premium packet forwarding would not enjoy rapid data transmission—or so the argument goes.)

While the building blocks for today's Internet were put in place almost half a century ago, it was not until the government turned the Internet over to the private sector in the 1990s that it became the dynamic engine for communication and economic growth, medium for collaboration, and mechanism for worldwide broadcasting capability that it is today.[22] Private investors have poured billions of dollars into the industry. Verizon alone invested an estimated $50 billion between 2009 and 2011 to build and improve its network infrastructure.[23] Such "facility investments" provide fuel for the engines of innovation at the network's edge and vice versa. After all, if the network cannot handle a particular type of application, because of data-traffic congestion, innovation in that area will grind to a halt. The reverse is also true: it is the Facebooks, eBays, Pandoras, and Hulus that keep people coming back to the Internet, and it is the Googles and Yahoos that make navigating the network efficient and enjoyable. Without the innovators on the edge, network providers really just have . . . well, bridges to nowhere.

This is a perfect example of why network neutrality is as short-sighted as it is stifling to the future of the Net. Continued innovation on both sides of the network (the core and the edge) propels the industry. Handicapping one side will inevitably cripple the entire ecosystem. Take network congestion, for example. Network-neutrality proponents argue that network providers' ability to use certain network-management practices, block certain applications at times, or offer tiered services should be heavily regulated or banned altogether. However, this position is erroneous. First, it ignores one major fact that is true about the Internet, just as it is true about any network: congestion is and will always be a problem, and, as with any other network, it is not a problem that can be managed by perpetually increasing capac-

---

22. *See* Barry M. Leiner et al., "Brief History of the Internet," Internet Society, http://www.internetsociety.org/internet/internet-51/history-internet/brief-history-internet/.

23. "Corporate History," Verizon, 2012, http://www22.verizon.com/investor/corporate history.htm.

ity. Whether you are talking about railway networks, electrical networks, traditional telephone networks, or the network of roads that runs through your hometown, engineers somewhere are aware of the usage patterns and are constantly attempting to maximize load and capacity in the most efficient and cost-effective way possible. Thus, in the most obvious case of a road network at rush hour, stoplight timings may change, two-way streets become one way (or vice versa), special lanes may be reserved for car-poolers, and so on. Similarly, Internet network operators must be able to manage their networks. And network operators have the ability to further maximize efficiency by, for example, making sure the packets carrying data for an emergency surgery always have a clear lane.

Even the Net's founding fathers recognized that congestion would increasingly become a barrier to optimal network performance and thus experimented with different traffic management techniques. In fact, "network neutrality" is a misnomer. The Net is not, and never was, neutral. Instead, routers at the heart of the Net's infrastructure "route" or make decisions about how data is transmitted. These decisions inevitably have implications that are not strictly uniform or neutral. As Christopher Yoo, one of the most prolific intellectuals of the non-neutral persuasion, writes, "Indeed, it would be surprising if any two similar packets would be treated exactly alike when traveling through a network consisting of more than thirty thousand autonomous systems that each determine their terms of interconnection through arms-length negotiations."[24] Active network management that includes data prioritization and quality-of-service assurances are needed to prevent a high-tech "tragedy of the commons" in which massive parts of the network could slow to a crawl or crash all together.

Besides keeping the networks running smoothly, network-management tools are necessary to support the cutting-edge content

---

24. Christopher Yoo, "The Evolution of Internet Architecture: Innovations in the Internet's Architecture That Challenge the Status Quo," *Journal on Telecommunications and High Technology Law* 8 (2010): 79.

and applications that ultimately benefit consumers. Examples include VoIP (Voice Over Internet Protocol), video downloads, streaming videos for movies and telemedicine, interactive network video games, and certain customized business applications. Forbidding network providers from managing their networks will inhibit the development of the kinds of exciting new technologies that we have come to expect, since an application is only as fast or robust as the network that supports it. While proponents site pro-consumer concerns in advocating their network-neutrality regime, it is consumers who will ultimately pay the highest price.

Put another way, network providers should be allowed to experiment—unfettered by regulatory constraints—with different business models and network-management practices, unless there is clear evidence that their practices are harming consumers or market competition. Such "network diversity" is particularly crucial in evolving markets like broadband, where network providers must be allowed to experiment with various business plans to best serve consumer needs and perpetuate incentives in network investment. It follows that prohibiting practices like tiered access or price differentiation could potentially preclude price reductions for consumers and lead to inefficient and unintended consequences.

And vertical integration (when a company expands its business into different points along the production path)—a phrase spit so violently from the lips of network-neutrality preachers you would think it the incarnation of Lucifer himself—will likely benefit consumers by offering cheaper and more dynamic service options, instead of the converse. And edge companies themselves are already experimenting with vertical integration. For example, Google is trying out Google+. While its effectiveness remains to be seen, it seems unfair to shrug off vertical integration by certain players while targeting others for doing the same. Moreover, while we argue that network access providers should be allowed to prioritize data, we will also argue that they have little incentive to perform content-based discrimination.

Finally, the best way to guarantee the rapid demise of American industry's position in the global Internet economy is to allow the Federal Communications Commission to assert itself at its center. The FCC has consistently hindered the evolution of the telecom industry, stifled competition, and cost consumers billions of dollars in the process: its sixty years of unabashed support for W. Bell's "natural monopoly" of the nation's telephone network; its complicated and arbitrary licensing procedures; its heavy-handed regulation of cable despite the absence of "scarcity" that supposedly justified its omnipresence in the broadcast arena; its mandating exclusive local franchises for cable providers; its twenty-plus-year delay in licensing the first cell service; among other examples.[25] Initially established under the Communications Act of 1934, the FCC was charged with regulating all non-federal use of the radio spectrum (both radio and television broadcast), all international communications that originate or terminate in the United States, and all interstate telecommunications including wire, satellite, and cable. The FCC's mission is to "make available so far as possible, to all the people of the United States, without discrimination on the basis of race, color, religion, national origin, or sex, rapid, efficient, nationwide and worldwide wire and radio communication services with adequate facilities at reasonable charges."[26] Along the way, however, it has anointed itself federal censor, leveling heavy fines on those who violate its rules.[27] It has also become an arbiter of ill-conceived affirmative-action mandates, and demonstrated a shocking inability to anticipate and encourage new innovations in the very industry it is charged to oversee and nurture.[28]

And the FCC keeps growing. Indeed, when Congress passed the Telecommunications Act of 1996—arguably the most important

---

25. *See generally* Peter W. Huber, *Law and Disorder in Cyberspace, Abolish the FCC and Let Common Law Rule the Telecom* (New York: Oxford University Press, 1997).

26. 47 U.S.C. § 151, 2012.

27. *See* Frank Ahrens, "FCC Indecency Fines, 1970–2004," *Washington Post*, 2005, http://www.washingtonpost.com/wp-srv/business/graphics/web-fcc970.html.

28. One commentator estimated that the FCC slowed competition in television service by decades by labeling cable a "supplemental service," thereby preventing cable operators from competing with broadcast providers. The same commentator notes that this was the FCC's first use of ancillary jurisdiction, which the agency now argues also extends its authority to broadband.

deregulatory piece of legislation in the twentieth century—to open markets and fuel competition in the industry, the FCC did not shrink from the spotlight. Indeed, competition increased, spectrum scarcity became less of an issue, and the FCC became well known for its repetitive blunders. For example, in a 2005 piece, CNET correspondent Declan McCullagh summarizes several examples of FCC bureaucratic malfeasance as follows:

> The FCC rejected long-distance telephone service competition in 1968, banned Americans from buying their own non-Bell telephones in 1956, dragged its feet in the 1970s when considering whether video telephones would be allowed and did not grant modern cellular telephone licenses until 1981—about four decades after Bell Labs invented the technology. Along the way, the FCC has preserved monopolistic practices that would have otherwise been illegal under antitrust law.[29]

Even more recently, there was the agency's unwavering five-year push for its broadcast flag requirements, which it eventually abandoned in 2011.[30] And in a case stemming from heavy fines levied on Fox and ABC for expletives and nudity in their broadcasts, the Supreme Court unanimously upheld a lower court's ruling that voided the FCC's indecency regulations as "unconstitutionally vague."[31] In doing so, the Court cast doubt on whether the FCC would be able to collect a $550,000 levy on CBS Corporation for the split-second exposure of Janet Jackson's nipple during a half-time performance at the Super Bowl in 2004.[32] If history is any lesson, given the chance, the FCC will

---

29. Declan McCullagh, "Why the FCC Should Die," CNET News, June 7, 2004, http://news.cnet.com/Why-the-FCC-should-die/2010-1028_3-5226979.html?tag=mncol;txt.

30. Brooks Boliek, "FCC Finally Kills Off Fairness Document," Politico.com, November 22, 2011, http://www.politico.com/news/stories/0811/61851.html.

31. Fox v. FCC, 129 S. Ct. 1800 (2012).

32. Greg Stohr and Todd Shields, "FCC TV Indecency Crackdown Limited by U.S. Supreme Court," Bloomberg, June 21, 2012, http://www.bloomberg.com/news/2012-06-21/fcc-s-tv-indecency-policy-limited-by-u-s-supreme-court.html.

saddle the Internet with the same regulatory baggage that has hobbled telephone, broadcast, and cable for years.

Indeed, in this new digital millennium, with the Internet at the center of a host of rapidly developing technologies, there is no place for the clumsy, bumbling, ballooning bureaucracy that is the FCC. And there is no more stark example of the danger of this audacious "unbridled, roving Commission" than its hijacking of the network-neutrality debate by which it has inserted itself into the center of an industry in which it has no jurisdiction, with no congressional mandate. In fact, more than three hundred members of Congress have warned the agency that it is exceeding its legal authority with regard to Internet regulation, and two other government agencies (the Federal Trade Commission and Justice Department) have each issued extensive reports concluding that there is no evidence of concentrations of abuse or abuses of market power in the broadband market that could possibly justify FCC interference.

Moreover, the Federal Trade Commission (FTC), the premiere federal antitrust authority, concluded not only that the broadband market is competitive, but that it was moving in the direction of increased competition, and that there was no evidence of "any significant market failure or demonstrated consumer harm from conduct by broadband providers." The FTC warned that "policy makers should be wary of enacting regulation solely to prevent prospective harm to consumer welfare, particularly given the indeterminate effects that potential conduct by broadband providers may have on such welfare."[33] The Antitrust Division of the Department of Justice reached a similar conclusion in comments filed with the FCC in early 2010, and warned against the temptation to regulate "to avoid stifling the infrastructure investments needed to expand broadband access."[34] As both organizations pointed

---

33. Federal Trade Commission, Internet Access Task Force, "Broadband Connectivity Competition Policy," June 27, 2007, 11, http://www.ftc.gov/reports/broadband /v070000report.pdf.

34. *See* "Economic Issues in Broadband Competition: A National Broadband Plan for Our Future," GN Docket No. 09-51, 2010, 28 (*ex-parte* submission of the U.S. Department of Justice).

out, there already exists a comprehensive body of law that is well positioned to deal with potential competitive and consumer-protection issues that may arise within the broadband sphere: antitrust. The FTC noted, "The competitive issues raised in this debate . . . are not new to antitrust law, which is well-equipped to analyze potential conduct and business arrangements involving broadband Internet access. In conducting an antitrust analysis, the ultimate issue would be whether broadband Internet access providers engage in unilateral or joint conduct that is likely to harm competition and consumers in a relevant market."[35]

In short, there is no problem that needs fixing, and if one materializes, additional regulation would be redundant and unnecessary. So why is the FCC obsessively pursuing the most radical regulatory overhaul of an industry since it declared the phone system a public utility? The answer in large part is because it cannot help itself.

---

35. *See supra* note 33, at 120.

Chapter Two
AN "UNBRIDLED AND ROVING COMMISSION"

THE FCC HAS BUMBLED its oversight of some of the most important industries it has sought to oversee, hindering their growth with short-sighted, over-reaching, and confusing policies of political appeasement. The agency's egregious mistakes in the realms of telephone, cable, and broadcast should leave us not just wary, but terrified of its interference on the Net. It is an agency failing on all cylinders, whose mistakes can be blamed on a trifecta of unfortunate, but not unpredictable—and definitely self-perpetuating—factors: lack of a clear congressional mandate, hunger for power, and political susceptibility.

Telephone

As previously noted, the FCC not only *stifled*, but effectively *banned* competition in telephony for years as it nurtured an AT&T monopoly wholly abhorrent to antitrust law. In furtherance of coddling the AT&T monopoly, the FCC created silos out of the various telecommunications mediums, failing to recognize the negative side effects of separating technologies. As a result, consumers were not only left without options, but were forced to wait decades for products such as answering machines, cell phones, and other complements or alternatives to traditional landline services. Moreover, the FCC's blunders with regard to telephony are not confined to the creation of AT&T's

monopoly. In telephony, the FCC enacted a universal service regime that was more corrupt than costly. Similarly, the FCC's broadcast and cable regulations were wrought with flaws, inconsistencies, and waste. In this chapter we will recount some of the agency's biggest and most costly flubs in these three sectors to support our argument that the Internet should not be left in the hands of the FCC. There is simply too much at stake to give history a chance to repeat itself.

Bell Telephone Company (later AT&T) was formed in Boston, Massachusetts, on July 9, 1877, by Alexander Graham Bell, his father-in-law, Gardiner Greene Hubbard, and businessman and investor Thomas Sanders.[1] The cornerstone of the Bell Telephone Company was Bell's master telephone patent.[2] The company's meteoric rise from fledgling to powerhouse was due in large part to the international fame Alexander Graham Bell's telephone display garnered at the Centennial Exhibition in Philadelphia in 1876. Bell won two gold medals at the exhibition, one for electrical equipment (the precursor to the telephone) and one for visible speech, a writing system (also known as the psychological alphabet) developed by his famous father Alexander Melville Bell, for use by deaf people to learn spoken language.[3] In addition to garnering a great deal of attention, the display earned Bell a reputation for forward thinking in communications technology.

In 1878, the first telephone exchange began operating in New Haven, Connecticut, under a license from Bell Telephone. By 1881 there were telephone exchanges in most major cities and towns in the United States. The following year, Bell acquired a controlling interest in Western Electric Company, which became its manufacturing unit,

---

1. "A Brief History: Origins," AT&T, 2012, http://www.corp.att.com/history/history1.html. Hubbard also helped organize a sister company called the New England Telephone and Telegraph Company.

2. Russell A. Pizer, *The Tangled Web of Patent # 174465* (Bloomington, IN: AuthorHouse, 2009).

3. Alexander Melville Bell, *Visible Speech: The Science of Universal Alphabetics* (London: Simpkin, Marshall & Co., 1867); *see also* "Visible Speech," Omniglot, http://www.omniglot.com/writing/visiblespeech.htm.

and gradually came to own most of its licenses. The collective enterprise became known as the Bell System.[4]

Even before the passage of the Communications Act of 1934, the Supreme Court viewed the telecommunications business as something resembling a public commodity. For example, in Western Union Tel. Co. v. Call Publishing Co., the Court held that telegraph companies had a common-law duty to provide service for all customers in a nondiscriminatory manner as a common carrier. The Court found:

> Common carriers, whether engaged in interstate commerce or in that wholly within the State, are performing a public service. They are endowed by the State with some of its sovereign powers, such as the right of eminent domain, and so endowed by reason of the public service they render. As a consequence of this, all individuals have equal rights both in respect to service and charges. Of course, such equality of right does not prevent differences in the modes and kinds of service and different charges based thereon. There is no cast iron line of uniformity which prevents a charge from being above or below a particular sum, or requires that the service shall be exactly along the same lines. But that principle of equality does forbid any difference in charge which is not based upon difference in service, and even when based upon difference of service, must have some reasonable relation to the amount of difference, and cannot be so great as to produce an unjust discrimination.[5]

Despite the Supreme Court's encouragement to adhere to a "principle of equality" with regards to telecommunications services, fledgling telephone companies were not initially bound by requirements to provide service.[6] There were many local-service telephone providers nationwide, but they did not interconnect.[7] Consequently, telephone users could only call people within their local loop. To call someone outside of the local loop, or long distance, a user needed two different

---

4. *See* "History," *supra* note 1 in this chapter.

5. Western Union Tel. Co. v. Call Publishing Co., 181 U.S. 92, 99–100 (1901).

6. Roger Noll, "The Economics and Politics of the Slowdown in Regulatory Reform," Brookings Discussion Papers in Domestic Economics, Brookings Institution, 1996.

7. Ibid.

telephone connections.[8] The lack of interoperability was unwieldy, particularly for long-distance callers, but the benefit was that it fueled cutthroat competition between rival companies that spurred them to build out infrastructure. Robust competition in the local loop was beneficial to consumers because it helped reduce prices.[9]

In an attempt to resolve the disputes between Bell and the smaller companies, thirty-four states began applying common carrier principles to the telephone industry, which bound telephone companies by interconnection obligations.[10] While Bell was the largest telephone company at the time, competition between different carriers was increasing dramatically. In the first few years of the twentieth century, more than three thousand competitors existed.[11] By 1907 non-Bell firms served 51 percent of the telephone businesses in local markets.[12] That same year, however, marked the beginning of Bell's new business strategy. Competition in the telephone industry would never be the same.[13]

"Alexander Graham Bell invented the telephone and Theodore Vail invented the telephone business."

Theodore Newton Vail was born on July 16, 1845, in Carroll County, Ohio. As a boy he was known as an avid reader and dreamer. Yet, his father, who had low expectations of young Vail, predicted he would need support through adulthood.[14] As a young man, Vail seemed destined to fulfill his father's prophecy, bouncing around from career to career. First he studied medicine, then telegraphy, and later went West with his father to farm. In 1868, merely two years after traveling West,

---

8. Ibid.

9. Ibid.

10. Michael Kende, "The Digital Handshake: Connecting Internet Backbones," Federal Communications Commission, Office of Plans and Policy Working Paper No. 32, September 2000, 10, http://transition.fcc.gov/Bureaus/OPP/working_papers/oppwp32.pdf.

11. Adam D. Thierer, "Unnatural Monopoly: Critical Moments in the Development of the Bell System Monopoly," *Cato Journal* 14 (1994): 2, http://www.cato.org/pubs/journal/cjv14n2-6.html.

12. Ibid.

13. Ibid.

14. Albert Bigelow Paine, *In One Man's Life* (New York: Harpers & Brothers, 1923).

Vail went to work for the Union Pacific Railroad. It soon became clear he had an incredible mind for business.

At Union Pacific, Vail started as an operator, but was quickly promoted to an agent. By 1869, he was appointed clerk of the railway mail service between Omaha and Ogden. His success getting the mail through the snow blockage of 1870 quickly won the attention and accolades of his bosses.[15] It was not long before he was promoted to the Chicago and Iowa City post office, which was one of the most important distribution points at the time. When the railway post office was established on the Union Pacific, he was promoted once again to head clerk. By 1876 he was the general superintendent of the Railway Mail Service, the highest grade in his branch of the federal government. Vail is credited with developing the mail-delivery system still used today by the U.S. Postal Service, a system that enabled mail to be delivered two weeks earlier than previously possible. He also helped to establish postal employees as civil servants.[16] Yet, at the pinnacle of his career with Union Pacific, he was lured away by Hubbard and appointed general manager of the then-fledgling Bell company.

Hubbard had opposed the Post Office Department before Congress on several issues, but took an interest in Vail and quickly learned that his faith in him was properly placed. Vail vehemently believed in the future of the telephone. He helped establish the Western Electric Company, a division of Bell that built telephone equipment and successfully defended Bell patents.[17] He also introduced the use of copper wire in telephone and telegraph lines and oversaw the establishment of the first long-distance network from Boston to Providence, Rhode Island.[18] By 1889, Vail felt he had done all he could for telephony and retired to spend time in Argentina making a fortune in mining,

15. Norris Taylor, "Vail, Alfred—Collaborator with Samuel Morse in Inventing Telegraph—1840's," *Tripod*, 1998, http://ntgen.tripod.com/bw/vail_ntbl.html.

16. "Heroes: Theodore N. Vail," Telecommunications Virtual Museum, http://www.telcomhistory.org/vm/heroesVail.shtml.

17. Tim Wu, *The Master Switch: The Rise and Fall of Information Empires* (New York: Knopf, 2010).

18. "Theodore N. Vail," PBS, http://www.pbs.org/transistor/album1/addlbios/vail.html.

railroads, and waterpower plants.[19] Vail did not anticipate that more than twenty years later he would return to Bell.[20] But in 1907 he did just that.

"One Policy, One System, Universal Service."

By the time Vail returned to the company, it was called the American Telegraph and Telephone Company (AT&T) and his prerogative was to eliminate AT&T's competition in the industry. He believed in the superiority of a monolithic telephone system and created a new AT&T slogan to reflect his belief: "One Policy, One System, Universal Service." Vail argued, "Effective, aggressive competition, and regulation and control are inconsistent with each other, and cannot be had at the same time."[21] Vail had in mind a single network that was unhindered by competition, lack of interoperability, or regulatory intrusions. In other words, Vail wanted for telephony what so many ambitious businessmen dream about: an unregulated monopoly.

Vail aggressively pursued his vision. Under Vail's command, AT&T began buying up numerous competitors, along with telegraph giant Western Union. AT&T throttled competition by refusing to interconnect its long-distance network—the most technologically advanced and extensive in the country—with local independent carriers. By buying local networks and refusing to interconnect with remaining companies, AT&T gained a stronghold on the market.[22] By 1910, AT&T served 81 percent of the market.[23]

Though that same year, the Mann-Elkins Act extended the Interstate Commerce Commission's (ICC) federal jurisdiction to include telephone companies, it was the Justice Department that threatened to

---

19. *See* Vail, *supra* note 16 in this chapter.
20. *See* Wu, *supra* note 17.
21. *See* Thierer, *supra* note 11, 4–5.
22. *See* Noll, *supra* note 6.
23. "Milestones in AT&T History," AT&T, http://www.corp.att.com/history/mile stones.html.

take action against AT&T's monopolistic practices.[24] With the threat of an antitrust suit looming, AT&T entered into agreement known as the Kingsbury Commitment. Under the commitment, essentially a letter from AT&T Vice President Nathan Kingsbury to the attorney general, AT&T agreed to sell $30 million in Western Union stock and to not acquire other independent companies, and allow its competitors to interconnect with its network. In return, the government would agree not to pursue its case against the company as a monopolist.[25]

While the commitment was thought to be pro-competitive, it actually gave AT&T greater control over the industry and established the company as a government-sanctioned monopoly. Furthermore, although AT&T *did* agree to connect its own long-distance service to independent local carriers, it did *not* agree to interconnect its local services with other local providers. The company also did not agree to interconnect with independent long-distance carriers. Consequently, independent telephone companies had little incentive to establish rival long-distance services, and AT&T was able to consolidate control over the most profitable urban markets and long-distance traffic.[26] Thus the Kingsbury Commitment essentially formalized Vail's "one system, one policy, universal service" ideal as federal policy. Commentator Thierer agrees: "This was hardly an altruistic action on AT&T's part. . . . The agreement was not interpreted by regulators so as to restrict AT&T from acquiring any new telephone systems, but only to require that an equal number be sold to an independent buyer for each system AT&T purchased. Hence, the Kingsbury Commitment contained a built-in incentive for monopoly-swapping rather than continued competition."[27]

---

24. *See generally* Kende, *supra* note 10, at 10; Mann-Elkins Act of 1910, Pub. L. No. 61-218, 36 Stat. 539.

25. *See* Thierer, *supra* note 11, at 5; *see also* "Milestones in AT&T History," AT&T, http://www.corp.att.com/history/milestones.html.

26. *See* "Milestones," *supra* note 23; *see also* Thierer, *supra* note 11, at 5; *see also* G. W. Brock, *The Telecommunications Industry: The Dynamic of Market Structure* (Cambridge, MA: Harvard University Press, 1981).

27. *See* Thierer, *supra* note 11, at 7.

If the Kingsbury Commitment set the stage for AT&T's monopolization of the telephone industry, government nationalization of the telephone and telegraph industries during World War I closed the deal.[28] Vail was initially hesitant about nationalization, but soon realized it was his salvation: the government takeover gave him an excuse to raise rates and increase profits. Government regulation ensured higher barriers to entry in the telephone industry and thus decreased competition. Additionally, government-determined rates meant AT&T could request rate increases without being chastised by consumers.[29] And that is precisely what happened; immediately after the terms of the government takeover were agreed to, AT&T applied for immediate and sizable rate increases.[30] As Thierer explains:

> By January 21, 1919, just 5.5 months after nationalization, long-distance rates had increased by 20 percent. In addition to being much greater than returns earned during more competitive years, the rates established by the postmaster during the year of nationalization remained in force many years after privatization. Consequently, AT&T's generous long distance returns continued to average near or above 20 percent during the 1920s.[31]

Rate regulation wiped out AT&T's competition. Standard long-distance rates were set throughout the country based on average costs, as opposed to actual costs. This means that some subscribers subsidized others. For instance, subscribers calling from large urban centers would pay above costs in order to subsidize rates in the more expensive rural areas. Subscribers had no choice in the matter: the government determined that the ability to communicate with subsidized subscribers was of value to those footing more than their fair share of the bill, and thus, "Vail's vision of a single, universal service provider was . . .

---

28. Ibid.
29. *See* Noll, *supra* note 6.
30. *See* Thierer, *supra* note 11, at 7.
31. Ibid., 7–8.

adopted and implemented by the government through discriminatory rate structuring."[32] By 1934, when Congress established the FCC
and transferred jurisdiction over all telecommunications companies
to the new agency, federal regulators had bought Vail's vision for the
telephone industry hook, line, and sinker.

The Communications Act of 1934

The Communications Act of 1934 was meant to provide a statutory
framework for U.S. communications policy, covering telecommunications and broadcasting. The act established the FCC as an independent agency:

> For the purpose of regulating interstate and foreign commerce in commu-
> nication by wire and radio so as to make available, so far as possible, to all
> the people of the United States a rapid, efficient, nationwide and worldwide
> wire and radio communications service with adequate facilities at reasonable
> charges.[33]

The act created the FCC, and charged it to protect the "public convenience, interest and necessity" by enforcing uniform regulation of
content.[34] The breadth of the act put the future of telecommunications squarely in the hands of the FCC. One commentator lamented,
"The FCC was simply told to go ahead and regulate in the public
interest . . . in the absence of congressional or popular mandate, with

---

32. Ibid., 8.

33. *See* McLaughlin, *supra* note 34, 2221 (claiming that even as early as the 1950s "the
regulatory regime developed by the 1934 Act was severely out of step with the demands
of consumers and the growth of new technology").

34. 47 U.S.C.A § 151 (West 2006). *See also* Duane McLaughlin, "FCC Jurisdiction
over Telephone under the 1996 Act: Fenced Off?," *Columbia Law Review* 97 (1997): 2210,
2213. FCC jurisdiction is a product of the interplay of sections 1 and 2(b) of the 1934 Act.
Section 1 creates the FCC and gives it authority over "interstate and foreign commerce in
wire and radio communication" with the goal, among others, "to make available . . . to
all the people of the United States a rapid, efficient . . . wire and radio communications
service with adequate facilities at reasonable charges."

the baffling and manifold complexities in that field."[35] What seemed clear, though, was that the FCC's powers were incredibly broad.

The act classified telephone networks as "common carriers," which in effect meant:

> . . . every American was henceforth found to be entitled to the right to tele-phone service, specifically cheap telephone service. To carry out this difficult policy objective, the FCC was given sweeping powers. Besides its powers to regulate rates to ensure they were 'just and reasonable,' the FCC was also given the power to restrict entry into the marketplace. Potential competitors were, and still are, required to obtain from the FCC a 'certificate of public convenience and necessity.' The intent of the licensing process was again to prevent 'wasteful duplication' and 'unneeded competition.' In reality, it served as a front to guard the interests of the regulated monopoly and the FCC's social agenda.[36]

Neither the 1934 Act nor the FCC invented the idea of a federally reg-ulated telephone industry, or AT&T's government-sanctioned monop-oly. The foundations for both were laid years before, but the FCC became chief implementer of both policies, and the act its foil. As Thierer notes:

> The overall hostility to competition by the FCC and the drafters of the legis-lation that gave birth to it is best illustrated by a 1988 Department of Com-merce report on the development of the telecommunications industry. The report notes, 'The chief focus of the Communications Act of 1934 was on the regulation of telecommunications, not necessarily its maximum develop-ment and promotion. [T]he drafters of the legislation saw the talents and resources of the industry presenting more of a challenge to the public interest than an opportunity for national progress.'[37]

---

35. Louis L. Jaffe, "The Effective Limits of Administrative Process: A Reevaluation," *Harvard Law Review* 67 (1954): 1105.

36. *See* Thierer, *supra* note 11, at 10.

37. Ibid.

This erroneous position that somehow national progress and maximization of the telecommunication/communication industries are at odds with each other, necessitating the need for heavy-handed federal interference, is one that is repeated throughout the FCC's approach to its oversight of the industries under its regulatory umbrella. And the FCC's strategy has almost invariably stymied growth and innovation in these industries, a fact that unarguably is *not* in the public or national interest.

The agency's position with regard to telephony stifled competition and crippled the industry for years—just as it was achieving greatness. In particular, the FCC has made three big mistakes with traditional voice telephone: 1) protecting the AT&T monopoly for nearly sixty years and, thus, stunting competition in the telephone industry; 2) creating silos out of the various telecommunication mediums and, thus, permitting itself to impose unevenly severe regulations on traditional voice telephone; and 3) failing to oversee a corrupt and wasteful universal service regime that ultimately imposed more social costs than benefits.

Protecting the AT&T Monopoly

Two related economic principles provided the purported rationale for imposing common carrier regulations on certain networks including early telecommunication services. The first was the idea that the telephone industry was a natural monopoly. The theory of natural monopoly is that "some industries function better without competition, especially those industries that are so critical to society as a whole that government regulation is necessary to ensure reasonable price points and widespread deployment."[38]

In telephony, natural monopoly was purportedly produced by *network effects*, which describes the tendency for certain industries to become monopolistic because one company or network can reach the most subscribers. By virtue of its reach, the network is perceived as the

---

38. Kevin Ryan, "Communications Regulations—Ripe for Reform," *CommLaw Conspectus* 17 (2009): 780, commlaw.cua.edu/res/docs/10-Ryan-out-to-publisher-FINAL.pdf.

only network worth joining and other networks are duly ignored by consumers. In industries susceptible to network effects, market power is self-perpetuating because a company's strength lies in the number of consumers and producers that participate in network build-out. In such industries, dominant companies quickly become monopolists by underselling their smaller competitors. *Economies of scale* are produced, where, as output increases, the cost per unit of providing service decreases. Whether such monopolies actually exist in other industries is beyond the scope of this book, but one thing is certain: "[T]he telephone monopoly has been anything but natural."[39] Instead, it was the manifestation of Vail's philosophy of closed systems, centralized power, and network control.

The FCC asserted that its protection of the AT&T monopoly was in the public interest and argued that rate regulation, which hurt competition, ensured a robust network and lower prices. The FCC imposed "rate of return" regulations, which ensured incumbents a return on infrastructural build-out by removing the threat of competition. Additionally, strict entry regulation protected against wasteful duplication.[40]

And the AT&T monopoly was not just limited to telephone networks; instead, the 1934 Act mandated that the FCC regulate all "instrumentalities," "facilities," and "apparatus" that were "incidental" to transmission. That meant that AT&T had the exclusive right to develop and sell all telephones (at the time customers leased their telephones from the company), wires on private premises, and any device that might attach to either.[41] As Huber points out, "Had they been around in 1934, every fax machine, every modem-equipped computer, and every video display, disk drive and keyboard—every last component of what is now the Internet would have been [protected]."[42]

---

39. *See* Thierer, *supra* note 11, at 2.
40. *See* Huber, *supra* note 25, at 36, in preceding chapter.
41. Ibid., 38.
42. Ibid.

Thus, the FCC's protection of the AT&T monopoly not only eradicated competition in the wireline markets, it also severely stifled the growth of would-be competitive technologies. For example, after World War II, microwave technology, which provided an alternative mechanism for domestic long-distance service, arrived as a potential competitor in the long-distance markets. In the late 1940s, the FCC accepted a few applications by independent companies to construct private long-distance microwave networks in areas where AT&T's service was unavailable, but the commission required these businesses to abandon their licenses once AT&T entered that market.[43] As Peter Huber remarks:

[The FCC] also refused to require Bell to interconnect with anyone else's microwave facilities. It backed and enforced Bell's own strict restrictions against piece-out and resale of long-distance services. The piece-out clauses in AT&T's tariffs prohibited anyone else from building competing parts of the long-distance network over flat terrain, for example, while reselling Bell services to carry traffic over mountains. AT&T would connect its private-line services only to ultimate customers. Customers and end users could buy AT&T's services. Competing carriers, resellers, and operators of private networks could not.[44]

For years, FCC regulation was backed, if not emboldened, by the courts. For example, in 1951 the Supreme Court rejected the commission's attempt to authorize a small radio-telegraph company to open competing circuits to Portugal and the Netherlands. In doing so, the Court held that the FCC had failed to demonstrate how competition was in the public interest and thus had "abdicate[d] what would seem to us one of the primary duties imposed on it by Congress."[45]

43. Ibid.

44. Ibid.

45. Ibid., 36–37 (quoting RCA Communications, Inc. v. FCC, 346 U.S. 86, 86, 93, 95 (1953)).

However, just a few years later, the high court began to offer AT&T's competitors some relief. The seminal Hush-A-Phone case marked the beginning of this trend. The Hush-A-Phone company began to manufacture and sell a metal cup that attached to the mouth-piece of a telephone to muffle external noise, bolster the sound quality of conversations, and reduce the risk of conversations being overheard. AT&T complained that the device degraded its network and should, therefore, be outlawed.[46]

The FCC considered the issue for *seven years*, and eventually agreed with the telephone giant. The FCC concluded:

> Gadgets like these might degrade signal quality or send destructive pulses of electricity through the network . . . they might impair the 'quality and efficiency of telephone service, [cause] damage to telephone plant and facilities, or injur[e] telephone company personnel.'[47]

The D.C. Circuit Court of Appeals eventually exonerated the Hush-a-Phone company and found that AT&T's prohibition of the device was not "just, fair, and reasonable," as required under the Communications Act of 1934, since the device "[did] not physically impair any of the facilities of the telephone companies," nor did it "affect more than the conversation of the user."[48] This victory for Hush-A-Phone is widely considered a watershed moment in the development of a secondary market for terminal equipment. Moreover, it was a victory for consumers, who were finally given a taste of what competition in any portion of the telephone industry could offer.

The FCC's *Carterfone* decision encouraged a similar change in the way that FCC treated the AT&T monopoly. The Carterfone was a device that interconnected landline telephones with radio systems to permit mobile and landline users to communicate with one another.[49]

---

46. Ibid., 38.
47. Ibid.
48. Hush-A-Phone v. United States, 238 F.2d 266 (D.C. Cir. 1956).
49. Joseph P. Fuhr, Jr., "Competition in the Terminal Equipment Market after Carterfone," *Antitrust Bulletin* 28 (1983): 669–71.

Once again, AT&T attempted to ban the device and complained that the device harmed the leased telephones and distorted the quality of the user's service. Taking a cue from the D.C. Circuit's position in the decade-old Hush-A-Phone decision, the FCC did not accept AT&T's complaint point-blank. After review, it found that, once again, AT&T had either fabricated or exaggerated the deleterious effects that the device had on both the service and the telephone equipment. Consequently, the FCC banned AT&T from interfering with interconnections between AT&T's terminal equipment and competitor terminal equipment.

Though many point to the *Carterfone* decision as a momentous break from the FCC's historic practice of protecting the monopoly, the decision occurred a staggering twelve years after the D.C. Circuit had boldly affirmed competition in the terminal equipment market. Consequently, the *Carterfone* decision does not mark a forward-looking break from a historically anti-consumer practice of maintaining a nationwide monopoly over the telephone; instead, the decision illustrates the FCC's slow uptake with regards to changes in the social and economic realities of the industry that it is meant to administer.

Creating False Silos between Telephone and Other Communications Services

From early on, the FCC embraced false differentiations or silos between telephone services and other communications devices. In doing so, the commission failed to identify facilities-based competition between closely related technologies (like that between wireless and wireline technologies) and imposed uneven regulatory regimes upon each. As a result, AT&T was isolated from the universe of computing for years, cable from telephone, and telephone from radio. The silo system undoubtedly stifled technological competition, and thus growth, in each market, and demonstrates the absence of FCC foresight into the convergence of the technologies under its regulatory umbrella.[50]

---

50. *See* Rob Frieden, "The FCC's Name Game: How Shifting Regulatory Classifications Affect Competition," *Berkeley Technology Law Journal* 19 (2004): 1; *see generally* Pierre de

Today, technology has converged in such a way that failure to recognize competition between previously separated modalities is increasingly considered ignorant:

> No longer can the cable, broadcasting, telecommunications and internet sectors be viewed in isolation. Cellular mobile telephony is replacing the fixed line telephone in many locations. (In the developing world, consumers are moving directly to mobile phones, bypassing the fixed lines altogether . . .). Many mobile phones are complements or substitutes for wireline access to internet: e-mail, web surfing, movies, photos are now available on most mobile phones. Not only are mobile phones becoming more sophisticated, they are becoming 'open source' as is the internet with the resulting promise of yet unthought-of applications and innovations.[51]

The previously separated worlds of broadcast, Internet, telephone, and cable are increasingly intersecting, so it is difficult to justify regulations in one sector where the other sector is exempt. Robust and true competition means that regulation cannot be the driving force or the mediator.

The Universal Service Faux Pas

The Communications Act of 1996 charged the FCC with implementing expensive new universal service subsidies for users supposedly neglected by the market. The FCC implemented the Act's universal service mandates by beginning a series of programs aimed at ensuring that consumers in all areas, and of varying means, had access to necessary telecommunications services and that schools, libraries, and rural medical facilities received discounts and federal support for their telecommunications services. There were thus five main universal service

---

Vries, "Notes on Reforming the Federal Communications Commission," December 2008, http://fcc-reform.org/response/notes-reforming-federal-communications-commission/.

51. James Allelman, Paul Rappaport, and Aniruddha Banerjee, "Universal Service: A New Definition?," *Journal of Telecommunications Policy* 34 (2010): 4.

programs: 1) high-cost program[52]; 2) low-income program[53]; 3) schools and libraries support programs, which include the E-Rate program[54]; 4) rural healthcare programs[55]; and 5) Native American initiatives.[56]

---

52. Ibid. The high-cost program was designed to ensure that consumers in rural, insular, or otherwise high-cost areas receive access to telecommunications services that are comparable in quality and price to urban areas. The program is premised on the goals of universal service and fulfills universal service mandates by subsidizing eligible carriers who service high-cost areas. In doing so, the program purportedly facilitates buildout and offsets rates charged to those consumers. *See* U.S. Government Accountability Office, GAO-08-633, "FCC Needs to Improve Performance Management and Strengthen Oversight of the High-Cost Program," June 2008, http://www.gao.gov/new.items /d08633.pdf.

53. "Universal Service Program for Low-Income Consumers," FCC, http://transition .fcc.gov/wcb/tapd/universal_service/highcost.html. The low-income program provides discounts on installation and service rates to qualifying consumers. There are two subprograms that are available to qualifying consumers: 1) Link-up America, which provides subsidies for telephone installation costs; and 2) Lifeline, which provides discounts on monthly service fees.

54. "Overview of Schools and Libraries Program," Universal Services Administration Company, http://www.universalservice.org/sl/about/overview-program.aspx. The Universal Service Administrative Company (USAC) administers the E-Rate program under the direction of the FCC. The program provides discounts to assist schools and libraries to obtain affordable telecommunications and Internet access. It is funded by the universal service fund, which is financed by companies that provide interstate or international traditional telecommunications services.

55. "Rural Health Care Program," FCC, http://transition.fcc.gov/wcb/tapd/rural health/welcome.html. The rural healthcare program provides funding to eligible healthcare providers in rural areas, in order to ensure the necessary provision of healthcare to rural communities and to improve the quality of healthcare in those communities. The program is funded through the universal service fund, which is financed by companies that furnish interstate or international traditional telecommunications services. The fund is used to purchase discount rates for rural healthcare providers and funding is capped at $400 million annually.

56. Ibid. The Native American Initiatives within universal service programs attempt to establish access to telecommunications services in remote tribal lands. The Link-up and Lifeline subprograms provide discounts on installation fees and monthly charges, respectively. They are paid for by the universal service fund, which is financed by traditional telecommunication service providers that furnish services interstate or on an international basis.

Despite the high cost of administering and distributing the fund, the FCC did not traditionally impose stringent reporting requirements or specific standards on universal service providers. Consequently, the programs received "heavy criticisms"[57] for "wasteful, corrupt, and fraudulent practices."[58] In 1998, for instance, the FCC initiated the E-Rate program that aimed to connect schools and libraries to the Internet. When the House Energy and Commerce Subcommittee on Oversight and Investigations examined the program's finances, it concluded that conspirators had rigged the bidding process in order to secure over $48 million in grants and funding that both grossly exceeded the costs of providing services to the school district at issue and that excluded competing bidders from having a fair chance to offer the services.[59] Even more alarming than the conspiracy itself was that the Universal Service Administrative Company (USAC), which the FCC erected to administer and oversee the program, failed to detect any wrongdoing.[60] In 2004, the Office of Inspector General (OIG) in the FCC reported that out of 135 E-Rate subsidy audits, 36 percent were noncompliant.[61] Thomas W. Hazlett argued that "an endemic problem has emerged" with regards to the FCC's oversight function and ability to eradicate fraud from its subsidy programs.[62]

In addition to "lax oversight," the FCC failed to specifically enforce the quality and affordability requirements in the 1996 Act and, instead, relied on state authorities to set benchmarks for reasonable quality

---

57. Ramsey L. Woodworth and Jared B. Weaver, "Camp Runamuk: The FCC's Troubled E-Rate Program," *Commlaw Conspectus* 14 (2006): 335–36.

58. Ibid.

59. Ibid.

60. Ibid., claiming "the program has been open to fraudulent and corrupt schemes—many of which in hindsight appear so obvious that one wonders how they were allowed to progress as far as they did."

61. *See* Federal Communications Commission, "Office of the Inspector General Semi-annual Report to Congress," 12, 2004 (hereafter "FCC, OIG Report 2004").

62. Thomas W. Hazlett, "'Universal Service' Telephone Subsidies: What Does $7 Billion Buy?," 53, Heartland.org, 2006, http://heartland.org/sites/all/modules/custom/heart land_migration/files/pdfs/19520.pdf.

and rates. One commentator contends, "the FCC determined that the federal program should guarantee that rates are comparable across states, but left it to the states to develop programs that would address intrastate differences."[63]

While there are arguments in favor of devolving authority to state regulators, doing so here resulted in inconsistencies across the nation in the effectiveness, administration, and costs of the program. In 2008, the Government Accounting Office (GAO) assessed the FCC's "high-cost program"[64] and reported that it "was unable to identify performance goals or measures for the program . . . [and] [i]n the absence of performance goals and measures, the Congress and FCC are limited in their ability to make informed decisions about the future of the high-cost program."[65] The GAO recommended that the FCC establish short- and long-term goals for the program and identify areas in which guidance or cost-effective mechanisms should be enforced to prevent inefficiency.[66] At the time, the FCC internalized the criticism but failed to enact any meaningful changes.

In 2007, Thomas W. Hazlett exposed the inefficiencies in the system by making the flow of payments from the universal service fund transparent. He found that many carriers were being overcompensated for their services and not necessarily improving national penetration rates. He argued that the $7 billion collected annually through universal service taxes "fail—on net—to extend network access . . . encourage widespread inefficiency and block adoption of advanced technologies."[67] Indeed, the universal service system that Hazlett surveyed was not benefiting the targeted constituencies. For example, subsidies meant to benefit low-income residents were instead received by

---

63. Gregory L. Rosston and Bradley S. Wimmer, "The State of Universal Service," Stanford.edu, http://www-siepr.stanford.edu/papers/pdf/99-18.pdf.

64. See "Universal Service," *supra* note 53, in this chapter.

65. See U.S. Government Accountability Office, GAO-08-633, "FCC Needs to Improve Performance Management and Strengthen Oversight of the High-Cost Program," 2008.

66. Ibid.

67. See Hazlett, *supra* note 63, Introduction.

landlords, landowners, and the already-subsidized telecommunications providers. Hazlett concluded that these inefficiencies were not surprising, but instead the predictable "outcome of a system that clings to existing technologies and rewards incumbent carriers for inefficiency, increasing payments as costs rise."[68]

The difficulty of formulating an efficient and effective universal service regime is partly a result of the multitudinous objectives embedded in the 1996 Act. The Act strives to "maintain artificially low monthly rates for local residential voice service . . . while professing to promote competition."[69] In addition, the act erected federal support for advanced services to schools, libraries, and rural medical facilities and required federal and state regulators to establish support levels for these programs.[70] Both the expense and difficulty of coordinating on both a federal and state level to provide adequate financial support and guidance for these ambitious universal service initiatives resulted in inefficiencies, high costs, and widespread complaints regarding the effectiveness of the programs.[71]

For more than fifteen years since its inception, the Universal Service Fund (USF) has been administered in roughly the same manner. Common carriers pay into the fund—generally by passing off the tax in a line item on consumers' bills—and the money is paid out to eligible carriers and rural carriers who use it to subsidize service for high-cost areas, low-income consumers, or educational and public healthcare institutions. The USF has been berated for its high cost and administrative inefficiencies.[72] Until 2011, the fund paid out roughly $7.5 billion

---

68. *See* Hazlett, *supra* note 63, at 70.

69. Robert W. Crandall and Leonard Waverman, "Who Pays for Universal Service? When Telephone Subsidies Become Transparent" (Washington, D.C.: Brookings Institution Press, 2000), 12.

70. Ibid.

71. Ibid.

72. *See generally* Scott Wallsten, "The Universal Service Fund: What Do High-Cost Subsidies Subsidize?," Technology Policy Institute Working Paper, 2011, 2, http://works .bepress.com/cgi/viewcontent.cgi?article=1117&context=scott_wallsten (arguing that the "existing high-cost program is ineffective, inefficient, and inequitable").

annually, more than half of which subsidizes telephone service in high-cost areas.[73] Additionally, the fund has supported rural consumers disproportionately more than urban consumers.[74] In 2008, the Office of Inspector General in the FCC found that many of these disproportionately higher payments were "erroneous," in that they were both unnecessary and unjustifiably excessive.[75] The "poor foundation" upon which universal service has been shaped has prompted commentators to question why the FCC's 2011 report and order overhauling the USF did not go even further in reshaping the universal service institution.

The FCC's gross mishandling of the universal service fund, its failure to recognize the deleterious effects of creating false silos between various telecommunications mediums, and its long-time, unabashed coddling of the AT&T monopoly caused considerable harm to the very industry it was charged with perpetuating. More importantly for our purposes, poor FCC oversight and decision-making with regard to telephony is not an unfortunate anomaly in the agency's history; it is, instead, its modus operandi. As we will demonstrate below, similar failures in its oversight of broadcast and cable should convince even the greatest skeptic that FCC regulation of the Internet, if permitted to go forward, will most assuredly follow the same unfortunate course.

Broadcast

As people prepared for Super Bowl XXXVIII, no one expected that the most memorable part of the 2004 championship would occur in a flash instant during halftime, when all the football players were off the field. Amidst close calls, bad plays, or rowdy audience members, nothing stood out quite like "nipplegate," the brief instant during which

---

73. Ibid., 6–7.

74. Ibid., 1. "About 60 percent of the total fund goes to programs in rural areas while only 40 percent goes to urban areas. The numbers tilt further in favor of rural areas when considering only programs targeting residential subscribers (high-cost and low-income support)—65 percent rural and 35 percent urban."

75. Ibid., 9.

Janet Jackson exposed her breast during her now-legendary halftime show with Justin Timberlake.[76] In addition to being seared into the annals of scandalous American history, the incident has since occupied court dockets and the minds of top legal scholars in the country. The question before the courts was whether the FCC, which had never imposed heavy fines on "fleeting indecency," could impose a $550,000 penalty on CBS for the incident.[77] After the case bounced back and forth between the Third Circuit and the Supreme Court, the courts concluded that the FCC's fine, inspired by public distaste for the incident, was "arbitrary and capricious" and, therefore, void.[78] But how did the FCC come to defend this supposedly unfounded penalty for nearly a decade? The courts noted that the issue with the penalty was that it was inconsistent with the FCC's past decisions and interpretations. Yet, the FCC pursued the fine to its bitter end. Why? Perhaps because the FCC has always attempted to push its jurisdictional limits and, consequently, can no longer tell when it is out of bounds.

Examples abound of how the commission's regulation of the broadcast industry has been uneven, inconsistent, and overaggressive. All the while, the agency has shown its susceptibility to political pressures, and an astounding inability to resist the urge to meddle in areas tangentially related to telecommunications but clearly beyond the bounds of its own expertise. As a result, the agency has repeatedly imposed rules and

---

76. *See* Clay Calvert and Robert D. Richards, "The Parents Television Council Uncensored: An Inside Look at the Watchdog of the Public Airwaves and the War on Indecency with Its President, Tim Winter," *Hastings Communications and Entertainment Law Journal* 33 (2011): 295.

77. Angela J. Campbell, "Pacifica Reconsidered: Implications for the Current Controversy over Broadcast Indecency," *Federal Communications Law Journal* 63 (2010): 248. "About six months after the Golden Globe decision, the FCC issued an NAL [Notice of Apparent Liability] against CBS in the amount of $555,000 for the 2004 Super Bowl Halftime show in which Janet Jackson's breast was exposed."

78. Shelly Rosenfeld, "An Indecent Proposal? What Clamping Down on Fleeting Expletives on the Airwaves Means for the TV Industry," *Texas Review of Entertainment and Sports Law* 12 (2011): 227 (citing the court's decision that the FCC's fine on CBS was arbitrary and capricious).

regulations that have had deleterious effect on robust expression over what has become an increasingly important mass-communications medium. As we will show later, the FCC's initial foray into Internet regulation, its Open Internet Order, is but a manifestation of many of these themes only applied to the Internet. We will briefly describe three areas of FCC failures with regard to broadcast—the Fairness Doctrine, obscenity/indecency regulation, and affirmative action—in order to demonstrate the type of regulatory oversight we should expect with regard to the Net.

Fairness Doctrine

Because the broadcast spectrum has long been considered a scarce but important public resource, the FCC, from its inception, has been charged with allocating that spectrum and ensuring that the programming for which it is used is well suited to the public interest. In furtherance of this objective, the commission articulated goals and guidelines for broadcast networks and affiliates. Among other things, the FCC mandated: 1) better children's programming, 2) more educational TV, and 3) greater public investment in the sort of technology that would keep the United States ahead of other nations, both commercially and militaristically. In many cases, the system comported with the objectives of the contemporaneous educational system.[79]

The mystery, however, is how these ideas, goals, and initial hopes for broadcast manifested themselves in the Fairness Doctrine, although the Doctrine must have been premised on public-interest concerns and dissatisfaction about the level of public-affairs coverage on the networks. Its origins are hard to pinpoint, but, once the Fairness Doctrine took hold, it attracted a political constituency that kept it afloat for forty years. The doctrine was simple in its requirements: 1) broadcasters had to cover important news issues and controversies or, in the commission's words, "controversial issues of public

---

79. http://www.fcc.gov/spectrum/.

importance"[80]; 2) the coverage had to be evenhanded, both through a balance of views and in terms of time allocated to each side of the policy under consideration[81]; and 3) broadcasters were required to charge identical rates for similar time on the air. Furthermore, individuals who were attacked on the air—generally in the context of a political campaign—were guaranteed equal time to respond. The commission announced that it would use keen scrutiny in overseeing broadcasters and ensuring that the networks fulfilled these obligations.

It was not long before the Fairness Doctrine fell into stunning disrepute. Ironically, the demise of the doctrine began with a case in which the Supreme Court, by an eight-to-zero vote, declared the doctrine constitutional. The case was *Red Lion Broadcasting v. FCC*. It all started when a political commentator named Fred J. Cook wrote a book about Barry Goldwater—the Arizona conservative and GOP presidential candidate in 1964—suggesting that some of Goldwater's positions bordered on insanity. When Cook was counterattacked by the right-wing preacher Billy James Hargis on Hargis' weekly radio show,[82] Cook demanded redress under the Fairness Doctrine.[83] Hargis' station, Red Lion Broadcasting, rejected the demand, so Cook sued. All justices voting favored Cook's view of the law and the proclaimed the Fairness Doctrine constitutional.[84]

The Fairness Doctrine smacked in the face of basic free-speech rights. As commentators point out, the Fairness Doctrine essentially

---

80. 47 C.F.R. § 73.1212 (2005).

81. 29 Fed. Reg. 10410 (July 25, 1964) (announcing the equal time requirement under the Fairness Doctrine).

82. *See* Dominic E. Markwordt, "More Folly Than Fairness: The Fairness Doctrine, the First Amendment, and the Internet Age," *Regent University Law Review* 22 (2010): 414. On November 25, 1964, WGCB, a radio station owned by the Red Lion Broadcasting Corporation, carried a fifteen-minute program in which Hargis spent two minutes accusing Cook of, among other things, working for the "left-wing publication [*The Nation*]" and seeking to "smear and destroy Barry Goldwater."

83. *See generally* Mark A. Conrad, "The Demise of the Fairness Doctrine: A Blow for Citizen Access," *Federal Communications Law Journal* 41 (1989): 169.

84. Red Lion Broad. Co. v. F.C.C., 395 U.S. 367, 375 (1969).

pit two important First Amendment rights against one another: 1) the right to speak, and 2) the right to refrain from speech.[85] The case, *Miami Herald Publishing Co. v. Tornillo*, demonstrates the conundrum within the Fairness Doctrine.[86] In that case, Pat Tornillo, boss of the Classroom Teachers Association and candidate for the state legislature in Florida, demanded equal space in the *Miami Herald* following publication of a highly critical piece.[87] Once again, the U.S. Supreme Court came to a unanimous decision, only this time it held the First Amendment prevented the *Miami Herald* from having to yield to Tornillo's, and the Fairness Doctrine's, demand.[88] The Court found that newspapers have a First Amendment right to editorial discretion and that legislation or regulations that require newspapers to permit equal time and equal space impinged on the First Amendment by penalizing the protected expression of editorial discretion.[89] Many constitutional scholars found it strange that the court would go one way on Cook and the other way in Tornillo—especially over a period of only eight years.[90] As far as important precedents go, very few have been reversed in such a short period of time.[91] After *Tornillo*, it was evident that the Fairness Doctrine would not pass constitutional muster and would have to either be repealed or severely limited in scope. In 1987, when the Fairness Doctrine's final embers of dignity were

---

85. Sir Edward Coke, "The Regulation of Competing First Amendment Rights: A New Fairness Doctrine Balance after CBS?," *University of Pennsylvania Law Review* 122 (1974): 1283, 1288.

"The conflict among the asserted first amendment rights of the broadcasters, individual citizens, and the general public (represented by the FCC) is, therefore, no closer to being resolved through an agency 'common law' than it was twenty-five years ago when the fairness doctrine was first systematized by the FCC."

86. *See* Miami Herald Pub. Co. v. Tornillo, 418 U.S. 241, 241 (1974).

87. Ibid., 241.

88. Ibid.

89. Ibid., 258.

90. *See* L. A. Powe Jr., *Tornillo*, 1987 S. Ct. L. R. 345, 345 (1987).

91. Ibid.

already burning out, the commission voted to repeal it.[92] Only a handful of the most liberal members of each house opposed the action.[93]

Obscenity and Indecency

The FCC of course did not disappear with its progeny. Down with the Fairness Doctrine, but long live control over cable television, obscene or indecent language on the air, and, most coveted of all, control over the Internet. During the years that the FCC dominated radio and television outlets, it could control much of what was put on the air. It could also decree the conditions under which producers and programmers remained eligible for a much-desired broadcast license. Not all of the FCC's efforts were without merit. The commission could, and did, for example, limit the content and duration of advertisements during children's programs and reviewed general advertisements for relevance, appropriateness, and overall quality.[94]

---

92. Ibid.

93. Ibid.

94. With cable, this power became more difficult to justify. Stringent content restrictions that imposed on the cable provider's editorial decisions seemed like relics of an era when commercial advertisement and entertainment programming had yet to pervade the social landscape. In the mid-1960s, as cable was rising to prominence, the FCC attempted to assert control over the cable industry. The FCC asserted its jurisdiction over cable television in the Second Report and Order. 2 F.C.C.2d 725 (1966). The FCC limited individual holdings on spectrum to stave off a long-range threat of media conglomeration and dominance. The commission also asserted that scarcity of spectrum justified municipal regulations that would prevent cable operators from charging unreasonable rates. But, in the 1980s, a number of lawsuits between the commission and would-be cable operators stripped the commission of most of its power over the cable industry. *See generally* Geoffrey A. Berkin, "Hit or Myth: The Cable TV Marketplace, Diversity and Regulation," *Federal Communications Law Journal* 35 (1983): 41. Cable operators argued that they should be treated like unregulated newspapers rather than like broadcasters. At that point, the regulatory status of cable operators had not been conclusively established. The courts sided with the cable operators and imposed stricter scrutiny on regulations that imposed on the cable operators' "editorial" discretion. Turner Broad. Sys., Inc. v. F.C.C., 512 U.S. 622, 623 (1994) (holding regulation cannot intrude on the "editorial control of cable-operators").

Perhaps the most entertaining battles between the FCC and content providers occurred over the issue of indecency. One can argue until eternity as to whether a particular program, image, or expression is offensive or obscene. Accordingly, parents differ widely over what programs they permit their children to watch. Yet, in regulating obscenity or indecency, the FCC attempts to impose a uniform standard for all audiences. At the outset, it was important to distinguish between obscenity—graphically spelled out in the 1973 *Miller v. California* decision—and words that might be crude or offensive, but do not satisfy the Supreme Court's definition of obscenity.[95] The former does not receive any constitutional protection, while the latter receives a malleable range of protection. Though the spectrum can be vague and confusing, it was developed by some of the finest judicial minds of the United States. In the *Miller* case, the defendant was convicted of mailing unsolicited, obscene materials because the materials, taken as a whole, appealed to "the prurient interest in sex."[96] The U.S. Supreme Court attempted to create a test for defining obscene materials:

> The basic guidelines for the trier of fact must be (a) whether the 'average person, applying contemporary community standards' would find that the work, taken as a whole, appeals to the prurient interest . . . , (b) whether the work depicts or describes, in a patently offensive way, sexual conduct specifically defined by the applicable state law, and (c) whether the work, taken as a whole, lacks serious literary, artistic, political, or scientific value.[97]

Caution was taken in formulating the definition of obscenity because the designation of an item as obscene deprives it of all constitutional legitimacy.[98] So long as that definition remains constant,

---

95. *See* Miller v. California, 413 U.S. 15, 15 (1973).
96. Ibid.
97. Ibid.
98. Ibid.

purveyors or purchasers of obscene material are on notice that they can be prosecuted at the will of local authorities.[99]

Though the Supreme Court has consistently held that the First Amendment does not protect obscenity, it has not offered a consistent method of separating obscenity from closely related, yet protected speech: indecency. On the spectrum between thinly protected indecency and fully protected expression are many opportunities for First Amendment violations. Accordingly, the FCC's attempt to regulate indecency has caused confusion regarding what constitutes protected expression and has incited controversy. As noted above, the dialogue on obscenity and indecency today is premised on the halftime performance of Janet Jackson and Justin Timberlake at Super Bowl XXXVIII. Though the incident incited some public outrage and attracted many complaints, the FCC went against its own definition of indecency in an overly aggressive attempt to penalize CBS. In June 2012, the Supreme Court refused to grant *certiorari* to the government after it lost its case in the circuit court of appeal, officially relieving CBS of the $550,000 fine.[100] In the end, the case cost the FCC eight years of resources and the embarrassment of losing a case premised on only a split second of television.

"Nipplegate" was not the only occasion in which the FCC attempted to micromanage content under the guise of policing indecency or obscenity. The outrageous but widely popular Howard Stern found that his sponsors were so pressured by the threat of FCC penalties and fines that he ultimately left public broadcasting in favor of satellite broadcasting.[101] Additionally, programs like the critically acclaimed *NYPD Blue* were hauled before the commission for display-

---

99. Ibid.

100. Joe Flint, "Supreme Court Refuses FCC Bid to Fine CBS for Janet Jackson Incident," *Los Angeles Times*, June 29, 2012, http://articles.latimes.com/2012/jun/29/entertainment/la-et-ct-janet-jackson-fcc-20120629.

101. Alexander Lindey and Michael Landau, *Lindey on Entertainment, Publishing and the Arts* § 4:36 (3d ed. 2012).

ing the rear end of a female actress, Charlotte Ross, in 2003.[102] The FCC pursued that case for nearly a decade before the Second Circuit ruled against the agency, finding that the FCC's rules on "fleeting expletives" are unconstitutionally "vague" and create an unjustifiable "chilling effect."[103]

The Supreme Court eventually granted *certiorari* and combined that case with a similar one brought by Fox after the FCC levied similarly steep fines against the network for swear words uttered by Nicole Ritchie and Cher during a live broadcast of Fox's *Billboard Awards*. In June of 2012, the Court agreed that the FCC fines were unfair, although it did not reach the network's constitutional claims. Instead, in a unanimous opinion penned by Justice Kennedy, the Court held that the networks "lacked notice at the time of their broadcasts that the material they were broadcasting could be found actionably indecent under then-existing [FCC] policies."[104]

These incidents indicate that FCC regulators were throwing indecent material under the bus with obscenity, even though the content was often entitled to First Amendment protections. Considering the subjective nature of determining whether material is indecent or not and whether it is indecent enough to warrant massive fines, it seems that a satisfactory solution will be difficult to achieve. This begs the question: should the FCC be trying to micromanage content by regulating indecency at all?[105]

---

102. Joe Flint, "Court Tosses Indecency Case against ABC's 'NYPD Blue,'" *Los Angeles Times*, January 4, 2011, http://latimesblogs.latimes.com/entertainmentnewsbuzz/2011/01/court-tosses-indecency-case-against-abcs-nypd-blue.html.

103. ABC, Inc. v. F.C.C., 404 F. App'x 530, 533 (2d Cir. 2011).

104. F.C.C. v. Fox Television Stations, 132 S. Ct. 2307 (2012).

105. If one ventures back to 1978 to the classic monologue of the late comedian George Carlin, it is especially clear that broadcast has become more receptive to crude or unsavory material. F.C.C. v. Pacifica Found., 438 U.S. 726 (1978). During the course of his twelve-minute shtick, Carlin listed seven words that, if uttered on radio or television, would subject the speaker to both a fine and, probably, temporary banishment. Ibid. In resisting the proposed penalty, Pacifica and the *Columbia Law Review* ran a lead article urging that protected words—those falling short of the court's definition of obscenity—should never

Either way, the FCC's handling of the issue serves as an example of the agency's seeming inability to restrain itself from the urge to micromanage the industries it is charged with overseeing, or to insulate itself from the political or social whims of the day. We will argue that the agency's confused affirmative-action policies and checkered regulatory history deserve similar commentary, while the agency's network-neutrality rules are simply the latest example of the FCC's either inability or unwillingness to exercise self-control. We believe an intervention is in order.

Affirmative Action

Had Aristotle been asked to critique the performance of the FCC on affirmative-action issues, say, over the past fifty years, he might well have rebuked the agency for failing miserably to find the golden mean between excess and deficiency, having never managed to strike a consistent policy that offered both fairness and predictability.

For years the agency did little or nothing to prevent white domination of the medium, particularly in the South, where a coalition of violent Klansmen and courtly committee chairmen held sway. In one particularly shocking case involving a Jackson Mississippi licensee, management suffered no FCC challenge when it decided to black-out broadcasting of the *I Spy* network TV show of the 1960s in which a white intelligence operator (Robert Vaughn) and his African-American colleague (Bill Cosby) teamed up to fight in the service of the United States.[106]

Following passage of the Civil Rights Act of 1964, and the diminution in the power of Southern legislators, the FCC moved 180 degrees in the opposite direction. Suddenly, instead of tolerating racism they

---

be the basis of a penalty given their protection status under the First Amendment. Michael Coenen, "Of Speech and Sanctions: Toward a Penalty Sensitive Approach to the First Amendment," *Columbia Law Review* 112 (2012): 991, http://www.columbialawreview.org /assets/pdfs/112/5/Coenen.pdf. The article was widely considered ahead of its time. Indeed, the article was so far ahead of its time that at least a generation would pass before the proposal would be ripe for debate.

106. Cosby v. Moyant, 55 Misc. 2d 393 (N.Y. Sup. Ct. 1967).

implemented their own variety of discrimination. They dispensed federal "set asides" in a number of government contracts, judged licensee compliance by implementing something very close to quota systems, and mandated elaborate procedures for considering potential minority job applicants, even after a number of barely disguised quota systems were struck down by the courts.[107] For example, in *Lutheran Church-Missouri Synod v. FCC*,[108] the Court found that the FCC had been issuing equal-employment opportunity requirements far beyond what was required by law. Moreover, the case demonstrates that micromanaging racism was both administratively difficult and inequitable.[109]

In *Synod*, the FCC mandated that a religious broadcaster hire women and minorities by issuing quota and numerical requirements. In order to enforce these mandates, the FCC had to incorporate a stringent and detailed record-keeping process.[110] The commission evaluated the number of minority employees that the station hired relative to the ratio of minorities in the community at large, whether or not the broadcaster was diligently searching for qualified minorities. The commission also evaluated whether the on-air programs were racially balanced. The FCC played this numbers game not only with on-air people and programming, but with technicians, cameramen, crews, and producers, as if by magic the station was supposed to conjure a perfectly balanced workforce.[111] The absurdity of this requirement is apparent when one recalls that this was a *religious* station, appealing to a defined *religious* community that had the right, if not the necessity, to put together a staff of like-minded people for the purpose of praying to God.

---

107. *See, for example,* Office of Communication of the United Church of Christ v. F.C.C., 359 F. 2d 994 (1966).

108. *See* Lutheran Church-Missouri Synod v. F.C.C., 141 F.3d 344 (D.C. Cir. 1998).

109. *See* Lutheran Church-Missouri Synod v. F.C.C., 141 F.3d 344 (D.C. Cir. 1998).

110. *See generally* Leigh Woodruff Marquardt, "Programming the Future of Equal Employment Opportunity in Broadcasting: Lutheran Church-Missouri Synod v. F.C.C.," *Villanova Sports and Entertainment Law Journal* 6 (1999): 351.

111. Ibid.

In enforcing its system, the FCC was asserting itself into the details of the broadcaster's proprietary interests and encroaching on the broadcaster's freedom to express itself through its broadcasting outlet as it saw fit. These overzealous intrusions into the broadcaster's business decisions and First Amendment freedoms were often unjustified and demoralizing. Considering the FCC's purported expertise in telecommunications technology and competition rather than race relations, however, it is unsurprising that the FCC's attempts to micromanage race relations within sectors of the telecommunications industry were unsuccessful. When considering the heavy costs of implementing, enforcing, and litigating these affirmative action regimes, one cannot help but lament over this tragic misuse of government resources.

Indeed, the clear guidance from the Supreme Court was that, contrary to the FCC's inclinations, the age of government set-asides and quasi-quotas was drawing to an end. This was made clear in *Croson v. City of Richmond*, where the city had passed legislation requiring approximately one-third of municipal contracts to go to minority applicants. A Supreme Court majority, led my Justice Sandra Day O'Connor, termed Richmond's actions unconstitutional.[112]

Still, the FCC pressed on, implementing procedures that favored minority ownership of stations hoping for FCC licenses. In a quirk of history, one Supreme Justice, Byron R. White, who had vigorously opposed racial favoritism over the years, changed his vote in *Metro Broadcasting v. FCC 497 U.S. 517* (1990) and bestowed a fleeting majority on the FCC's practice of minority preferences in competition for FCC licenses. The new precedent lasted only five years, when in *Adarand Constructors Inc., v. Pena*, a case involving a federal road-building contract, the Supreme Court once again held preferences for women and minorities unconstitutional.[113] While there has been a great deal of judicial activity on racial issues, subsequent to *Adarand*, none has involved FCC or related broadcasting issues. Instead the Supreme Court has focused on such issues as school busing, police

---

112. Croson v. City of Richmond, 488 U.S. 469 (1989).
113. Adarand Constructors Inc., v. Pena, 515 U.S. 200 (1995).

and firefighter exams, and university admissions.[114] It would be hard to imagine anything in the FCC's record regarding race or otherwise that begs for additional authority. To the contrary, the agency's record has been confusing, inconsistent, illogical, and demanding of constant judicial oversight and review. In fact, it would be hard to imagine an agency that has earned less public confidence, let alone a fresh injection of authority over a yet unblemished industry. And yet that is precisely what the Open Internet Order purports to do.

Cable

The only consistent aspect of the FCC's regulation of the cable industry has been its inconsistency. In fact, the history of the FCC's relationship with cable providers is one of peaks and valleys. One commentator describes FCC regulation of the cable industry as "on-again, off-again."[115] Other scholars claim, "Regulation of the cable television industry was marked by remarkable periods of re-regulation, and re-deregulation during the 1980s and 1990s."[116] Indeed, the FCC harnessed jurisdiction over the cable companies in one fell swoop, then alternated each decade thereafter between heavy-handedness and total deregulation. Perhaps, then, the greatest fault of the agency's oversight of cable has been its failure to imagine a coherent vision for the industry and to implement sound policy as a means by which that vision might be realized. We will show that the FCC's shortsightedness meant it failed to recognize cable's potential as a facilities-based competitor in telecommunications. Instead, the agency confined each sector of telecommunications to an isolated silo, preventing competition between the sectors while bumbling oversight of each. Cable suffered particularly

---

114. *See* Regents of the University of California v. Bakke, 438 U.S. 265 (1978); *see also* Parents Involved in Community Schools v. Seattle School District No. 1, 551 U.S. 701 (2007); Ricci v. DeStefano, 129 S. Ct. 2658, 2671, 174 L. Ed. 2d 490 (2009).

115. Gregory S. Crawford, "Cable Regulation in the Satellite Era," 2007, http://www.nber.org/books_in_progress/econ-reg/crawford10-24-07.pdf.

116. Mary T. Kelly and John S. Ying, "Effectiveness of Regulation and Competition on Cable Television Rates," Villanova School of Economics, Working Paper 3, 2001.

mercilessly at the hands of the FCC, and the agency's inconsistent regulatory schemes thwarted its growth.

Agency regulation of the cable industry was introduced as a mix of common carrier and broadcast services. As a result, it fell outside the traditional boundaries of FCC jurisdiction. Initially, the FCC was reluctant to cast cable into its purview of regulation because it viewed cable as "a passive transporter of broadcast" and that it should be left to local regulators.[117] Cable television developed parallel to broadcast television, which was regulated by the FCC.[118] In fact, when cable was first developed in the 1940s, its purpose was to "enhance" broadcast television rather than replace it.[119] By 1962, however, it was clear that cable was a forerunner in over-the-air entertainment. By the late 1960s, the FCC was eager to take control.

In the 1968 Supreme Court case *United States v. Southwestern Cable Co.*, the Court affirmed the FCC's control over cable by asserting that its organic statute (the 1934 Communications Act) conferred power to regulate industries that may not have been contemplated at the time the statute was enacted.[120] The Supreme Court determined that the FCC had "regulatory power over all forms of electrical communication, whether by telephone, telegraph, cable, or radio," meaning the FCC had definitive authority to regulate the budding cable industry.[121] The FCC's newfound control over cable would have significant effects on the entire telecommunications industry.

---

117. *See* Huber, *supra* note 25, at 55, in preceding chapter. "The Commission was expected to serve as the single Government agency with 'unified jurisdiction' and 'regulatory power over all forms of electrical communication, whether by telephone, telegraph, cable, or radio.'"

118. *See* Huber, *supra* note 25, at 31, in preceding chapter.

119. Jim Chen, "The Last Picture Show (on the Twilight of Federal Mass Communications Regulation)," *Minnesota Law Review* 80 (1996): 1459–60. Chen writes, "[C]able technology emerged in the 1940s as a way to bring broadcast television signals to remote or mountainous communities." "The purpose was not to replace broadcast television but to enhance it. . . ."

120. Ibid., 53.

121. United States v. Southwestern Cable Co., 392 U.S. 157 (1968).

Though perhaps unforeseen at its inception, cable providers literally laid the foundation for unprecedented facilities-based competition.[122] Facilities-based competition has been heralded as the most effective means of inducing meaningful competition among telecommunications providers.[123] Unlike terminal equipment competition, discussed in the telephone section of this chapter, facilities-based competition forces competitors to be more self-reliant and, thus, more traditionally competitive. The reason independence offers more effective competition is because "facilities-based competition breaks down incumbents' bottleneck control over existing networks . . . [and] enables new entrants to innovate without restraint."[124] In addition, facilities-based competition, in so much as it is premised on proprietary control over network facilities, creates incentives for providers to maintain and improve facilities.[125]

How did the cable companies provide a new avenue of facilities-based competition? Quite simply, they installed a second pipeline to people's homes. Before the cable industry laid wires, copper wires from

---

122. Verizon Communications, Inc. v. F.C.C., 535 U.S. 467, 491 (2002). "First, a competitor entering the market (a 'requesting' carrier, § 251(c)(2)) may decide to engage in pure facilities-based competition, that is, to build its own network to replace or supplement the network of the incumbent."

123. See "FCC Chairman Michael Powell's Comments on AT&T's Proposal to Transition to Facilities-Based Competition," 2004 WL 912270 (F.C.C. Apr. 29, 2004). The FCC now recognizes the importance of encouraging facilities-based competition. In 2004, Chairman Michael Powell explained that "in the long run, the transition to facilities-based competition holds out the best promise of real benefit to America's telephone consumers."

124. See Alexandra M. Wilson, "Harmonizing Regulation by Promoting Facilities-Based Competition," George Mason Law Review 8 (2000): 729, 731. Facilities-based competition has not been fully realized because the FCC has traditionally encouraged access between competitors in order to encourage competition at other layers of the industries. For instance, the Telecommunications Act of 1996 includes an access regime, which requires telephone companies to lend their facilities to competitors as needed and so long as it does not result in undue hardship. Though this strategy has since been abandoned, its effect has been to retard the development of facilities-based competition.

125. Ibid.

telephone companies were the only tangible connection to individual residences. At the time, the cable industry was not viewed as a competitor to telephones. Indeed, if it were, the effort of connecting a second wire to residential homes would have seemed lavish and unnecessary. After all, regulators and industry leaders alike viewed the telephone industry as a natural monopoly that would not embrace market competition.[126] Consequently, the cable industry occupied its own sphere, which was viewed with similar natural monopoly status.

Regulation

The FCC struggled deeply in its attempt to regulate cable. As commentator Jim Chen points out:

> As of 1984, the cable industry had survived no fewer than four FCC initiatives designed to cabin the explosive growth of cablecasting: (1) mandatory origination, (2) access channel requirements, (3) distant signal and program exclusivity, and (4) the rule against the 'siphoning off' of attractive feature films and sports events into premium cable venues.[127]

The commission experimented with both content-based and access-based structures, but "virtually every effort to reshape cable in the image of television floundered."[128] As a result, history is pockmarked with the FCC's self-conscious stabs at formulating effective regulation of the cable industry.

At first the FCC thought it best to leave the cable industry under the auspices of local authorities. These authorities were given the opportunity to select and franchise their local cable carrier and to operate services for their constituents within a framework of rules provided by the FCC.[129] It was not long before the process resulted in corruption and graft. Cable providers forged underhanded relationships with

---

126. *See supra* note 49 in this chapter, and accompanying text.

127. *See* Chen, *supra* note 119, at 1463.

128. Ibid.

129. Mark I. Wallach, "Whose Intent? A Study of Administrative Preemption: State Regulation of Cable Television," *Case Western Reserve Law Review* 25 (1975): 258.

regulators in hopes of receiving bids. Local officials, who reaped the fruits of the corruption, allowed the industry to develop free of competition. As a result, issues of monopolization became as salient in the cable industry as it had within telephony.

As noted above, cable—like telephony—was initially regarded as a natural monopoly[130] and competition was considered wasteful and duplicative.[131] Consequently, the FCC did not attempt to encourage competition with the cable industry, but rather (as described above), attempted to separate the various components of the whole telecommunications industry in order to create silos of services. This meant keeping telephone companies out of the cable industry and vice versa, to ensure that each household would have access to one provider of the service rather than a choice of providers.[132] In addition, instead of ameliorating the rising price of cable through the promotion of market competition, the FCC artificially adjusted prices for consumer protection.

The FCC first imposed price regulations on the cable industry in 1972.[133] Using a combination of rate regulation and public service requirements, the FCC sought to serve the public interest in maintaining non-monopolistic prices, while allowing cable companies to make returns on their initial investments.[134] The FCC also "imposed a host of other requirements, including Must-Carry, franchise standards, network program non-duplication, and cross-ownership rules."[135] Though these requirements suggest the FCC was interested in sparking competition within the cable industry, they were mere precautionary regula-

---

130. Duane McLaughlin, "FCC Jurisdiction over Local Telephone under the 1996 Act: Fenced Off?," *Columbia Law Review* 97 (1997): 2210, 2221.

131. Leland L. Johnson, *Toward Competition in Cable Television*, 2 (Cambridge, MA: MIT Press, 1994).

132. Ibid., 3.

133. Donald J. Boudreaux and Robert B. Ekelund, Jr., "Cable Reregulation," *Cato Journal* 14, no. 1: 1–3, http://www.cato.org/pubs/journal/cj14n1-8.html.

134. *See* Johnson, *supra* note 131, at 4.

135. Gregory S. Crawford, "Cable Regulation in the Satellite Era," 2007, http://www.nber.org/books_in_progress/econ-reg/crawford10-24-07.pdf.

tions meant to "leave open the possibility of competition."[136] When competition *was* introduced to the cable industry, the FCC watched as its former regulatory regime was rendered "increasingly unnecessary and inappropriate."[137]

In 1974, only two years after their initial implementation of price regulations, the FCC deregulated much of the industry. After the FCC's anti-siphoning rules, "designed to keep cable from taking sports and movie programming away from broadcasters," were judicially rebuked in the 1977 case *Home Box Office Inc. v. FCC*, the FCC began a full-scale deregulation of the cable industry, announcing publicly that its new strategy would not have a serious economic effect on broadcasting.[138]

For a long time thereafter, the FCC stopped trying to regulate the industry. Regulation trickled out in the late 1970s and was formally vanquished by the deregulatory policies embedded in the Cable Act of 1984. The act promoted competition and heralded deregulation, and aimed to "establish guidelines for the exercise of Federal, State, and local authority with respect to the regulation of cable systems."[139] It adopted the deregulatory goals of the FCC, but promoted regulation when the market forces were unable to encourage "effective competition."[140] Under the FCC's guidelines for what constituted effective competition,[141] most cable companies qualified for rate deregulation and, by 1986, rates were largely unregulated.

The outgrowth of the 1984 Act was a desolate regulatory landscape. Even when the industry faced unprecedented obstacles, the FCC stayed out of the issue. In order to overcome new issues, the cable companies and their adversaries turned to judicial review. For example, a "serious problem" ensued when landowners refused to give easements to cable

---

136. *See* Johnson, *supra* note 131, at 3.

137. Ibid.

138. 567 F.2d 9 (D.C. Cir. 1977).

139. 47 U.S.C.A. § 521 (West 1984) (describing the purpose of the Cable Communications Act of 1984).

140. *See* Johnson, *supra* note 131, at 4.

141. Ibid. The FCC found there was effective competition if there were three or more unduplicated broadcasting signals within the service area.

providers to lay wire.[142] Many of these landowners were in cahoots with other broadcasters and did not want to help cable providers compete. Others were homeowners who simply did not want to relinquish control over their property. Such behaviors created substantial setbacks for the young cable industry and called for a series of adjudications to alleviate the situation. The courts responded by giving cable companies permission to provide service without easements from the non-tenant landlords, indicating a general supportive attitude toward the budding industry.[143]

As rates climbed, so did "competitive pressures and complaints by cable operators."[144] Broadcasters, who had been pushed to the wayside, demanded reregulation of the cable industry in order to curtail the growth of cable and gain a competitive edge. The FCC attempted to resume its role as rate regulator for the cable industry. The commission created a cumbersome "six-signal" test to determine whether competition effectively ruled out abusive market-power behaviors.[145] The test still left much of the cable industry unregulated. The problem was that cable, in and of itself, was fiercely competitive in the mid- and late 1980s. While cable operators competed vigorously for cable franchises, however, broadcasters were walking away with a proverbial black eye. Such broadcasters, who certainly competed for the same audiences as the cable operators, still functioned under the licensing regime governed by the FCC. Perhaps this misalignment made it difficult to stimulate competition between these overlapping industries, but it is certain that, as far as broadcasters were concerned, the FCC failed to respond adequately.[146]

Consequently, Congress stepped in. The Cable Act of 1992 was Congress' response to broadcasters who complained about rising pressure

142. *See generally* Russell G. Donaldson, 113 A.L.R. Fed. 523 (1993).

143. Richard D. Harmon, "Co-Use of Compatible Private Easements by Cable Television Franchisees under the 1984 Cable Act: Federal Refinement of an Established Right," *Golden Gate University Law Review* 22 (1992): 1–2.

144. *See* Johnson, *supra* note 131, at 3.

145. Ibid., 5.

146. "Cable Television, Fact Sheet Information Bulletin Transition," FCC, 2000, http://transition.fcc.gov/mb/facts/csgen.html.

and rising costs of competing against the vigorous cable industry. The act aimed to "promote the availability of diverse views and information . . . to ensure cable operators do not have undue market power, and to ensure consumer interests are protected in the receipt of cable service."[147] The FCC was charged with regulating under these new guidelines, and thus the agency promulgated rate regulations, access regulations, and franchising fee regulations. It also embraced the act's odd commitment to retransmission regulation, which regulated cable by distinguishing it from broadcast so it would not supplant broadcast. As commentators point out:

> Without viable competition in most markets and with cable prices rising more than two times the rate of inflation, Congress effectively re-regulated the industry by passing the 1992 Cable Act. Congress directed the FCC to design regulations to ensure that basic cable rates were reasonable. Accordingly, the Commission, in April 1993, adopted a benchmark approach to regulate prices in markets without effective competition.[148]

The FCC also sought to diminish undue market power. Despite the restrictive tone of the "reasonable limits" provision,[149] the FCC attempted to create caps on the market power assumed by any single cable operator. The reasonable-limits provision prevents the FCC from placing unreasonable limits on the number of subscribers cable operators are allowed to reach. Yet, the FCC made multiple attempts to promulgate hard caps on the market share of any individual cable company. This was a strategy disfavored by the courts, and though never formally outlawed, such rules did not overcome judicial scrutiny. As recently as 2009, the FCC attempted to rehash this technique of stifling monopolization by capping cable operators' market shares at 30 percent. The D.C. Circuit threw this rule out, as it had done

---

147. Ibid.

148. *See* Kelly, *supra* note 116, at 2.

149. "Cable Television Industry Is Handed a Legal Setback," *New York Times*, September 17, 1993, http://www.nytimes.com/1993/09/17/business/the-media-business-cable-television-industry-is-handed-a-legal-setback.html.

with similar rules in the past.[150] The court's response is not surprising given the current landscape of cable television. Indeed, in an age where cable is robustly competitive, the desire to promulgate heavy-handed market caps seems laughable.[151]

The FCC's failure to implement long-lasting regulations that were either effective or could overcome judicial scrutiny left the cable industry in a confusing situation. "Without strong evidence that regulation was effective in containing cable rates and with indications that cable rates were significantly lower," the FCC's continued regulation instigated perverse reactions from the cable industry. Cable operators were "accused of putting newer, cheaper, less-watched channels on the basic tier and moving many of the more popular services onto unregulated, higher programming tiers." Operators negotiated for deregulation by promising the FCC that they would issue customer rebates and invest in capital-improvement projects.[152] Despite evidence cutting in favor of deregulation, the FCC continued to experiment with regulation and, once again, Congress had to step in by passing the Telecommunications Act of 1996.

The Telecommunications Act of 1996 "eliminated price caps for the majority of cable service bundles," meaning the cable industry has been able to charge consumers whatever it has felt like charging since 1999, when the provision took effect.[153] More importantly, the 1996 Act opened the door to media cross-ownership, allowing both cable operators and telephone networks to engage in the once-isolated silos of the telecommunications industry. One commentator notes:

> Enactment of the Telecommunications Act of 1996 dramatically altered the regulatory and public policy landscape for telecommunications services, spurring new competition and greater choice for consumers . . . a

---

150. "Another Video Smackdown: The FCC's Anti-Cable Campaign Gets Whacked," *Wall Street Journal,* September 2, 2009, http://online.wsj.com/article/SB10001424052970204 731804574387120029467020.html.

151. Ibid.

152. *See* Kelly, *supra* note 116, at 3.

153. *See* Crawford, *supra* note 115.

> deregulated environment for cable operating and programming companies enabled the cable industry to accelerate deployment of broadband services, allowing consumers . . . to have more choices in information, communication, and entertainment services.[154]

Though initial cross-ownership was modest, most cable companies today offer multiple basic services. Between 1996 and 2002, cable operators invested roughly $65 billion to build higher-capacity hybrid networks that could provide multichannel video, two-way voice, high-speed Internet access, and high-definition video.[155] In 2007, cable high-speed Internet gained 24.3 million subscribers and digital cable customers increased as well.[156] By 2009, broadband subscriptions exceeded one billion globally and some began calling for a redefinition of broadband that transcends the specific type of network connectivity or speed.[157] Consequently, cable has been forced to morph.

In the past, cable operators relied on superior or exclusive programming to gain a competitive edge. Today, the ability to access programs from a variety of sources is more important to consumers than the programs themselves. For example, children simply do not use the television set to access cable programming. So long as they have Internet access, they can watch whatever programs they want. As a result, cable operators have had to change their strategy. The rise of IPTV (Internet protocol television) has further eroded the distinctions between cable, broadcast, and other forms of information service technology. IPTV is digital television delivered to television sets through

---

154. Satish K. Moorthy, "U.S. Cable Television Industry: The Multi-Service Operator Organizational Structure as a Bundle of Competencies," 9, Materials Science and Engineering, University of Pennsylvania, 2009, http://dspace.mit.edu/bitstream/handle/1721.1/49770/457057912.pdf?sequence=1.

155. Ibid., 10.

156. Ibid., 11.

157. Yongsoo Kim, Tim Kelly, and Siddhartha Raja, "Building Broadband: Strategies and Policies for the Developing World," xxi, The World Bank, January 2010, http://site resources.worldbank.org/EXTINFORMATIONANDCOMMUNICATIONAND TECHNOLOGIES/Resources/282822-1208273252769/Building_broadband.pdf.

high-speed Internet (broadband services). Such technologies obviate the need for exclusive programming and should, ideally, encourage cable operators to enhance broadband services by abandoning the old television entertainment model in exchange for converged services delivered via broadband.

The result would be a whole new scheme of maximizing profits and soliciting subscriptions. Cable providers are reluctant to embrace the change, but consumers have left the aging cable industry in their dust. While "pay-TV operators are finding different ways to improve customer growth," cable TV is left with price innovation and programming to stay competitive.[158] Analysts estimate "IPTV service revenues will approach $14 billion in 2012, growing from $694 million in 2007."[159] In 2010, David Calarusso announced in the *Huffington Post* that he "stopped paying for cable . . . despite the fact that half of the first-run shows [he] watch[es] are cable series."[160] He expressed concern that content providers would end up with the short straw in this structural mix-up, but came to the realization that most of the cable shows that he cared about were available online free and legally. Apparently, everyone except the cable companies is aboard the broadband wagon. In August, Time-Warner CEO Glenn Britt said broadband was the future of the cable industry, suggesting cable operators are becoming more attuned to the changing landscape of their industry. Time-Warner is the second-largest cable operator in the United States, so their new direction is telling.

Whatever the future holds for the telephone, broadcast, and cable industries, it will certainly be brightest if not eclipsed by the FCC's regulatory shroud. The same is absolutely true of the Internet.

---

158. Mike Robuck, "Report: Worldwide pay-TV revenue to hit $236B at end of 2012," cedmagazine.com, 2011, http://www.cedmagazine.com/news/2011/12/report-worldwide-pay-tv-revenue-to-hit-236b-at-end-of-2012.

159. Ibid.

160. David Calarusso, "The Future of Cable Television," *Huffington Post*, 2010, http://www.huffingtonpost.com/david-colarusso/the-future-of-cable-telev_b_501895.html.

Chapter Three
THE "INTERGALACTIC NETWORK"

ON OCTOBER 4, 1957, the Soviet Union launched Sputnik 1, the world's first artificial satellite into orbit. With this remarkable achievement, the Soviets took the early lead in the so-called "space race" between the United States and the Soviet Union, and forcibly opened the Space Age.[1] While the Eisenhower administration's initial reaction was low key, if not dismissive, the American public was shocked and outraged. In fact, the depth and breadth of the Soviet achievements impact on American society's psyche cannot be understated. After all, the space race was not only a competition between the two Cold War adversarial superpowers for supremacy in space exploration, but dominance was seen as imperative for national security supremacy during what was quickly becoming a long and bitter Cold War. Moreover, leading the charge was symbolic of nationalistic technological and ideological superiority. As a result, the launch of Sputnik not only refocused the American government's efforts into developing a serious, concerted program to achieve manned space flight, it inspired a whole new generation of engineers and scientists, and led to an unprecedented increase in U.S. government spending on scientific research and education. The impact of both is still being felt today.[2]

---

1. L. S. Swenson, Jr., J. M. Grimwood, and C. C. Alexander, "This New Ocean, A History of Project Mercury," National Aeronautics and Space Administration, 71, 1966.

2. Neal Homer, *Beyond Sputnik* (Ann Arbor: University of Michigan, 2008), pp. 3–4.

An immediate response to the Sputnik launch was the U.S. Department of Defense's creation of the Advanced Research Projects Agency (ARPA) in February 1958. (ARPA was renamed the Defense Advanced Research Projects Agency, DARPA, in 1972.) The agency was tasked with regaining the technological lead in the arms race. DARPA, in turn, created the Information Processing Technology Office (IPTO) to continue, among other areas of interest, research of the Semi-Automatic Ground Environment (SAGE) program, the first computer-based command-and-control air defense system for tracking and intercepting enemy bomber aircraft and other space-based weapons. The SAGE system, an automated network of radar sites spanning both U.S. coasts and Canada, was connected to a central computer over telephone lines. NORAD used SAGE from the late 1950s until the early 1980s. The radar systems were designed to send the computer information (presumably about incoming enemy bombers), which could then be interpreted by a human operator. That operator would then choose the appropriate response, for example, instructing the computer to attack specific targets.

In 1962, J. C. R. Licklider was appointed to head the new IPTO organization. His original mandate was to extend the research that had successfully computerized the SAGE program into other military command-and-control systems. In particular, the IPTO, under Licklider's guidance, was to build a survivable electronic network to interconnect key Department of Defense sites at the Pentagon, and Strategic Air Command (SAC) Headquarters. There is much debate among Internet historians as to the underlying purpose for creating the network—some contend that its purpose was to ensure the president would have the capability of conveying a "launch" order to nuclear missile installations around the country, even if a preemptive nuclear strike by the Soviets wiped out much of the country and its communications systems. Others claim that the network would serve the much more mundane purpose of connecting the various government-supported computer labs across the country to facilitate communications and to aggregate the processing power of the mainframe computers housed in each lab.[3] For our purposes, the precise motivations are of little importance; either way the move would plant the initial seed for what would become the modern-day Internet.

Licklider (or Lick, as he insisted on being called) was a major proponent of universal computer networking and had worked on a committee at MIT (where he had served as an associate professor since 1950) that established the Lincoln Laboratory to work on the SAGE project. Before becoming interested in information technology, he earned a PhD and made valuable contributions to the field of psychoacoustics.[4] Yet, Licklider's most valuable contribution to the world of computers was his vision for the future. He has been justifiably called "computing's Johnny Appleseed" for having planted the seeds of computing in the digital age. In his various positions atop some of the most cutting-edge organizations, Licklider distributed funding to bring his many ideas to fruition. As his friend and colleague, Robert W. Taylor put it, "Lick had a vision of a better way of computing. Once upon a time, to get a computer to do your bidding, you had to punch holes in paper cards or tapes, give the paper to someone who fed it to the machine, and then go away for hours or days. Lick believed we could do better and, more than any other single individual, saw that we did."[5]

Two years before Licklider was appointed to run the IPTO, he published a paper entitled "Man-Computer Symbiosis," which outlined the need for simpler interaction between computers and their users,

---

3. Jonathan E. Nuechterlein and Philip J. Weiser, *Digital Crossroads, American Telecommunications Policy in the Internet Age* (Cambridge, MA: MIT Press, 2005). *See also* Paul Baran, "On Distributed Communications," RAND Corporation, RM-3767, 1964, http://www.rand.org/pubs/research_memoranda/RM3767.

4. In the field of psychoacoustics, Licklider is most remembered for his 1951 paper, "Duplex Theory of Pitch Perception." The paper, which has been cited hundreds of times and reprinted in 1979 in the form of a book, formed the basis for modern models of pitch perception. Robert Taylor, "In Memoriam: J. C. R. Licklider, 1915–1990," Digital Systems Research Center, August 7, 1990, http://www.hpl.hp.com/techreports/Compaq-DEC/SRC-RR-61.pdf.

5. Ibid.

foreshadowed interactive computing, and would provide a guide for decades of computer research to follow. Unlike many of his contemporaries who envisioned man being replaced by artificial intelligence, or computer-based beings, Licklider, as the title of his paper suggests, envisioned a symbiotic relationship between man and machine, where

> Men will set the goals, formulate the hypotheses, determine the criteria, and perform the evaluations. Computing machines will do the routinizable work that must be done to prepare the way for insights and decisions in technical and scientific thinking. Preliminary analyses indicate that the symbiotic partnership will perform intellectual operations much more effectively than man alone can perform them.[6]

Licklider argued that prerequisites for the achievement of this "effective, cooperative association" between man and computer included developments in computer time sharing, in memory components and organization, in programming languages, and in input and output equipment.[7] Licklider's paper was based on the work of a small research group he headed at Bolt, Beranek, and Newman, which a few years earlier had designed and built one of the earliest time-sharing machines.

Initially, others in the computer establishment criticized Licklider's ARPA program and argued time sharing was an inefficient use of computer resources and should be abandoned.[8] But Licklider persevered, and under his, and his successors', tutelage, "the IPTO funded research into advanced computer and network technologies, and commissioned thirteen research groups to perform research into technologies related to human-computer interaction and distributed systems."[9] As such, Licklider was the architect of Project MAC at MIT, which developed

---

6. "Man-Computer Symbiosis," MIT.edu, March 1960, http://groups.csail.mit.edu/medg/people/psz/Licklider.html.

7. Ibid.

8. Robert Taylor, "In Memoriam: J. C. R. Licklider, 1915–1990," (*supra* note 4).

9. "Semi-Automatic Ground Environment (SAGE)," Mitre Corporation, January 25, 2005, http://www.mitre.org/about/sage.html.

some of the first time-sharing computers, helped to conceive and fund the ARPANET, the first wide-area packet-switching network (more on this later), and funded the work of Douglas Engelbart, who founded the Augmentation Research Center at Stanford Research Institute, where he developed the On-Line System. These projects and others played pivotal roles in shaping the field of information technology and computer science, and, as Robert Taylor put it, "The leaders he chose twenty-five years ago now read like a Who's Who of computing research."[10]

In 1962, the same year he began his tenure at the IPTO, Licklider composed a series of memos that he disseminated to the other members of the office describing his ideas for a global, distributed, computer network he called the Intergalactic Computer Network. He addressed some of the memos to "Members and Affiliates of the Intergalactic Computer Network," and the memos not only describe almost all of the characteristics of today's Internet, but also had such a powerful influence on his successors at the IPTO, they generated the intellectual excitement that led to the realization of the ARPANET just seven years later.[11]

ARPANET

Understanding the history that led to ARPANET is crucial to understanding the technological underpinnings of the Internet. In many ways the ARPANET is the Model T of the Internet, but many network-neutrality proponents go even farther and regard it as the "natural state" of the Internet, which must be preserved or rediscovered through regulation. However, we argue, and believe history demonstrates, that the ARPANET is as man-made as the network congestion or algorithms that attempt to coordinate data efficiently. Like the Model T, the ARPANET is an important relic from the past,

---

10. *See* Taylor, *supra* note 4.

11. "J. C. R. Licklider and the Universal Network," Living Internet, http://www.living internet.com/i/ii_licklider.htm.

but not a practical mode of transportation in the twenty-first century. In fact, we hope to show that the modern Internet itself is not a static technology, but a constantly evolving consortium of technologies. It is that metamorphic quality that makes the Internet great, and thus any policy—like network neutrality—which seeks to "preserve" the Net in a particular state is antithetical to its stated goal.

The ARPANET was the world's first operation packet-switching computer network, the mother of today's Internet.[12] It was the original core network of a number of networks that today make up the Internet. ARPANET was based on designs by Licklider and Lawrence Roberts of MIT's Lincoln Laboratory and funded by DARPA. By the time of its completion, it incorporated the ideas, research, and inventions of many of the greatest computer scientists of the day.[13]

In commissioning the development of ARPANET, DARPA's ultimate goal was to create and test architecture for interconnected computer networks that could connect to, and communicate with, each other despite differences in architecture and interfaces of the individual networks.[14] ARPANET was to become the first of these networks. This key technological concept of "open architecture" networking, the idea that individual networks could choose their own technology according to their specific environment and use requirements, and would still be able to interwork with other networks through a meta-level "Internetworking architecture," remains the fundamental characteristic of the Internet as we know it today. Survivability of the interconnected networks was also of tremendous importance; it was essential that communications on the larger Internet would not be disrupted even if individual networks, or the gateways between them, should fail.[15]

---

12. Michael Hauben, "History of ARPANET," http://www.dei.isep.ipp.pt/~acc/docs/arpa.html.

13. *See* Waldrop, M. Mitchell, *The Dream Machine: J. C. R. Licklider and the Revolution That Made Computing Personal* (New York: Viking Press, 2001).

14. *See* Leiner, *supra* note 22 in Chapter 1.

15. As we will see, it was survivability due to national-security concerns that dictated the end-to-end architecture. Today both are outdated.

Packet Switching

At the core of ARPANET was a brand new technology called "packet switching." Today, packet switching is the dominant basis for worldwide data communications, but prior to the ARPANET, such communications networks had been based on circuit-switching technology, including the military's own communications infrastructure. Circuit switching, as utilized by the traditional telephone circuit, requires that a dedicated circuit be allocated exclusively for the duration of each communication. As such, communication is only possible between the two interconnected parties. Circuit-switched networks also require a highly centralized network with a rigid hierarchy of switches.[16] At the time work began on ARPANET, the U.S. military's communications infrastructure was largely contained within AT&T's circuit-switched network. It is easy to see why they were so eager to develop a new communications infrastructure that would not be rendered useless by one or two strategic attacks by the Soviets on central switches.

Unlike circuit-switched networks, networks using packet-switching technology disassemble information into pieces of data called "packets" and forward them through a connecting medium to a recipient computer that then reassembles them into their original form. Each data packet is an individual entity, containing its own source, destination, and reassembly information. Thus, unlike a traditional circuit-switched network, the packets comprising an e-mail message, for example, may be dispersed and transmitted via multiple paths, only to be reassembled after arriving at their final destination.[17] The idea is analogous to buying a bed or some other huge piece of furniture from IKEA. It looks like a single (and sturdy) object on the showroom floor. Then they give it to you in multiple boxes (like a thousand) and you are supposed to reassemble it into an actual bed before you die. It is the same idea with packet-switched networks, but the networks are

---

16. For a complete discussion of the architecture of circuit-switched networks, see Nuechterlein and Weiser, *supra* note 3 in this chapter.

17. *See* Leiner, *supra* note 22 in Chapter 1.

much better at the reassembly part.[18] Therefore, a data system on a packet-switching network can use one communications link to communicate with multiple computers by transmitting data as packets on the attached network link whenever that link is not in use. In this way the link is like a mailbox through which multiple pieces of mail, all addressed to different destinations, may be sent.[19] The result is that the nodes in a packet-switched network can be linked to other nodes in a nonhierarchical way that maximizes the number of routes the data can take between two points. It might sound inefficient, but you want as many different routes as possible if you're concerned the Soviets might nuke half of them. There is also no need to have a direct path; one node can hand off the data to another, and so on, until the data reaches its intended destination. It follows that if one or several nodes are not working properly, the message can simply be rerouted.[20] This is precisely how communication over ARPANET worked.

Digital versus Analog

While packet-switching technology made the transmission of data over the ARPANET (and its predecessors) efficient by allowing portions of that data to be broken up into small packets and transmitted individually from node to node over available links without tying up specific dedicated "circuits," digital technology made communication in this manner feasible. That is, it was essential that ARPANET (and any other packet-switched network for that matter) use digital rather than analog signals to actually transmit the data. Understanding the

---

18. *See* Federal Trade Commission, "Broadband Connectivity Competition Policy," 14–15, June 2007, http://www.ftc.gov/reports/broadband/v070000report.pdf [hereafter "FTC Broadband Report"].

19. David Clark, "Design Philosophy of the DARPA Internet Protocols," MIT Laboratory of Computer Science, 1988, http://groups.csail.mit.edu/ana/Publications/PubPDFs/The%20design%20philosophy%20of%20the%20DARPA%20internet%20protocols.pdf.

20. *See* Nuechterlein and Weiser, *supra* note 3.

differences between analog and digital transmissions on a basic level is not only key to understanding how the ARPANET and its successor, the Internet, work, but is fundamental to comprehending technology in general in the digital age.

Analog and digital technologies are both methods of transmitting data, in the form of an audio or video signal (although digital technology can be used to transmit virtually any kind of data) from point A to point B. However, they both use different means for accomplishing the same goal. Analog technology takes an audio or video signal, which is fundamentally continuous pressure waves of air particles, and translates it into electronic pulses. Once the communication reaches the intended receiver, it is converted back into the original waves. This is precisely how all telephone networks (which, remember, were circuit-switched networks) worked from the momentous occasion on March 10, 1876, when Alexander Graham Bell placed his first call to his assistant Mr. Watson in the next room—uttering those famous words, "Mr. Watson, come here, I want to see you"—until the mid-1980s, when digital technology was incorporated into telephone networks.[21] So, when you spoke into your phone in the 1970s or '80s—let's say to call you mother at her retirement home in Florida—your voice was carried via an analog signal through a copper wire to a transmitter, which converted the audio waves into analogous variations of electrical current. When that electrical current reached her receiver, it was converted back into audio waves, which—if her hearing aid was turned up—came out as audible sounds.

Digital technology, on the other hand, breaks the audio or video signal (or any type of data, for that matter) into a binary format, such that the data is represented by a series of 1s and 0s called bits. A series of bits is essentially an encoding of that data, just as one could describe the topography of a mountain range using a series of numbers

---

21. See Nuechterlein and Weiser, *supra* note 3, at 116. Not all telephone networks continue to be circuit-switched. For example, 4G cell-phone networks are solely packet-switched for both voice and data.

representing the longitude, latitude, and altitude of every peak, valley, crest, or slope in the range.[22] So, let's go back to your call to your mother in Florida. Nowadays, as you speak, your call might still begin with an analog transmission over a copper wire, but a digital device would rapidly convert it into an abstract mathematical representation. The digital device at your mother's end of the network would then decode the stream of 1s and 0s and translate it back into an analog sound, which presumably your mother could hear.

The device that converts the data transmission into bits is the silicon chip that is at the heart of a computer. The chip is an integrated circuit, composed of an intricate network of microscopic transistors, which opens and closes a series of individual circuits. If a circuit is open it is "on" and if it is closed it is "off." The 1s and 0s correspond to these respective states. Using this mathematical shorthand to represent data, it is easy to see how digital technology can describe *any* information, not just audio and video signals. Its potential is virtually limitless. It can describe voice, video, photographs, a single-page letter, or a two million-page document, all in a series of 1s and 0s.[23]

One tremendous benefit of digital technology over analog, and a characteristic that makes digital transmission essential over a packet-switched network, is that the quality of the transmission does not

---

22. ASCII is an example of this encoding. There are 256 characters in ASCII, most of which are letters and numbers (256 characters because that is how many different numbers you can get in a byte (8 bits): 00000000 (0) to 11111111 (255)). It is a table of 256 characters and a number for each. Someone decided that 65 should be capital A, so 65 "means" A. Sixty-five is a base 10 (decimal) number, but as a base 2 (binary) number it is 01000001 (for 8 bits). So 01000001 is A on the ASCII table (http://www .asciitable.com). Just like 01000010 (66) is B. Without the ASCII table, 01000010 could mean something entirely different. All data is encoded somehow, but audio and video use much more complicated encoding systems. *See also* Nuechterlein and Weiser, *supra* note 3, at 116.

23. Note "describe" is the right word here. There can be many different descriptions of something. My rocky ledge can be your craggy cliff, for example, and data encoding just captures one particular representation of an object.

noticeably degrade, irrespective of how far the data has to travel.[24] Digital symbols are just a series of numbers, so the sequence can be "repeated" from one device to another or from point to point to point without suffering quality. As you probably remember from making long-distance calls in the "olden days," this is not the case with analog transmissions. When you placed those calls to your mother in the 1970s or '80s, her voice often sounded distant or less clear. Sometimes she was holding the receiver upside down, but usually it was simply due to signal degradation. And overseas calls to your brother living on the Ashram in India could become very frustrating—for more than one reason. The degradation is due to the fact that the only way to transmit an analog signal long distances is to amplify the signal. The farther between the points of transmission and reception, the more the signal has the potential to fade. Additionally, any background noise or other distortions in the original signal are amplified with the rest of the transmission.

Another benefit of digital technology is that it can be compressed, meaning the information contained in the original transmission can be encoded so that elements of the transmission that remain unchanged do not have to be retransmitted. It is best to visualize this in a video transmission. Let's say you are watching—God knows why—an interview with the latest celebrity "it" girl. She is promoting her new movie, seated in a chair, in front of the promotional poster for the film. Despite her Botox, she moves—her hands at least—while she is speaking, but most of the background remains static. The encoded data that describes the background, then, does not need to be continuously retransmitted. Only short subsequent placeholders telling the receiving device that the background remains unchanged need to be retransmitted. Or you might just think of it like this: "hhhhhhhh-heeeeeeeeeelllllllllllllloooooooooooooo" can more efficiently be encoded

---

24. In fact, the quality does degrade, but so-called "error-correcting codes" check whether data has been received incorrectly and try to fix it, or trash it and ask for a new unvarnished copy. The codes are not perfect, but they generally work well.

as "h9e10l13o12."[25] Conversely, in an analog transmission, that static background information must be transmitted over and over again, many times a second. As you can imagine, compression makes digital technology extremely efficient since it conserves bandwidth, making it available for other purposes. Digital technology revolutionized the telecommunications industry, and together with packet-switching technology, formed the technological core of the ARPANET and later the Internet.

ARPANET Goes Online

UCLA student programmer Charley Kline transmitted the first communications over the ARPANET at 10:30 p.m. on October 29, 1969, from Boelter Hall 3420. Under the supervision of professor Leonard Kleinrock, Kline sent a text message from UCLA's Sigma 7 host computer to the Stanford Research Institute's SDS 940 host computer. The message was "login." But as Leonard Kleinrock describes, the first test did not go off without a hitch: "At the UCLA end, they typed in the 'l' and asked SRI if they received it; 'got the l' came the voice reply. UCLA typed in the 'o', asked if they got it, and received 'got the o'. UCLA then typed in the 'g' and the damned system CRASHED! Quite a beginning. On the second attempt it worked fine!"[26] Less than a month later, a permanent ARPANET link was established between the Interface Message Processors (IMPs) at UCLA and Stanford. Several weeks later, two more nodes, one at UC Santa Barbara and one at the University of Utah, were added to the network.

In order for computers on a network or two different networks to communicate with each other, they must use a communications

---

25. This type of encoding is also lossless, in that no data is lost when the information is encoded. This is not always the case; some compression algorithms, like those for MP3s and YouTube videos, *are* "lossy," so quality does degrade. However, the 192 Kbps bitrate used by most MP3s for sound is sampled at a rate designed to sound lossless to the human ear.

26. "ARPANET—The First Internet," Living Internet, 2000, http://www.livinginter net.com/i/ii_arpanet.htm.

protocol, or a system of digital message formats and rules for the exchange. Think of a communications protocol as a common language that each computer agrees to speak to the other when working together. In order for any two digital devices to communicate with one another, they must both use the same communications protocol.[27] Remember that digital technology allows for a sending device (say a computer in a network) to convert a signal, or encode it into a mathematical shorthand of 0s and 1s, and the communications protocol tells the receiving device (a second computer in the network) how to decode the information.[28]

The ARPANET initially used a host-to-host protocol called the Network Control Protocol (NCP), developed by S. Crocker with the Network Working Group (NWG). A functionally complete version of NCP was finalized in December 1970, and ARPANET sites completed implementing the protocol between 1971 and 1972. The adoption of NCP by ARPANET meant network users could begin to develop applications, computer software that enables the computer to perform specific tasks (like e-mail). At the same time, additional computers were being added to the ARPANET, and in October 1972, Robert Kahn organized the first large public demonstration of the ARPANET at the International Computer Communication Conference (ICCC). The demonstration was extremely successful, and that same year the first ever "hot" network application, electronic mail (e-mail), was introduced. E-mail quickly became, and remained, the largest network application for over a decade.[29]

---

27. Or to be more technical, at the least the new system must have backwards compatibility for an older system's legacy protocol.

28. *See* Nuechterlein and Weiser, *supra* note 3, at 116. Transmission Control Protocol/ Internet Protocol (TCP/IP) does not tell the receiving device how to decode *all* of the information. Instead, it tells the device how to convert the packets into a file; it does not necessarily tell the device what to do with the file once it is reassembled. The latter is handled at the application layer by a different protocol, like FTP.

29. Barry M. Leiner et al., "Brief History of the Internet," Internet Society, 2012, http://www.isoc.org/internet/history/brief.shtml.

Still, the NCP protocol had some major shortcomings that researchers knew would become serious impediments to the growth of the now rapidly expanding ARPANET network. Most notably was the protocol's complete dependence on ARPANET to provide end-to-end reliability, meaning that hosts on the ends of the network bore sole responsibility for the reliability of data transfer throughout the network. Thus, if any node within the network were disabled, the integrity of the network would be compromised.[30] Kahn, along with then assistant Stanford professor Vinton Cerf, began work on developing a versatile protocol system that would support a wide range of hardware on various networks, and provide a resilient, redundant, and decentralized system for delivering data across what they envisioned would one day be a global network of networks.[31] The result was the Transmission Control Protocol/Internet Protocol (TCP/IP) suite, which remains today the communications protocol for the Internet.

TCP/IP

The TCP/IP protocols not only define the network's communication process, they define how each unit of data should be configured and what information it must contain so that it can be interpreted correctly by the receiving computer, located somewhere else on the network. The TCP/IP protocols are, therefore, a complete system that defines how the data should then be processed, transmitted, and received on the network. The TCP component of the suite controls the disassembly and reassembly of the data packets sent from the computer server, while the IP component provides the formatting and addressing scheme for transmitting data between the sender and recipient computers.[32] While User Datagram Protocol (UDP) has gained prominence because of its capacity to achieve the steady throughput rate necessary for video,

---

30. Ibid.

31. Joe Casad, *Sams Teach Yourself TCP/IP in 24 Hours* (4th ed.) (Sams Publishing, 2008).

32. *See* "FTC Broadband Report," *supra* note 18, at 15.

voice, and gaming, it does not include any mechanism to control the integrity of its data stream. TCP is still vital for the transportation of data for which integrity is important, such as e-mail.

The TCP/IP protocol suite performs error control and flow control so that computers are able to communicate reliably with each other. In addition to controlling the flow of data, the protocols ensure that the computers on the network can identify and correct faulty data transmissions.

Layered Model of the Internet

In order to accomplish its many tasks, TCP/IP uses a modular design, which divides the system into separate components, so that each is responsible for a specific piece of the communication process, and each can function independently of one another. The individual modules are then subdivided into layered components. The most typical TCP/IP model contains five protocol layers: the Application Layer, the Transport Layer, the Network Layer, the Data Link Layer, and the Physical Layer.[33]

Each of these layers performs specific functions, and when the TCP/IP protocol software prepares a piece of data for transmission over the network, each layer on the sending computer adds a layer of information to the data that will be relevant to the corresponding layer on the receiving computer.[34]

Networks using the TCP/IP protocol suite are connected to each other through infrastructure that carries the data between the various

---

33. Note that the ARPANET model as described in RFC 871 actually describes only three layers: the Network Interface Layer, the Host-to-Host Layer, and the Process-Level/Applications Layer. M. A. Padlipsky, "Perspective on the ARPANET Reference Model," Mitre Corporation, September 1982, http://tools.ietf.org/html/rfc871; *see also* Casad, *supra* note 223, 23; *see also* Adam Thierer, "Are 'Dumb Pipe' Mandates Smart Public Policy? Vertical Integration Net Neutrality, and the Network Layers Model," *Journal on Telecommunications and High Technology Law* 3 (2005): 279–80.

34. *See* Casad, *supra* note 31, at 23–28.

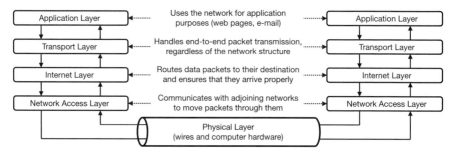

DIAGRAM 1: The four layers of the TCP/IP networking model, on top of the physical link that carries the signal transmissions.

computers. In its most simplistic form, this infrastructure is composed of gateway interface devices, called routers (they usually just look like metal boxes with electronics inside), that connect to each other by links (communication wires). So, for example, if you want to send a thank-you card via e-mail, here is how that works: The data is created at the Application Layer. The Application Layer creates connections between processes. Here, the application layer protocol, FTP, encodes your thankful message, and passes it on to the Transport Layer in a form that is readable by your recipient's e-mail client.

The Transport Layer turns those data packets into segments and creates connections between hosts. The two primary methods of doing this are with the TCP and the UDP. TCP uses a series of ports to direct data streams to correct processes, and informs both hosts through a series of messages, first, that a connection should be established, and second, which ports will be used. Under TCP, every message must return with an acknowledgment, within a certain latency window, or it will be resent. Some applications, however, are sensitive to latency, such as voice and streaming video. For these applications, it makes more sense to just deal with a garbled message than to wait for ACK commands to time out. UDP does just that; it does not wait for the ACK response. So, generally, applications that are reliability sensitive and can tolerate delay, use TCP, while applications that are latency sensitive and can tolerate unreliability, use UDP.

In the Network Layer segments are converted into datagrams. This layer facilitates the interconnection of autonomous systems to one another. Network Layer protocols are only absolutely necessary in gateways-connections between networks, not within autonomous networks. Because this layer serves as the connection vehicle for multiple networks, it must contain one agreed-upon protocol, and this is the IP. IP encompasses only a minimal amount of information, and importantly contains a type-of-service flag that promotes traffic prioritization.[35]

The protocol at the Data Link Layer is designed to govern how packets are transmitted within an autonomous network. Here, datagrams are encoded as frames. Although nodes that direct traffic are called routers at the Network Layer, at the Data Link Layer, they are known as switches. Ethernet is the most widely used Data Link protocol.

The Physical Layer is the most intuitive of all. This is the actual electrical circuitry that moves packets from one node to the next. When your message is received by your intended recipient, it is unwrapped in reverse order of its packaging so that only infrastructural elements at the same layer need to understand each other's protocol.

As previously described, networks using the TCP/IP protocol suite are connected to each other through systems of links and routers. Therefore, packets of data on the Internet are passed from one router to another via links until they reach their intended destination.[36] Most routers have several incoming and outgoing transmission links through which data arrives and is deployed. When a data packet arrives, the router uses an algorithm to decide through which outgoing link that packet should be routed. If that link is free, the packet is immediately sent out, but often the link will be busy. In such a case, the packet must be temporarily held or "buffered" in the router's memory.[37] It will be released once the designated link is finished transmitting other packets. Buffering is therefore a way that a router deals with temporary surges in traffic common on the Net. In fact, Internet traffic is often

---

35. Ibid.

36. Edward W. Felton, "Nuts and Bolts of Network Neutrality," July 2006, 1–2, http:// itpolicy.princeton.edu/pub/neutrality.pdf.

37. Ibid., 3.

described as being "bursty," characterized by periods of relatively low activity punctuated by occasional bursts of packets.[38] The reason is that when an individual is surfing the Web, for example, he or she generates little or no traffic while reading individual pages. However, once he clicks on a link, for example, the browser then needs to fetch that new page from the server and send it back to you. This generates a burst of data packets.[39] Because the router does not have unlimited buffering capabilities, continued congestion may mean that the router is forced to either reroute the packets or drop them all together. Such on-again, off-again delay in individual packet transmission is called "jitter."

The resulting characteristics of the TCP/IP protocol are that it typically routes traffic on a first-in, first-out basis, unless the network is queued to individual IP addresses. So, if it is buffering packets because a particular link is busy, once that link is free it will release the packets in the order in which they were received, unless it detects that one IP address has opened several streams to strategically gain more bandwidth than its fair allocation.[40] However, as we will discuss later, first-in, first-out is not *mandatory*, and packets can be prioritized. Additionally, the TCP/IP protocol typically functions on what is called a "best-efforts" basis. This means that the protocol does not guarantee a particular quality of service, or that the "network makes no specific commitments about transfer characteristics, such as speed, delays, jitter, or loss."[41] As we will see, many proponents of network neutrality argue that these two characteristics of the TCP/IP protocol—its first-in, first-out and best-efforts transmission features—demonstrate an inherent neutrality of the Internet that must be preserved. We disagree.

While the collaboration between DARPA and academic researchers had initially developed the ARPANET for Department of Defense and research purposes, the utility of computer networking, particularly as

---

38. Ibid., 4.

39. Ibid., 4.

40. Bittorrent, for example, engages in this practice to achieve higher throughput rates.

41. David Clark et al., "New Arch: Future Generation Internet Architecture," December 2003. 25, http:/www.isi.edu/newarch/iDOCS/final.finalreport.pdf.

e-mail applications became more sophisticated, was not lost on other governmental and academic organizations. Throughout the 1970s and 1980s governmental agencies, including the Department of Energy and NASA, built their own networks. In 1985, the United States National Science Foundation (NSF) commissioned the construction of the NSFNET network, a long-distance, wide-area network. Initially, the network was created to provide long-distance access to five supercomputer centers around the country.[42] Working in collaboration with a number of private-sector organizations, including Merit Network, Inc., IBM, and MCI, NSF soon set a goal of connecting thirteen geographically dispersed sites. NSFNET was completed in 1988.

As we will discuss below, the physical infrastructure of the modern Internet, born in the NSFNET era, consists of pipes, called links, and switches, called nodes or routers. The pipes themselves fall into two categories. There are *transport* facilities, which are also called Internet *backbone* facilities, and *access* facilities. *Backbone* facilities, like NSFNET, connect one node to another and one network to another. Access facilities are the "last mile" pipes that connect an end user's computer to a network node, which in turn connects that user to the Internet.[43]

As work on the NSFNET backbone was being completed, so too was work on several other commercial backbones or networks. And while the NSFNET was the largest backbone of the day, it enforced an "acceptable use policy" that precluded its use for purposes "not in support of Research and Education," which meant that the growing number of privately owned networks were not permitted to exchange commercial data traffic with each other using the NSFNET backbone.[44] The direct, and intended, result was that in 1991, several commercial backbone operators, including PSINet, UUNET,

---

42. Michael Kende, "The Digital Handshake: Connecting Internet Backbones," FCC, Office of Plans and Policy, Working Paper No. 32, September 2000, 5, http://transition.fcc.gov/Bureaus/OPP/working_papers/oppwp32.pdf.

43. *See* "Digital Crossroads," *supra* note 3. *See also* Kende, *supra* note 42, at 3.

44. *See* Leiner, *supra* note 22 in Chapter 1, at 7.

and CerfNET, banded together to establish the Commercial Internet Exchange (CIX) to interconnect their own networks via a router housed in Santa Clara, California.[45] The NSF, in order to encourage the growth of overlapping competing backbones, designed a system of geographically dispersed Network Access Points (NAPs) similar to the CIX configuration. The backbones could interconnect with each other at any or all of the NAPs. The four original NAPs were in San Francisco (operated by PacBell), Chicago (operated by BellCore and Ameritech), New York (operated by SprintLink), and Washington, D.C. (operated by MFS), and each consisted of a shared switch, or local area network (LAN), which was used to exchange traffic.[46] In 1993, the NSF had determined that the Internet was outpacing the organization's own ability to manage it, and turned management of the backbone to competing commercial backbone operations. By 1995, these commercial backbones had permanently replaced the NSFNET. And so, by 1996, the Internet was effectively privatized.

The World Wide Web

Throughout the 1990s, the exponential growth of the Internet was fueled in large part by the invention of the World Wide Web by British computer scientist Tim Berners-Lee. Many people use the terms Internet and World Wide Web (or web) interchangeably, although incorrectly. The Internet, as previously discussed, is a global system of interconnected computer networks. The web is but one of the services (or applications) that runs on the Internet. "It is a collection of textual documents and other resources, linked by hyperlinks and URLs, transmitted by web browsers and web servers."[47]

The World Wide Web was not an instant success since it was initially difficult to maneuver from website-to-website. The tipping point

---

45. *See* Kende, *supra* note 42, at 5; *see also* Leiner, *supra* note 22, at 7.

46. *See* Kende, *supra* note 42, at 5.

47. Lucian Polo, "World Wide Web Technology Architecture: A conceptual analysis," GNU, 2003, http://newdevices.com/publicaciones/www/.

for the application was the introduction in 1993 of the web browser Mosaic by a team led by Marc Andreessen at the National Center for Supercomputing Applications at the University of Illinois.[48] A web browser is a software application for receiving, presenting, and travers- ing an information resource (like a web page, image, or video) on the World Wide Web. Websites are really collections of files posted on web servers, high-capacity computers that store or host the material. When a user wants to access a website, he or she typically clicks on a link, or types in the address of that website (like www.google.com). That address is called a URL, or a uniform resource locator. Browsers cannot directly access an address like www.google.com because it is not descriptive enough. Domain Name System (DNS) servers con- vert www.google.com into a specific IP address, like 72.14.204.103 (or even more accurately, something like 2001:4860:b002::68, which is an IPv6 address). So, when you type in www.google.com, the browser first asks the DNS server what IP it means, then contacts the server at that IP and asks for the web page hosted there. There are only so many DNS servers out there, so the browser knows which they are and how to get in touch with them. It identifies the server address and file location where a particular web page can be found. A browser translates the request into code that the server can understand; the server then sends out a burst of code in response, and the browser translates the code into words, images, and even sounds that the user can understand.

The Mosaic browser was the first user-friendly browser, because it was the first to incorporate graphics into the user interface. This made it more intuitive for laypeople to use. And this was precisely as Marc Andreessen intended, as he wanted to democratize the web.[49] But what Andreessen did not foresee was the impact of his application on the industry. At the time, Andreessen did not take his Internet-related work

---

48. *See* "Mosaic—The First Global Web Browser," Living Internet, http://www.living internet.com/w/wi_mosaic.htm.

49. David Sheff, "Crank It Up," *Wired* 8.08, August 2000, http://www.wired.com /wired/archive/8.08/loudcloud.html?pg=1&topic=&topic_set=.

that seriously, since the next big thing—and the technology that all the big companies, from Microsoft to Silicon Graphics, were working on—was interactive TV. As Andreessen describes, "The work was fun, but no one was taking it seriously. It was nerds and scientists and typing. All that crap. That's what everyone thought—Microsoft and everybody else. I just thought, 'I may as well work on this now, and then when I get out of college I can go work for Silicon Graphics or Time Warner or TCI.'"[50]

Funding for Mosaic came from the U.S. High-Performance Computing and Communications Initiative and the High Performance Computing and Communication Act of 1991. The High Performance Computing Act, known as the "Gore bill," was developed by then-Senator Al Gore and led to the establishment of the National Information Infrastructure, which came to be known as the "information superhighway."[51] The information superhighway was, and continues to be, a "seamless web of public and private communications networks, interactive services, interoperable hardware and software, computers, databases, and consumer electronics to put vast amounts of information at users' fingertips."[52] Then-President George H. W. Bush predicted that the national information infrastructure would "unlock the secrets of DNA, open up foreign markets to free trade, and a promise of cooperation between government, academia, and industry."[53] So, to clarify, Al Gore did *not* invent the Internet, but he *did* play a pivotal role in establishing the infrastructure and funding that would support it.

Mosaic was released free to the public. This was key, not only for Mosaic's success, but for the success of the Internet in general: so little was patented that anyone could take a platform and add onto it, improve it, or develop other applications to work with it. For example, around this time there were two protocols for accessing the web:

---

50. David Sheff, *supra* note 49.

51. 15 U.S.C. § 5527 (1991).

52.   http://www.sccs.swarthmore.edu/users/08/ajb/tmve/wiki100k/docs/National _Information_Infrastructure.html.

53. "Remarks on Signing the High-Performance Computing Act of 1991," George Bush Presidential Library, December 9, 1991, bushlibrary.tamu.edu.

Gopher and HTTP. HTTP was released free of royalty, and Gopher was patented and licensed for profit. Long story short, web page URLs begin with http://, not gopher://. Many network-neutrality proponents, Jonathan Zittrain most notably, argue that the increase of patented technology in the Internet and related markets today threatens to turn the Net into a maze of "walled gardens," where one's access to Internet features will be limited to the proprietary technologies of the service provider. We disagree (and will discuss in greater detail later) with the probability of the walled-garden scenario, and believe the goal of improving service is equally if not more important than interface technologies.

After releasing Mosaic, Andreessen went to work for a small software company in California. But he was soon approached by Jim Clark, the man who had famously founded Silicon Graphics. Clark, of course, had heard about Andreessen's work on Mosaic, and wanted to speak with him about new business ideas. The two met, and one night, after several bottles of Burgundy, in what would become a piece of industry folklore, Andreessen suggested, "We could always create a Mosaic killer—build a better product and build a business around it."[54] Clark would quickly become one of Andreessen's foremost mentors, and soon after, the two founded Netscape, a computer services company that did just that—dramatically improved upon Mosaic— with its Netscape Navigator browser.[55]

On August 9, 1995, Netscape went public in what proved to be an incredibly successful initial public offering (IPO). Initially, Netscape's stock was set to be offered at $14 a share, but at the last minute, a decision was made to double the offering to $28 per share. The stock's value quickly soared to $75 on the first day of trading, eventually closing at $58.25 with a whopping market value of $2.9 billion.[56] The company's revenues continued to double every quarter in 1995, with its overwhelming success landing Andreessen on the cover of

---

54. *See* Sheff, *supra* note 49.
55. Ibid.
56. Ibid.

Time magazine.[57] Netscape had become the fastest-growing software company in history, and its success directly led to the Internet boom of the 1990s, spawning hundreds of Internet start-ups and galvanizing the computer mega-corporations like Microsoft, Sun, Oracle (now SunOracle), SGI, and others, to refocus their energy away from interactive TV and toward the Internet.[58] Furthermore, the combination of the availability of this great new browser, with the billions of dollars suddenly being poured into the industry, resulted in the rapid advancement and availability of Internet-based applications for public consumption.[59] And the public was hungry. The growth of the Internet has continued to burgeon over the last decade. By the beginning of 2011, it was estimated that the number of Internet users had reached 2.08 billion.[60] That growth will be stymied if the Internet is not left to evolve freely, without the FCC and its restrictive Open Internet Order. We hope to have shown that the Internet was born and continued to develop through the cooperation of individuals, academic institutions, and government agencies. As we will show next, the modern Internet has evolved in adherence to certain design principles and protocols that themselves have evolved as new technologies and ideas became available. The only way to ensure the continued growth of the Net is to permit it to flourish freely, without mandating network neutrality and forcing it to conform to the singular vision of the FCC, an agency that has already proven itself frightfully shortsighted.

The Internet Today

The Internet is not a single network, but a network of networks, operated and owned by a variety of companies, varying in size and function and connecting millions of end users. Generally, there are four catego-

---

57. "The Golden Geeks," *Time*, February 19, 1996, http://www.time.com/time/covers /0,16641,1101960219,00.html.

58. *See* Sheff, *supra* note 49.

59. Ibid.

60. "Number of Internet Users Reaches Two Billion," PHYS.Org, January 26, 2011, http://www.physorg.com/news/2011-01-internet-users-worldwide-billion.html.

ries of Internet participants: end-users (individual people who connect to the Net); Internet content providers (ICPs) (like YouTube, *New York Times*, and Facebook); Internet Service Providers (ISPs), which provide your Internet service; and Internet backbone providers (backbones that connect network to network). When a user logs on to the Internet with the intent of purchasing something from Amazon.com (a content provider), the user accesses the Internet via an ISP, which could be a cable company (such as Comcast, RCN, or Verizon) or a content storage company (such as EarthLink). Amazon.com, in turn, is connected to its own ISPs through a dedicated line. ISPs are generally connected to other ISPs through backbone providers. Backbones own or lease national or international high-speed fiber-optic networks connected by routers, which deliver traffic to and from their customers.[61]

Narrowband to Broadband

Until very recently, users connected to the Internet using a so-called narrowband dial-up connection. An individual's computer was connected to a computer modem, which connected to an ordinary phone line. To connect to the Internet, the modem placed a phone call. Remember that annoying beeping followed by various degrees of fuzz? That was the sound of your computer dialing up the ISP's local access number through the phone circuit switch. The ISP then converted the call's analog signal to a digital one and sent it onto a packet-switched network, which connected the user to the Internet. Since these dial-up connections used the phone companies' networks, the speed of the connection was limited to the network's narrow bandwidth, which typically ranged between 28.8 Kbps and 56 Kbps.[62] The relatively slow speed of such a connection meant delays in connects and loading time.

In recent years, faster and more robust connections have become available to the public through broadband connections. Cable modem

---

61. *See* Kende, *supra* note 42, at 3.
62. *See* Nuechterlein and Weiser, *supra* note 3, at 135.

or a digital subscriber service (DSL) allows end users to connect directly to a packet-switched network, without that intermediate stop at the circuit switch. The FCC defines broadband as "services that enable consumers to download content at actual speeds of at least 4 Mbps and to upload content at speeds of at least 1 Mbps over the broadband provider's network."[63] Unlike dial-up connections, a broadband connection is always "on," so you can access the Internet almost instantly. It is also much easier to surf the web and download content off the Net, since everything happens more quickly. Most importantly, broadband allows users to use bandwidth-intensive applications like games, video streaming, and even make phone calls over the Internet using VoIP (voice over Internet protocol). And of course, it is true that these applications were only developed once broadband became available, since you simply cannot stream video or place a phone call over the Internet using a dial-up connection.

"Open" Internet Architecture and the End-to-End Design Principle

The layered model is related to two other key design principles that characterize—or at least have largely characterized—the architecture of the modern Internet: its open architecture, and its end-to-end design. The two are closely related. First, the architecture of the Internet is "open" in the sense that no one owns the core protocols—TCP/IP, HTTP, SFTP, or SCP—at the logical layer of the Internet. Thus, anyone who wishes to develop a website incorporating content, or develop a new application like a web browser, or develop a search engine can do so using TCP/IP. It also means that anyone is free to develop complementary products or services on the other layers.[64]

---

63. Federal Communications Commission, "Seventh Broadband Progress Report," 2010, http://www.fcc.gov/reports/seventh-broadband-progress-report.

64. *See generally* Nuechterlein and Weiser, *supra* note 3, at 120.

The next key characteristic of early Internet architecture is its "end-to-end" design principle. The idea is that complex application functions, or intelligence, should not be built into the routers and links at the core of the Internet but should be reserved for applications running on computers at the edges of the network. To preserve the end-to-end design principle, proponents of neutrality contend that the routers and links should be "dumb," so that the only thing they do is transmit data packets. The argument in favor of the end-to-end principle is that it minimizes the potential for transmission and interoperability problems that could arise by introducing technological complexity into the middle of the network.[65] The principle also gives maximum control to the users, and content and application providers at the edge of the networks.

It is fair to say, as network-neutrality proponents will argue, that the original characteristics of the Internet—including its decentralized open architecture, its equally decentralized, resilient, and redundant TCP/IP communications protocol, and its end-to-end design—were inherent to the Internet's success and phenomenal growth. However, we will argue that elevating these principles to *philosophies* requiring a *regulatory mandate*, as network-neutrality proponents do, is a grave mistake. Mandating adherence to the traditional modes of Internet interaction or interconnection will—without a doubt—stifle competition, and ultimately harm all aspects of the Internet experience for businesses and end users alike.

Adherence to the end-to-end principle makes sense in many cases; it is appealing because it makes communication over the Internet via TCP/IP the quintessential form of common carriage.[66] But it is an incredibly inefficient, seemingly archaic medium for a plethora of new real-time applications like VoIP, video conferencing, interactive

---

65. *See* Felton, *supra* note 36.

66. *See* Nuechterlein and Weiser, *supra* note 3, at 124; *see also* Christopher S. Yoo, "Would Mandating Broadband Network Neutrality Help or Hurt Competition? A Comment on the End-to-End Debate," *Journal on Telecommunications and High Technology Law* 3 (2004): 26, http://www.jthtl.org/content/articles/V3I1/JTHTLv3i1_Yoo.PDF.

gaming, and telemedicine, because it provides no assurance that data will arrive in time for such applications to function properly. In many respects, end-to-end is simply out of date.[67] It seems intuitive that congestion should be managed by an arbiter with the ability to see congestion throughout the network. Yet end users who bear the responsibility for congestion management have no ability to see any network traffic besides their own.

The fact is the Internet has evolved at a mind-shuddering pace, perpetually growing more complex and dynamic. New technologies— either not imagined in the Net's nascence, or at that time seemingly the stuff of science fiction—today pose equally perplexing challenges to network providers and engineers. Consider again VoIP, fifteen or even five years ago, would you have envisioned yourself making telephone calls over the Internet? What about watching television shows or movies on the Net? And maybe today you are still content with leaving such indulgences to the true "techies," or your kids for that matter, and will remain satisfied with your landline telephone and good old-fashioned high-definition flat-screen TV; however, the fact is that these technologies are already widely available to the masses. Moreover, to some extent now, and certainly in the not-so-distant future, telemedicine will play a large role in how your maladies are diagnosed and treated. As these technologies evolve and more people depend on the Internet for a wider variety of applications, the Internet—from its architecture and topology to the business relationships that characterize it—must be allowed to evolve as well. Network neutrality will hinder the growth of the Net and thus stifle improvements that benefit anyone who logs on.

The Evolving Internet

Let us begin with the architecture of the Internet. The architects of the NSFNET backbone designed it as a tripartite structure.[68] At the top

---

67. *See* Nuechterlein and Weiser, *supra* note 3, at 124.

68. Christopher S. Yoo, "Innovations in the Internet's Architecture That Challenge the Status Quo," *Journal on Telecommunications and High Technology Law* 8 (2004): 81,

of that structure was the NSFNET backbone itself, which at its peak connected sixteen research facilities across the country. The middle of the structure consisted of regional networks that initially were typically operated by university consortia or state-university partnerships.[69] These regional networks linked campus networks to the major computing centers. At the bottom of the structure were campus networks run by the individual universities.[70] As a consequence of this tripartite structure, packets traversing the network would follow a parallel path up and then back down the hierarchy as they moved from their initiator to their intended recipient. For example, let's say a researcher at one university requested a document from another. The request would move from the campus network where it was initiated, to the regional network with which the campus network was associated. The regional network would then hand off the request to the NSFNET backbone, which in turn would hand it off to the regional network with which the recipient campus network was affiliated, and finally to the recipient campus network.[71]

When the NSFNET was privatized in 1997, the network (the Internet) retained that same basic structure, although the NSFNET backbone itself was replaced by a series of private backbone providers that interconnected with each other at four public network access points called NAPs. The regional networks in the middle tier of the hierarchy evolved into regional Internet Service Providers (ISPs). The campus networks at the bottom of the hierarchy were replaced by last-

---

http://lsr.nellco.org/cgi/viewcontent.cgi?article=1293&context=upenn_wps&sei-redir
=1&referer=http%3A%2F%2Fwww.google.com%2Furl%3Fsa%3Dt%26rct%3Dj
%26q%3Dchristopher%2520yoo%2520innovations%2520in%2520the%2520
internet%27s%2520architecture%2520that%26source%3Dweb%26cd%3D3%26
ved%3D0CDYQFjAC%26url%3Dhttp%253A%252F%252Flsr.nellco.org%252
Fcgi%252Fviewcontent.cgi%253Farticle%253D1293%2526context%253
Dupenn_wps%26ei%3D56aGT9TKKaaI8gGyuYi_CA%26usg%3DAFQjCNHE
QySJNQd6gWL-4RlNYzilR9V3MQ#search=%22christopher%20yoo%20
innovations%20internets%20architecture%22.

69. Ibid.
70. Ibid.
71. Ibid., 82.

mile providers that transported traffic from local distribution facilities, in individual cities, to the residences and businesses of end users.[72] So, traffic on the newly privatized Internet continued to follow the hierarchical path of its precursor. Thus, a request initiating from an end user would travel from the last-mile provider to the regional ISP, which was still connected to a single backbone. The regional ISP would hand the traffic off to the backbone, which in turn would hand it off to a regional ISP, who would hand it to the last-mile provider associated with the recipient.[73]

The early Internet was also characterized by relatively simplistic business relationships. End users purchased Internet access for flat-rate pricing, meaning they could use as much bandwidth as they wanted and the price would remain the same (however, many early ISPs charged hourly rates).[74] In today's world, where users are reluctant to switch wireless providers lest they lose their legacy limitless data plans, the notion of a flat-rate price for bandwidth is enticing. Indeed, most wireless providers are even abolishing legacy limitless data plans.

Additionally, relationships between network providers and backbone providers generally fit into two categories: *peering* and *transit* relationships. While such arrangements are still common, as we will see, they no longer amount to an exhaustive categorization of business relationships on the Net. Tier 1 backbones (or backbones of relatively the same market stature) typically entered into *peering* agreements in which they exchanged traffic on a settlement-free basis, with no money exchanging hands.[75] Tier 1 backbones are the largest network providers and include AT&T, Centurylink (formerly Qwest), and Sprint, among others. This hand-off normally occurred using a strategy called "hot potato routing," which forwards the packet down the path with the most minimal delays.[76] Since no money changes hands, peering relationships reduce transaction costs for both "peers" involved in the arrangement. It fol-

72. Ibid.
73. Ibid., 82.
74. Ibid., 82.
75. Ibid., 84; *see also* Nuechterlein and Weiser, *supra* note 3, at 132.
76. Nuechterlein and Weiser, *supra* note 3, at 132; *see* Kende, *supra* note 42.

lows that such a relationship works only if the backbones are relatively the same size, exchanging similar levels of traffic. Thus, the agreements typically stipulate that each peer must maintain a minimum amount of traffic and that inbound and outbound traffic not exceed a certain ratio.[77] Smaller network providers who are unable to meet the standards of a peering agreement typically entered into *transit* agreements with larger providers, in which they paid the larger backbone to provide connectivity to the rest of the Internet. In this sense, the smaller backbone becomes a wholesale customer of the larger network. Additionally, the larger backbone then routes traffic from its customer to its own peering partners.[78] Yet, the architecture of the Internet, with regard to both its topology and the business relationships that characterize the interconnection between these networks, is rapidly changing.

Backbones and ISPs have increasingly begun to enter into more complex interconnection agreements, which deviate both from the strict tripartite hierarchy of the early Internet and from network neutrality. Still, backbone agreements are generally immune from network-neutrality requirements, a distinction that is as fortuitous for the parties involved as it is arbitrary.

Because of increased congestion in the NAPs, the backbones themselves began to exchange traffic at private interconnection points.[79] Smaller, regional ISPs have also begun to enter into two new kinds of interconnection relationships called *multihoming* and *secondary peering*. Multihoming can generally be described as a practice in which regional ISPs, in order to protect themselves from service outages and limit their vulnerability to potential exertions of market power by the respective backbones, connect to more than one backbone.[80]

---

77. *See* Yoo, *supra* note 63, at 84; *see also* Vincent T. Cerf, "Computer Networking: Global Infrastructure for the 21st Century," Computing Research Association (CRA), 1997, http://www.cs.washington.edu/homes/lazowska/cra/networks.html; *see also* Kende, *supra* note 42, at 3.

78. *See* Kende, *supra* note 42, at 7.

79. *See* Yoo, *supra* note 68, at 86; *see also* Kende, *supra* note 42, at XX.

80. Yoo, *supra* note 68, at 86.

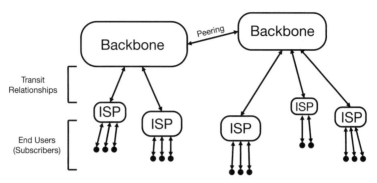

DIAGRAM 2: Example of the early Internet tripartite hierarchy, based on peering and transit relationships between backbones, ISPs, and end-users.

As discussed above, not all ISPs maintain enough volume to peer with Tier 1 backbones. Instead of entering into transit agreements, which obligate the ISPs to pay for the interconnection with a backbone, these ISPs entered into peering relationships with other regional ISPs and agreed to exchange traffic on a settlement-free basis. This practice is known as *secondary peering*, and is particularly beneficial to the ISPs because they are ostensibly able to pass their savings on to their end users. Secondary peering provides the ISP with additional control over the quality of its network. Consequently, secondary peering provides two additional benefits to ISPs and consumers: 1) it often reduces the number of hops needed for a particular packet to reach its intended destination; and 2) it subjects ISPs to bilateral rather than multiparty negotiations.[81] Multihoming and secondary peering collectively are beneficial to the entire network since they necessarily make the network more robust by creating an increased number of paths through which network nodes can interconnect, and decrease the market power of the top-tier backbones.[82]

Compare to:

81. Ibid.
82. Ibid.

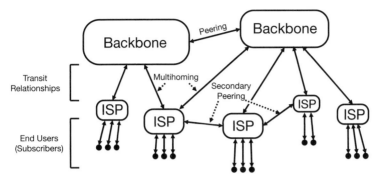

DIAGRAM 3: A more modern Internet architecture illustrating multihoming and secondary peering relationships.

These new interconnection relationships have also changed some of the business relationships entered into by ISPs. For example, secondary peering reduces the scope of transit services an ISP needs to purchase since that relationship provides the ISP access to the customers served by its secondary peering partner. As a result, instead of entering into traditional transit agreements, the ISP will often negotiate a partial transit agreement that allows it to purchase transit only to the portions of the Internet not covered by its secondary peering relationships.[83] Partial transit agreements are also beneficial to ISPs already engaged in peering contracts but who find that, for example, its inbound traffic far exceeds its outbound to the point that it risks violating the terms of its peering agreement. Such an ISP may increase its outbound traffic by entering into a partial transit agreement with another ISP that covers outbound traffic only. Conversely, it may reduce its inbound traffic by buying partial transit for its outbound traffic.[84]

Paid peering, also called settlement-based peering, is identical to free peering in terms of function, but requires one party to submit payment to the other. Such arrangements are particularly useful when the Tier 1 ISPs involved share similar costs associated with traffic flow.

---

83. *See* Yoo, *supra* note 68, at 95.
84. Ibid.

As the Internet has evolved, backbones have begun to serve two different categories of Tier 1 ISPs: "eyeball"-heavy broadband access networks that serve end users, such as AT&T, Verizon, and Comcast; and "content"-heavy networks that serve content providers, such as Abovenet and Cogent.[85]

The cost of operating the content networks is relatively low, since they typically only require a single high-speed line to a small number of businesses. However, the costs associated with operating an "eyeball" network are high, since it requires wiring and upgrading equipment in hundreds of neighborhoods. Additionally, the networks have asymmetric traffic flows. End users on "eyeball" networks send relatively small amounts of traffic upstream to content networks, which in turn send rather traffic-dense replies. Since the two types of networks have symbiotic relationships—end users connect to the Internet to access the content, and content providers depend on end users for advertising or subscription revenue—paid peering allows network providers to charge differential prices to both end users and content and application providers to balance out the differing costs associated with the two-sided market.[86]

New business relationships are also emerging between network providers and end users. A tremendous force influencing the desirability and necessity of such relationships is the growing importance of peer-to-peer (P2P) technologies.[87] P2P is a favorable platform for supporting a wide and increasingly important array of Internet-based applications. Unlike the traditional client-server architecture, P2P technologies use architecture in which each user at the edge of the network simultaneously serves as both an end user and a mini-server.[88] In a client-server architecture, end users send data requests for content stored on large servers at central locations, to which the servers respond with larger bursts of data. In P2P architecture, the rate of

---

85. Faratin et al., "The Growing Complexity of Internet Interconnection," *Communications and Strategies* 72 (2008): 58.

86. Ibid.; Yoo, *supra* note 68, at 90–91.

87. *See* Yoo, *supra* note 68.

88. Ibid.

traffic between connected computers ranges from steady streams to rapid bursts of activity. Consequently, it is difficult to systematically predict congestion.[89]

The peer-to-peer architecture is particularly desirable for users interested in downloading media-rich content like audio and video because P2P applications can obtain portions of the data from hundreds or thousands of different computers on the network instead of relying on transmission from a single, possibly distant server. Thus, in P2P networks, end users provide resources, including computing power, storage space, and even bandwidth. As more end users, or nodes, join the network, its capacity increases.

The problem with P2P technologies, at least from the network provider's perspective, is that their networks are not built to support the amount of bandwidth P2P networks enable users to consume. The result is that users on a P2P network can cause significant increases in congestion in certain areas of the network.[90] Remember that traditional "eyeball" networks are built with a lot of bandwidth from the servers to the end user, but little bandwidth going in the opposite direction. The reason, again, is because traditional applications only require bursts of traffic from end user to server (when downloading a web page, for example), and larger amounts of traffic (in the form of the requested information) from server to end user. Since computers using P2P applications act as mini-servers themselves, the users and thus the P2P architecture can put a lot of strain on the uploading capacity of the network. Furthermore, unlike traditional applications that require a user to actually click on links for example to generate traffic, as long as a computer in a P2P network is on, it can continue to generate traffic.

Congestion from P2P technologies is particularly taxing on last-mile networks that share bandwidth locally, such as cable modem and wireless broadband systems. For example, users connecting to the Internet via cable modem share bandwidth with the other households

89. Ibid.
90. Ibid.

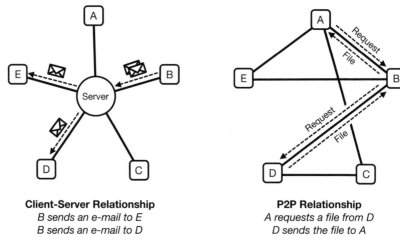

Client-Server Relationship
B sends an e-mail to E
B sends an e-mail to D

P2P Relationship
A requests a file from D
D sends the file to A

DIAGRAM 4: Comparison of client-server (centralized) relationships vs.
peer-to-peer (decentralized) relationships. In the client-server example,
if B wants to send e-mails to D and E, B first sends the messages to the
server, and the server relays the messages to their destinations. In the P2P
model, since A and D are not directly connected, if A wants a file from D,
A must first relay the request through B, and D must relay the file back to A
through B.

in their neighborhood connected to the same ISP's network. Service
can slow down significantly, even if only a handful of neighbors are
using P2P applications at the same time.[91]

As beneficial as P2P technologies are, their bandwidth-hogging
characteristics have forced network providers to search for, and experiment with, new ways to price their services and manage congestion.
Traditionally, network providers have charged end users a flat fee for
their services, and charged content and application providers prices
that increase according to bandwidth consumed.[92] These models fail
when P2P technologies are involved. With regard to end users, as
discussed above, a single end user using a P2P application can use
a tremendous amount of bandwidth and therefore degrade service
for a great many other users in his or her immediate area. Since that

---

91. Ibid., 93–94.
92. Ibid.

user pays a flat fee—the same flat fee that his computer-challenged neighbor pays—his financial burden is not proportional to his use of network resources. The result is that there is no pricing mechanism in place to deter congestion, and no increased revenues to the ISP that might allow for build-outs in the bandwidth capacity of the network.[93]

Moreover, ISPs have traditionally charged content and application providers incremental fees based on bandwidth consumption associated with downloading the content or application from the server. In the traditional client-server architecture, that download would have to pass through one link (at the server) and was thus measurable. So, this pricing model also reflects a reasonable approximation of that content or application's contribution to network congestion.[94] However, this model also fails when P2P technologies are involved. For example, let's say end user Tom downloads a song off of iTunes and stores it on his computer. The content provider, iTunes, would then be charged by the service provider for the resulting traffic. However, let's say that Tom then joins a P2P network where 100 other end-users ask for and are able to download that same song from Tom's computer. Since those downloads no longer pass through the link, the network provider is unable to charge the content provider for the significant additional network congestion attributable to that content. Considering these unique characteristics of P2P technologies, it is easier to see why they pose such a challenge to network operators trying to manage congestion on their networks. It is also not surprising that the same network operators have been experimenting with new pricing models and congestion-management practices in response to this unique set of challenges. They must be permitted to continue to do so as they strive to improve their networks for all users. Yet, as we will show, the FCC's network-neutrality rules threaten to severely limit their ability to do so, since many of these models are not "neutral."

P2P technology is also being used in another increasingly important development in Internet architecture, the advent of content delivery

---

93. Ibid.
94. Ibid.

networks (CDNs). It is useful to think of the Internet as divided into three different kinds of networks. As we have already discussed, the first would be the backbone networks that use fiber-optic cable to connect networks—including other backbone providers, the networks of large businesses, and access provider networks—all over the world.[95] The second kind of network would be the access providers' networks, which bridge the gap at the "last mile" between most end users and the backbone network. The third kind of network would be the edge networks. Edge networks can be divided into two subcategories: end-user networks, which would include home WiFi networks, and corporate private networks, called local area networks (LANs). The second category of edge networks is composed of those networks operated by major Internet services companies. Such networks are composed of giant server farms and caching facilities, and are also referred to as overlay networks because they are massive and are built over the backbone networks (P2P networks are overlay networks).[96] The edge companies that own these networks are typically mega online retailers like Amazon.com and eBay, Internet behemoth Google, or service providers like Akamai and Level-3.[97] A CDN is one type of such network and consists of strategically placed and geographically dispersed servers at various nodes of a network. Popular CDNs include Akamai and Limelight. The CDNs contain copies of data from specific content providers. The CDN stores or "caches" the copies of this data, making it available upon demand from end users. When an end user requests data (say a web page) from a content provider using a CDN, that request is redirected to the CDN, which because of its strategic placement is often much closer to the requesting end user than would be the case if the content provider used a central server.

---

95. Jonathan E. Neuchterlein, "Antitrust Oversight of an Antitrust Dispute: An Institutional Perspective on the Net Neutrality Debate," *Journal on Telecommunications and High Technology Law* 7 (2009): 23.

96. Ibid.

97. Ibid.

The benefits of CDNs are enormous, and we will discuss CDNs in more detail later. For now, it is enough to note that because CDN servers are strategically placed on the edges of the network, they decrease the load on interconnects between networks, peers, and backbones. The resulting benefits for the content and network providers and end users include a freeing up of network capacity, lower delivery costs, and increases in access bandwidth and network redundancy and reduced access latency.[98]

While P2P technology is not a traditional CDN technology, it is being used increasingly in this context. It is particularly valuable when a content provider must quickly deliver data in high demand like the latest episode of a television show or a software patch. The benefits of CDN technology are enormous to network providers at the core of the Internet, to content and application providers, and to end users at the edges of the network. Still, it is important to note that use of CDNs necessitates that similar packets traversing the Internet will not necessarily do so in a totally neutral fashion, although it is unclear whether network neutrality would actually apply to CDNs.

As we have seen, the development of new technologies like VoIP, interactive gaming, P2P platforms, and telemedicine have necessitated changes in many of the features thought to define and distinguish the Internet itself. This is also true with the Net's communication protocol: TCP or UDP/IP. For example, as discussed earlier, routers dealing with continued congestion are sometimes forced to either reroute packets or drop them all together, causing an on-again, off-again delay in individual packet transmission called "jitter." Jitter was generally thought to be a fact of life with regards to the TCP/IP protocol suite, inherent in its first-in, first-out and best-efforts methodology for transmitting data. And initially, at least, jitter was just not a huge issue for end users. But some of the newest Internet technologies are

---

98. *See* Markus Hofmann and Leland R. Beaumont, *Content Networking: Architecture, Protocols, and Practice* (Amsterdam: Elsevier Science, 2005).

less forgiving. As Edward W. Felton, director of Princeton University's Center for Information Technology Policy (CITP), describes:

> If you're downloading a large file, you care more about the average packet arrival rate (the download speed) than about when any particular packet arrives. If you're browsing the web, modest jitter will cause, at worst, a slight delay in downloading some pages. If you're watching streaming video, your player will buffer the stream so jitter won't bother you much. On the other hand, applications like online gaming or Internet telephony (VoIP), which rely on steady streaming of interactive, real-time communication, can suffer a lot if there is jitter. Users report that VoIP services like Vonage and Skype can become unusable when subjected to network jitter.[99]

The Internet is an ever-evolving and increasingly dynamic network of networks, and the emergence of new applications and technologies accessible over the Net often simultaneously create an explosion of benefits and equally dynamic challenges. Many of these challenges, like congestion, were predictable to the Net's founding fathers, but equally as many were unimaginable. While the distinct characteristics that defined the early Internet undoubtedly led to its tremendous success, it is also clear that the Internet must be allowed to continue to evolve unobstructed. None of the new business relationships or technologies discussed in the latter part of this chapter are "neutral." Mandating network neutrality would thus not only halt further development of Internet topology, business relationships, and technology, but would force us to devolve into the Internet of the past. And who wants to relive the 1990s?

---

99. *See* Felton, *supra* note 36.

Chapter Four
FROM DEREGULATION TO NETWORK NEUTRALITY
A Tale of Radical Politics, Ivory Tower Rock Stars, and Regulatory Creep

THE SUCCESS OF the modern Internet is due to a symbiosis of private-sector risk, investment, innovation, and pro-competitive, deregulatory policies of the federal government. These policies were seeded in an early recognition by the FCC that the intrinsic value of a computer was not its functionality as an autonomous processing machine:

> The modern day electronic computer is capable of being programmed to furnish a wide variety of services, including the processing of all kinds of data and the gathering, storage forwarding, and retrieval of information—technical, statistical, medical, cultural, among numerous other classes. With its huge capacity and versatility, the computer is capable of providing its services to a multiplicity of users at locations remote from the computer. Effective use of the computer is, therefore, becoming increasingly dependent upon communication common carrier facilities and services by which the computers and the user are given instantaneous access to each other.[1]

---

1. In the Matter of Regulatory & Policy Problems Presented by the Interdependence of Computer & Commc'ns Services & Facilities, 7 F.C.C.2d 11, 11 (1966) [hereafter "First Computer Inquiry"].

Based on this recognition, beginning in the 1960s, the FCC itself helped to plant the seeds for the exponential growth of the industry with its *Computer Inquiries*, which sought to explore the regulatory and policy issues raised by the nascent interdependence of computer and telecommunications technologies.[2] Specifically, the *Inquiries* were instituted to govern the relationship between telephone companies (defined under the Communications Act of 1934 as "common carriers") and the fledgling data processing or information service industries. While the commission's myopic delineations between technologies undoubtedly stymied the development of many, because the Internet was spared FCC oversight—at least until recently—the fledgling industry was also spared the ill fate met by the telephone industry twenty-five years prior. In the case of the latter, the heavy-handed FCC, under the auspices of its common-carrier designation, regarded the telephone industry a natural monopoly, at once crushing competition and stifling its growth for years to come.[3]

As described in the quote above, in its first *Inquiry*, the FCC foreshadowed not only the emerging and growing importance of computers in our lives, but some of the characteristics that would make the Internet such a valuable tool.

In establishing its parameters for regulation of the new technologies, the FCC distinguished between "basic services," which provide pure "transmission capacity for the movement of information," from "enhanced services," which "employ computer processing applications that act on the format, content, code, protocol, or similar aspects of the subscriber's transmitted information." The distinctions between these services also delineated how the commission would regulate them. Basic services would be treated as telecommunications services subject to Title II common-carrier requirements under the Communications Act, while enhanced services would denote services:

---

2. Michael Kende, "The Digital Handshake: Connecting Internet Backbones," *Comm-Law Conspectus* 11 (2003): 45.

3. *See* Adam D. Thierer, "Unnatural Monopoly: Critical Moments in the Development of the Bell System Monopoly," *Cato Journal* 14 (1994).

Offered over common carrier transmission facilities used in interstate communications, which employ computer processing applications that act on the
format, content, code, protocol, or similar aspects of the subscriber's transmitted information, provide the subscriber additional, different, or restructured
information; or involve subscriber interaction with stored information.[4]

Enhanced services would not be subject to Title II requirements.
Specifically, basic services are communications pathways, like telephone lines, while enhanced services are computer-enhanced services
that operate via the communications pathway. Such services include
voicemail services, gateway services, electronic publishing, and Internet services.

The FCC's distinction between computer and telecommunications
technologies is important, not only in in terms of the functionality of
the underlying technologies, but in understanding the current debate
about whether the FCC even has the authority to impose its network-
neutrality rules under the Communications Act, which, you may have
surmised, we believe it does not.

Telecommunications Services vs. Information Services.

Beginning with its *Computer Inquiries*, the FCC—until recently, that
is—has taken a decidedly different approach to the computer, and
later, Internet industries. The common-carrier regulatory model under
Title II of the 1934 Act (as amended by the 1996 Act) was born out of
the natural monopoly theory of public utilities, which until that time
included the railroads and electricity. Because the telephone network
was considered a natural monopoly, the FCC attempted to regulate
prices instead of working to stimulate competition.

Thus, under the act, telecommunications industries were, and to a
large extent still are, subject to stringent regulation and oversight. In
1996, the Communications Act went through its first major overhaul
in sixty-two years. As amended, the act loosened some of the regulations on common carriers. Still, these common carriers were, and still

---

4. 47 C.F.R. § 64.702(a) (2012).

are, required to offer their services on demand to the public without "any unjust or unreasonable discrimination in charged, practices, classifications, regulations, facilities, or services. . . ."[5] They are also bound to enable functional physical connections with competing carriers at "just and reasonable" rates,[6] which may be prescribed by the FCC.[7]

However, beginning with the *Computer Inquiries*, the FCC made clear distinctions between *telecommunications* services, which are "basic," common-carrier services and *information* services, which are "enhanced" services, which included Internet services. Basic services deliver voice or data to their destinations unchanged, that is, in raw form; they do nothing to change or otherwise modify the format between the point of origin and final destination. Information services, on the other hand, sell content or data-processing services to the public by means of underlying transmission facilities, but this content is processed along the way.[8] Thus, the FCC recognized that ISPs do not just provide "a physical connection [to the Internet], but also . . . the ability to translate raw Internet data into information [consumers] may both view on their personal computers and transmit to other computers connected to the Internet."[9] Consequently, the FCC consigned the Internet to a silo separate from the telephone industry.

Apart from the differences in functionality of these two types of services, in its *First Computer Inquiry*, the FCC determined there were "no natural or economic barriers to free entry into the market for [computer] services."[10] Thus, the commission sought to shield information services from the strict common-carrier obligations by subjecting such

---

5. 47 U.S.C. § 202 (1989).

6. 47 U.S.C. § 201(b) (1938).

7. 47 U.S.C. § 205 (1989).

8. *See* Nuechterlein, *supra* note 3 in Chapter 3, at 152; *see also* Steven Titch, "Google and the Network Neutrality Fallacy," The Reason Foundation, December 14, 2008, http://reason.org/blog/printer/google-and-the-network-neutral.

9. In re Fed.-State Joint Bd. on Universal Serv., 13 F.C.C.R. 11501, 11531 (1998) [hereafter "Universal Service Report"].

10. *See* First Computer Inquiry, *supra* note 1 in this chapter, at ¶18.

services only to regulation under Title I of the Communications Act. Under Title I, the FCC has catch-all jurisdiction over interstate communications, but the title contains very few rules delegating specific regulatory power to the commission over these services. Additionally, in the early years, state regulators maintained a great deal of control over interstate competition, since they controlled some of the interstate communications.

As noted in a report by the House Committee on Energy and Commerce:

> In the pre-broadband era of dial-up services, the FCC required telephone companies that provided enhanced services over their own facilities to make basic transmission service available on a nondiscriminatory basis to competing enhanced service providers. The FCC did not, however, regulate the retail provision of these enhanced services. Thus, the FCC regulated the dial-up telecommunications service a phone company provided to connect subscribers to an Internet service provider. It did not regulate the Internet access service that the phone company or a competing Internet service provider offered to connect the subscriber to the Internet.[11]

The FCC recognized that its deregulatory approach to enhanced services was responsible for the phenomenal growth of the data-services industry, and thus codified "enhanced services" as information services in the 1996 Telecommunications Act. It also added section 230 of the Communications Act, making it the policy of the United States to "preserve the vibrant and competitive free market that presently exists for the Internet and other interactive computer services, unfettered by Federal or State regulation."[12]

In its Universal Service Report in 1998, the FCC further clarified that "non-facilities-based" ISPs—service providers that do not own

---

11. Committee on Energy and Commerce, Report 112-51, 3, 112th Congress, 1st Session, April 1, 2011.

12. 47 U.S.C. § 230(b)(2) (1998).

their own transmission facilities—are also "information services."[13] And in a declaratory ruling in 2002, the commission concluded that broadband cable Internet access services were also information services, and thus not subject to common-carrier regulation under Title II of the act. This finding was upheld by the Supreme Court in its *National Cable & Telecommunications Association v. Brand X Internet Services ("Brand X")* decision in 2005.[14]

The FCC deregulatory approach to the Internet paralleled the industry's own successful tradition of self-governance. In fact, as early as 1986, the key standards associated with the Net, including its protocols that constitute the Web, Internet applications, and the Internet itself, have evolved under the supervision of the Internet Engineering Task Force (IETF). In its own words, the IETF is "a large open international community of network designers, operators, vendors, and researchers concerned with the evolution of the Internet architecture and the smooth operation of the Internet. It is open to any interested individual."[15] Thus, the IETF is an independent, nongovernmental body, which, despite lacking any formal authority to mandate standards for the Internet, has successfully managed this monumental task.

The Internet's tradition of self-governance stems from the philosophies of many of its founding fathers, that this new frontier should remain free and unfettered by government intrusion. One of the most famous rallying cries for Internet autonomy came from cyber-libertarian and former Grateful Dead lyricist John Perry Barlow, who, in his "Declaration of Independence of Cyberspace," wrote in part:

> Governments of the Industrial World, you weary giants of flesh and steel, I come from Cyberspace, the new home of Mind. On behalf of the future, I ask you of the past to leave us alone. You are not welcome among us. You have no sovereignty where we gather.

---

13. *See* Universal Service Report, *supra* note 9 in this chapter, at 11531.

14. National Cable & Telecommunications Association v. Brand X Internet Services, 545 U.S. 967 (2005).

15. *See generally* Nuechterlein, *supra* note 3 in Chapter 3, at 128.

We have no elected government, nor are we likely to have one, so I address you with no greater authority than that with which liberty itself always speaks. I declare the global social space we are building to be naturally independent of the tyrannies you seek to impose on us. You have no moral right to rule us nor do you possess any methods of enforcement we have true reason to fear.[16]

But Barlow and other like-minded libertarians were not the only ones adamant that the Internet should remain unregulated by the government. In fact, as until recently, Democratic and Republican administrations alike have adopted a hands-off-the-Net policy.

For example, during his tenure as FCC chairman between 1997 and 2001, William Kennard witnessed what he called the "explosive growth of the Internet, the digital economy, and the entire communications industry."[17] Just as industrial America was built on the strength and ubiquity of the railroad network, Kennard predicted that in the new information age, America's economic prosperity would rely on high-speed access to the critical network of information and commerce. "That network is the Internet," he declared, "and the type of access needed is broadband."[18]

In numerous speeches, Kennard repeatedly and emphatically stressed that the growth of these industries was not happenstance, but due in large part to the two touchstones of FCC policy: "competition and deregulation." "Competition," he said, "is our mantra." And, at a speech in 1999, Kennard proclaimed, "the best decision government ever made with respect to the Internet was the decision that the FCC made 15 years ago NOT to impose regulation on it. This was

---

16. John Perry Barlow, "A Declaration of the Independence of Cyberspace," 1996, https://projects.eff.org/~barlow/Declaration-Final.html. Barlow is also a founding member of the Electronic Frontier Foundation (EFF), a libertarian, nonprofit digital-rights advocacy organization, and a fellow at Harvard University's Berkman Center for Internet and Society.

17. Remarks of William E. Kennard, chairman Federal Communications Commission, before the National Cable Television Association, Chicago, Illinois, on June 15, 1999.

18. Ibid.

not a dodge; it was a decision NOT to act. It was intentional restraint born of humility. Humility that we can't predict where this market is going."[19] This deregulatory approach, he said, "will let this nascent industry flourish."[20]

Kennard pointed out that since passage of the Telecommunications Act of 1996, which made competition "the foundation of the nation's communications industry," revenues in the communications sector had grown by $140 billion. This growth in revenues came about by breaking down the legal barriers to entry by phone companies into the cable television marketplace, paving the way for facilities-based competition on local telephone service and stimulating similar competition in multi-channel video services. By 1998, revenue in the industry had hit $500 billion, creating more than 200,000 jobs in five years. Kennard insisted that this competitive, market-driven approach is the same strategy the FCC should take in "building the broadband networks of the next century."[21] "We can have openness and competition by allowing this market to develop unfettered by regulation. We can have openness and competition by following the FCC's tradition of 'unregulation' of the Internet. We can have openness and competition by having an FCC vigilant in its monitoring of anti-competitive behavior and bottlenecks, swift in its enforcement of the rules of the game, and humble in the use of its power."[22]

FCC Chairman Michael Powell, son of General Colin Powell, reemphasized the FCC's interest in continuing to foster a vibrant and competitive landscape for the continued growth of the Internet when he articulated his "four Internet freedoms." The four freedoms were aimed at allowing consumers to: 1) access legal content subject to reasonable network management; 2) run applications that do not exceed their service plan limits or harm the network; 3) attach devices that operate within their service plan limits, do not harm the network, or

---

19. Ibid.

20. Ibid.

21. Ibid.

22. Remarks by FCC Chairman William E. Kennard before the Federal Communications Bar, Northern California Chapter, San Francisco, California, July 20, 1999.

enable theft of service; and 4) obtain meaningful information about their service plans. While Powell's freedoms would eventually form the basis of the FCC's Open Internet Order, this was not his intention. In fact, Powell was clear: his freedoms were meant to apply to "all facets of the [Internet] industry" and were specifically intended in lieu of regulations. "The case for government-imposed regulations regarding the use or provision of broadband content, application, and devices is unconvincing and speculative," he said. "Government regulation of the terms and conditions of private contracts is the most fundamental intrusion on free markets and potentially destructive, particularly where innovation and experimentation are hallmarks of an emerging market." Therefore, "such interference should be undertaken only where there is weighty and extensive evidence of abuse," he warned.[23] Powell later insisted, "There are reasons to be concerned about making sure that the fundamentals of the Internet—that is, its open-ended nature—continue to be preserved." But, he warned, "be careful what you wish for with respect to the government in fast-moving industries. . . . I've never been confident in the government's ability to both predict and to move quickly enough to maintain relevancy and accuracy in the regulation of markets like this."[24] Powell's determination that the government would not be able to adequately keep up with the evolving telecommunications industry demonstrates the main issue with relegating control to a government agency: the pace of technological innovation will be tied to the government.

Comcast's Big Mistake, Chairman Martin, and the Far Left

It was not until Powell's successor, Kevin Martin, took the helm at the FCC that the tides truly began to turn for advocates of network

---

23. FCC Chairman Michael K. Powell, Address at Silicon Flatirons, University of Colorado School of Law, February 8, 2004. *See also* House of Representatives, Report 112-51, Committee on Energy and Commerce, http://www.gpo.gov/fdsys/pkg/CRPT -112hrpt51/pdf/CRPT-112hrpt51.pdf.

24. Bianca Bosker, "Former FCC Chairman Criticizes 'Religious' Commitment to Net Neutrality," *Huffington Post*, September 8, 2010, http://www.huffingtonpost.com/2010 /08/20/michael-powell-net-neutrality_n_688732.html.

neutrality. It may seem surprising that this new Republican chairman—a Bush appointee—would have set the course for the most dramatic reversal in federal policy toward the Internet ever, but Chairman Martin, many observers would come to believe, was no fan of the cable companies—the foremost group of broadband providers—and one of the largest of such companies, Comcast, would soon give Martin the impetus he needed to hit them where it hurt.

But let us not forget that network-neutrality proponents had been rallying their forces since at least 2002. This was the year that Silver, Nichols, and McChesney founded Free Press, and the same year that the latter penned his book *Our Media, Not Theirs: The Democratic Struggle Against Corporate Media*, in which he declared the "need to promote an understanding of the urgency to assert public control over the media." From its inception, the group had not-so-convincingly masked its socialist media ideology with buzz words like "Internet freedom," "preservation," and "neutrality," while the voices of Free Press, Public Knowledge, and their growing roster of ivory-tower supporters were a constant presence in Chairman Martin's ears.

The Network-Neutrality Proponents

By the time Chairman Martin took office in 2001, network-neutrality proponents had established a united front—except, perhaps, with regard to defining "network neutrality." It is clear they are all for it, but pinning down a precise definition of network neutrality, or the regulatory framework that would ensure its dominion, has been dizzying. As one might expect with such a group of intellectual powerhouses, each one has deeply thought about and conceptualized his or her own definition and scope of the term.[25] That the term network

25. Eli Noam identifies seven different "related but distinctive meanings in which the term is used." They are: "No different quality grades ('fast lanes') for internet service; no price discrimination among internet providers; no monopoly price charged to content and applications providers; nothing charged to the providers for transmitting their content; no discrimination on content providers who compete with the carriers' own

neutrality has been a moving target since its inception is one of the greatest difficulties in attempting to truly understand the contours of the network-neutrality debate, and ultimately take a position on it.

Tim Wu

For Tim Wu—the man attributed with actually coining the phrase "network neutrality"—network neutrality is a design principle. As he explains:

> The idea is that a maximally useful public information network aspires to treat all content, sites, and platforms equally. This allows the network to carry every form of information and support every kind of application. The principle suggests that information networks are often more valuable when they are *less* specialized—when they are a platform for multiple uses, present and future.[26]

Wu presents himself as a pragmatist. He frames his arguments in favor of network neutrality with questions regarding the import of his ideas, and encourages his reader to focus on the user rather than the network when considering Internet law.[27] By setting the stage for the

---

content; no selectivity by the carriers over content they transmit; no blocking of the access of users to some websites." Eli Noam, "A Third Way for Net Neutrality," FT.com, August 29, 2006, http://www.ft.com/cms/s/2/acf14410-3776-11db-bc01-0000779e2340 .html#axzz1araJiZZt.

26. Tim Wu, "Network Neutrality FAQ," http://timwu.org/network_neutrality.html.

27. Tim Wu, "Why Have a Telecommunications Law? Anti-Discrimination Norms in Communications," *Journal of Telecommunications and High Technology Law* 5 (2006): 26 (Wu pragmatically writes: "[I]f the goal is to maximize the value of the information networks as a catalyst for commercial, political, and personal activities, it would be useful to speak of the dangers that face the telecommunications regulator"); *see also* Tim Wu, "The Broadband Debate, A User's Guide," *Journal of Telecommunications and High Technology Law* 3 (2004): 89 (Wu describes how heeding "user rights" will lead to desirable deregulation because "user-centered NN rule is . . . deregulatory in spirit . . . [in that] it prevents government from . . . agreeing to regulations that block application or network attachment."); Tim Wu, "Network Neutrality, Broadband Discrimination," *Journal of Telecommunications and High Technology Law* 2 (2003): 155 (Wu also writes,

movement, he played an integral part in its evolution. Still, his own ideas of network neutrality have undergone mild changes over the decade that he has encouraged government-mandated neutrality.

Wu has always framed his argument for network-neutrality regulation from the perspective of "user rights." In 2003, Wu wrote, "The basic principle behind a network anti-discrimination regime is to give *users* the right to use non-harmful network attachments or applications, and give innovators the corresponding freedom to supply them."[28] Wu's goal is universal and undifferentiated access for consumers. Thus, his concern with innovators or content providers is usually overshadowed by a broader determination in their ability to serve consumer needs and demand. Wu writes:

> NN rules are, ideally, users' rights to use the equipment or attachments that they want, following directly the open, deregulatory spirit of Hush-A-Phone. Neither side should have much reason to oppose a rule that creates a right of users to use whatever legal and non-harmful application 'attachments' they want.[29]

Wu's emphasis on consumer and user rights appears facially enticing, particularly to those otherwise unfamiliar with the costs and potential repercussions that broad regulatory regimes often impose on industry. Wu's zealous support of network neutrality, however, apparently makes the assumption that most people are, or should be, supportive of the initiative.

Wu therefore couches his arguments in provocative rhetoric, such as comparing network-neutrality regulation to the preservation of

---

"as a baseline, the attractiveness of broadband service is a function of the applications it offers the consumer. Hence, any restriction on use will lower the value of the service, and consequently either the price the operator can charge or the number of customers who will sign up . . .").

28. Tim Wu, "Network Neutrality, Broadband Discrimination," *Journal of Telecommunications and High Technology Law* 2 (2003): 142.

29. Tim Wu, "The Broadband Debate, A User's Guide," *Journal of Telecommunications and High Technology Law* 3 (2004): 88.

"Darwinian competition among every conceivable use of the Internet so that the only the best survive."[30] The comparison ostensibly attempts to allude to an open market without mentioning the artificiality that an overlay of regulation would impose on competition, or lack thereof, within the industry. Though Wu has attempted to play the role of a moderate, he has steadfastly encouraged content-based regulation of the Internet, a concept that has lost much support within scholarship. As a result, Wu has recently suggested that the use of neutrality and open-access principles will lead to an industry landscape more ripe for deregulation. He writes, "The key point is that creating rights in users can and will serve deregulatory purposes" and attempts to dress neutrality regulation as a negative form of government oversight, which actually provides greater freedoms to industry players.[31] In the past, however, this has taken form in his discussion of "negative" anti-discrimination rules, which punish industry actors ex-post for unjustified discrimination of content. He writes, "NN rules are, in short, like other rights against government: a form of pre-commitment rule for both government and industry. They prevent now what may be temptations tomorrow."[32] Despite Wu's seemingly unobtrusive notion of neutrality regulation, one of his proposed regulations is a total ban on "broadband carriers from blocking or degrading *any* Internet application" (emphasis added).[33]

Since promoting this stringent regulation of all Internet service providers, Wu has changed his perspective considerably. For the past year, he has worked at the FTC and has been uncharacteristically quiet on the network-neutrality front. He has not proposed or pushed regulation, though a good reason for this may also be that everyone is waiting to hear how the D.C. Circuit will rule on the FCC's jurisdiction to do so. Still, Wu's silence is curious and one cannot help

---

30. *See* Tim Wu, "Broadband Discrimination," *supra* note 28 in this chapter, at 142.

31. *See* Tim Wu, "The Broadband Debate," *supra* note 29, at 89.

32. Ibid.

33. Tim Wu, "The World Trade Law of Censorship and Internet Filtering," *Chicago Journal of International Law* 7 (2006): 287.

but hope that his new post at the FTC has him questioning his previous determination to promote ex-ante rules for the telecommunications industry.

Lawrence Lessig

Lawrence Lessig is perhaps the only other equally well-known intellectual champion of network neutrality. His current associations reveal his sympathies and persuasions with regards to the regulation of cyberspace. He serves on the boards of organizations such as the Creative Commons, MAPLight, Brave New Film Foundation, Change Congress, The American Academy, Berlin, Freedom House, Free Software Foundation, the Software Freedom Law Center, Electronic Frontier Foundation, the Public Library of Science, Free Press, Public Knowledge, and iCommons.org, all of which are dedicated to promoting open access for both network users and content providers.[34]

Lessig's early writings advocated an incremental approach to regulation of the Internet.[35] His initial misgivings with regard to Internet regulation was that technology and social perceptions of the Internet had not fully developed and needed room to evolve.[36] Lessig wrote, "We know very little about how this market functions," and argued the government's principles of regulation should be guided by the Internet's initial infrastructure.[37] Yet, his current work argues the time for development and progress has ended. Indeed, according to Lessig, the Internet has matured to a point when comprehensive regulation can be imposed without stifling continued development in the technological and social underpinnings of the Internet.

---

34. Lessig, "Short Bio," http://www.lessig.org/info/bio//.

35. *See* Lawrence Lessig, *Code and Other Laws of Cyberspace* (New York: Basic Books, 1999).

36. *See generally* Lawrence Lessig, "Architecting Innovation," *Drake Law Review* 49 (2001): 397.

37. Mark A. Lemley and Lawrence Lessig, "Open Access to Cable Modems," *Whittier Law Review* 22 (2000): 34.

In 2003, Lessig and Tim Wu filed a letter with the Federal Communications Commission "promoting fair competition among applications on a neutral network."[38] Lessig's letter outlined:

> [First, how a] neutrality regime might relate to more general goals of the
> Commission's broadband policy. Second, it addresse[d] two arguments made
> by the cable industry. It explain[ed] why a regulatory solution is preferable
> to self-regulation in this instance, and refute[d] the occasional arguments
> that the First Amendment would prohibit neutrality regulations. Finally, it
> introduce[d] a sample neutrality regime designed to be simple while promot
> ing the security of investments in broadband applications and fair competi
> tion in the market.[39]

In short, Lessig made clear all the reasons he favored a neutrality
regime and encouraged the FCC to adopt one that encompassed all
aspects of the burgeoning Internet industry. Lessig made evident in
his writing that he distrusted industry to engage in self-governance
and that government oversight was necessary to avoid corruption.[40]

Lessig initially recommended that network-neutrality regulation
be implemented in increments because he feared that regulation might
stifle the still-infantile version of the Internet. As late as 2005, "[he]
believe[d] that with respect to networks, there is a gap in our understanding about when regulation makes sense."[41] In articles dating back
to the 1990s, Lessig claims that regulatory regimes, which attempt
to translate objectives from the real world, would fail in cyberspace.
Lessig explained, "our ideas, or intuitions, about how to preserve the
space of liberty that our framing document left, do not translate well

---

38. *See* Letter from Tim Wu, associate professor, University of Virginia School of Law,
and Lawrence Lessig, professor of law, Stanford Law School, to the F.C.C., August 22,
2003 (on file with author), http://www.freepress.net/docs/wu_lessig_fcc.pdf.

39. Ibid.

40. Ibid.

41. Lawrence Lessig, "Re-Marking the Progress in Frischmann," *Minnesota Law Review*
89 (2005): 1031.

when confronted by code. Code confuses us."[42] His response to this dilemma was to open the forum of discussion on who should govern cyberspace. Indeed, at the time, Lessig admitted he did not know who should be responsible and alluded to the idea that the community occupying the space should ultimately decide. He wrote:

> [W]e need to think about who is making the code. If code is political, then it is not the task of engineers alone. If there are fundamental questions about how cyberspace is to be structured, these are questions that should be addressed by the citizens of cyberspace.[43]

In 2008, Lessig wrote a retrospective article discussing his perspective of Internet regulation in the 1990s and claims, "I was one of those reluctant regulators." He describes his realization that government should "do something" by contending that there became "universal impatience with the notion that the market would solve the problem."[44]

Despite his early uncertainty about who should govern cyberspace, Lessig eventually expressed great confidence in the government's ability to regulate and improve the Internet. He began pushing for the adoption of industry-wide, *ex ante* regulation aimed at preserving network neutrality. He supported network neutrality, perhaps more as a concept to start, because he believed, "It [nondiscrimination or neutrality] is a guarantee—a constitutional guarantee, if you will— that innovation will be rewarded if the innovation is one that markets respect."[45] Though he recognized the major costs associated with broad and restrictive regulatory regime, he maintained, and continues to maintain, the benefits can outweigh the costs. In an article from 2005, Lessig wrote:

---

42. Ibid., 6. *See also* Lawrence Lessig, "The Constitution of Code: Limitations on Choice-Based Critiques of Cyberspace Regulation," *CommLaw Conspectus* 5 (1997): 191.

43. *See* Lessig, "Constitution of Code," *supra* note 42, at 15.

44. Lawrence Lessig, "I Blew It on Microsoft," *Wired*, January 2007, http://www.wired .com/wired/archive/15.01/posts.html?pg=6.

45. Lawrence Lessig, "Foreword," *Stanford Law Review* 52 (2000): 991.

[T]he mechanics of a 'network neutrality' policy are not simple . . . neutral network has produced spam and viruses, as well as instant messaging and Voice over Internet Protocol. The network begs for more discrimination, but where and how, consistent with neutrality, is impossibly hard to specify. More importantly, any rule that aims to specify such neutrality needs to avoid persistent intervention in market operations. The rule needs to be clear ex ante, so ex post enforcement is feasible.[46]

As the excerpt suggests, Lessig's calling for neutrality regulation vacillates between designating a need for broad restrictions and suggesting that a free market is both economically and socially desirable. Still, Lessig urges network-neutrality regulation as a means of ensuring continued innovation and competition among Internet providers. He contends the Internet's initial design, which uses a first-come, first-serve access architecture, is the optimal mechanism to encourage a socially and economically desirable future in cyberspace.

In 2007, Lessig wrote, "The innovation and explosive growth of the Internet is directly linked to its particular architectural design."[47] In this way, Lessig's vision of network-neutrality regulation is premised on the best-efforts Internet architecture, since he believes that innovation up until this point in time has been a result of this scheme. According to Lessig, a proper neutrality regime would be a broad, *ex ante* restriction on ISP content discrimination, with a few exceptions. These exceptions include: 1) complying with "duly authorized government directives"; 2) preventing physical harm to the network by attachment or network usage; 3) preventing broadband users from interfering with other broadband uses, such as through unsolicited e-mail, dissemination of computer viruses, and other such cyber "attacks"; 4) ensuring, as necessary, the quality of broadband service; 5) preventing security violations, commonly referred to as unauthorized "hacking"; and

---

46. Lessig, "Re-Marking the Progress in Frischmann," *supra* note 41, at 1042.

47. Lawrence Lessig, "In Support of Network Neutrality," *Journal of Law and Policy for the Information Society* 3 (2007): 186, http://moritzlaw.osu.edu/students/groups/is/files/2012/02/lessig-formatted.pdf.

6) serving purposes "specifically authorized" by the FCC. These seemingly broad exceptions are actually rather narrow, as they are all subject to government mandate or authorization. In this way, Lessig's neutrality regime is truly subject to the whim of the FCC.

Most recently, Lessig has couched his skepticism toward non-neutral networks by criticizing the lack of transparency in the way ISPs manage networks. This notion of "transparency" comes from the European Union Commission, which has proposed to codify transparency requirements toward the fulfillment of network-neutrality requirements in Europe.[48] Lessig compares America's regulatory regime to other countries with developed broadband accessibility, and criticizes America's unilateral movement toward deregulation of the Internet. He claims the rest of the world continues to regulate the Internet toward an objective of universal and affordable service.[49] He claims that absent government policy, "the rest of the world got better broadband and we [America] got worse broadband."[50] He further asserts that the move toward deregulation has been largely a result of lobbying efforts by industry incumbents. As a result, he assumes a new strategy toward network-neutrality reform: freeing Congress from the talons of special interests.

Lessig's distrust of industry leaders and market players is a consistent theme throughout his career. Indeed, Lessig's current academic work focuses on the issue of "institutional corruption," demonstrating his distrust of industrial or corporate organizations and complementing his early desire to put the regulation of the Internet in the hands of the government rather than industry market players.[51] Furthermore,

---

48. Body of European Regulators for Electronic Communications, "BEREC Guidelines on Network Neutrality and Transparency: Best practices and recommended approaches," October 2011, http://www.erg.eu.int/doc/berec/consultation_draft_guidelines.pdf.

49. Lawrence Lessig, "America's Broadband Policy," April 14, 2010, http://www.channels .com/episodes/show/12909555/America-s-Broadband-Policy?page=5.

50. Ibid.

51. *See* Victoria Baranetsky, "Lessig's Focus on Corruption May Have Uncomfortable Implications for Harvard," *Harvard Law Record*, November 19, 2009, http://hlrecord

in 2008, Lessig ran for Congress on a platform to "Change Congress." Lessig openly campaigned with the objective of fighting special interests on the Hill with the help of grassroots support.[52] In his online blog, Lessig explained his decision early on by claiming:

> We've all been whining about the 'corruption' of government forever. We all should be whining about the corruption of professions too. But rather than whining, I want to work on this problem that I've come to believe is the most important problem in making government work.[53]

He continues to push his message through mass media and attempts to garner younger, grassroots audiences through online campaigns.[54] Lessig's activism, both politically and academically, reveals a simultaneous distrust of industry and government. It seems almost ironic that, at least with respect to network neutrality, he believes the latter can save the former.

Jonathan Zittrain

Jonathan Zittrain might not enjoy the rock-star status of Lessig and Wu in network-neutrality circles, but his work has been equally influential. A Harvard law professor and self-proclaimed enthusiast of "open Internet" policies and regimes, Zittrain funnels his perspective on telecommunications policy through a dichotomy of Internet tech-

---

.org/?p=10100. *See also* Lawrence Lessig, "Institutional Corruption—Opening Lecture," Edmond J. Safra Foundation Center for Ethics at Harvard, Cambridge, Massachusetts, October 8, 2009, http://www.youtube.com/watch?v=0-lEDiUFXUk.

52. *See* "Lawrence Lessig: Change Congress," *Forum Network*, October 13, 2010, http://forum-network.org/lecture/lawrence-lessig-change-congress. *See also* David Weigel, "Change Congress: The Larry Lessig Launch," *Reason*, March 20, 2008, http://reason.com/blog/2008/03/20/change-congress-the-larry-less.

53. Lawrence Lessig, "Required Reading: The Next 10 Years," June 19, 2007, http://lessig.org/blog/2007/06/required_reading_the_next_10_y_1.html.

54. Lawrence Lessig, "Change Congress—We're Bringing Sexy Back," *Huffington Post*, October 19, 2011, http://www.huffingtonpost.com/lawrence-lessig/change-congress--were-b_b_160961.html.

nology: 1) generative platforms and 2) walled-garden platforms. These two ideas inform his vision of the Internet and propel his recommendations for creating efficient infrastructures for a progressive, valuable, and user-friendly Internet.

Zittrain's book *The Future of the Internet—And How to Stop It* encapsulates his perspective on the "generative"–"walled-garden" dichotomy.[55] The book, which is heralded by Lessig in its foreword,[56] discusses the threat of surrendering Internet innovation rights and abilities to firms or corporations. His anecdotal description of this phenomenon is a comparison between Steve Job's Apple II product and the original iPhone. Zittrain characterizes the first as a "generative" platform, which lends itself to users and application providers for customization, innovation, and spin-off technologies. The latter, Zittrain argues, is "walled-garden" or proprietary software that resists foreign innovation unless approved by the original software designer.[57] Zittrain critiques walled-garden technologies as stagnant and antagonistic to effective and user-friendly innovation.

Though Zittrain recognizes issues associated with generative technology—namely, that it can be "too open"[58] and, therefore, impede on the device's reliability—he maintains that it is preferable to corporate control, which would render technology stagnate and "sterile."[59] Zittrain explains that complete openness increasingly interferes with reliability because there are fewer restrictions on individuals than on firms in terms of updating, revamping, or using the devices on the Internet. As a result, individuals are free to use the information that is there for either good or evil. In other words, the same openness that

---

55. Jonathan Zittrain, *The Future of the Internet—And How to Stop It* (New Haven, CT: Yale University Press, 2008).

56. Ibid., 89.

57. Ibid., 2.

58. *The Future of the Internet*, "Ahead of the Curve," April 10, 2008, http://www .youtube.com/watch?v=yt4rLVdSQ5E&feature=related. *See also* Zittrain, *supra* note 55, at 101.

59. *See The Future of the Internet, supra* note 58, at 5:44–5:50*; see also* Zittrain, *supra* note 55, at 63.

provides household creations such as Facebook, Skype, or Wikipedia also invites viruses, spam, and unwanted use of personal information.

Zittrain offers a middle-ground solution to this dilemma: the Internet users should police unwanted and detrimental innovation through filtering devices. In other words, self-help. In an interview on *ABC Now*, in which Zittrain discussed his book, Zittrain claimed, "openness on the Internet needs to be tempered . . . [because] people want an Internet with the same kind of reliability that they expect from an automobile, or a refrigerator, or a hairdryer."[60] Zittrain continued, "I am not calling for massive government regulation of the Internet . . . yet."[61] Rather, he maintains his book is an appeal to the Internet users to use their resources to deflect unwanted repercussions of a totally free Internet.[62] To that end, Zittrain recommends firewalls, spyware devices, and other intelligent filtering devices in order to block content on an individual basis rather than appealing to firms for protection. Yet, Internet gurus have repeatedly contended that self-help mechanisms will not be effective because they will be "routinely cracked, and the counter-technologies that defeat encryption may well proliferate as easily as computer users exchange copyrighted works on the Internet."[63] Moreover, network providers could offer more "intelligent"[64] systematic protocols to filter unwanted malicious

---

60. See *The Future of the Internet, supra* note 58, at 2:40–3:17.

61. Ibid.

62. See *The Future of the Internet, supra* note 58, at 5:03–5:14.

63. *See* Jonathan Zittrain, "Exploitative Publishers, Untrustworthy Systems, and the Dream of a Digital Revolution for Artists," *Harvard Law Review* 114 (2001): 2456.

64. In the context of data conveyance, "intelligent" data-traffic management refers to traffic-control mechanisms that permit network providers "to prioritize the transmission of certain data or provide quality-of-service assurances for a fee in the same way that consumers pay for priority mail service." *See* FTC Broadband Report, *supra* note 18 in Chapter 3, at 64. *But see* Bill D. Herman, "Opening Bottlenecks: On Behalf of Mandated Network Neutrality," *Federal Communications Law Journal* 59 (2006): 107 (arguing for a "stupid" network that will "faithfully carry [sic] all data and place [sic] the intelligence at the ends of the network 'smart.'" Moreover arguing that "smart networks predestine certain uses, [while] stupid—or neutral—networks liberate 'large amounts of innovative energy'").

content. Even network-neutrality proponents generally agree that targeted data discrimination is justified when it comes to malicious data, but Zittrain's attempt to salvage even the worst of Internet transmissions (i.e., viruses, terrorists attacks, and malicious content) demonstrates the extremity of his position. Ultimately, Zittrain concedes that failure to implement the community-policing plan may require some systematic data discrimination.

While one might be tempted to dismiss team network neutrality as a group seemingly divided by different ultimate objectives and varying underlying philosophies, it has proven itself to be a united and lethal force when faced what it perceives as a mutually disdainful adversary: broadband behemoth Comcast.

The Comcast Debacle

Even from the first days of FCC Chairman Martin's reign, seasoned observers and industry insiders could sense a storm brewing on the horizon. First, to the delight of network-neutrality proponents, he formally adopted Powell's Internet freedoms as "principles" in a September 2005 policy statement. Still, Martin reassured the industry that the policy statement did "not establish rules" and was not enforceable. But, just three years later, Martin announced that he *was* going to enforce the rules against Comcast in a debacle and resulting legal battle that, to many, ignited the network-neutrality debate anew.

It all started in early October 2007, when Comcast subscriber and computer consultant Matthew Elvey noticed that his uploads using the popular BitTorrent application were being stifled. BitTorrent is a peer-to-peer file-sharing application in which individuals' computers serve as both mini-servers and end users, allowing for the rapid transfer of large, or media-rich, files like music and video. Peer-to-peer applications like BitTorrent had been at the center of much public debate for some time because of their popularity with individuals illegally sharing copyrighted material (such as on Napster), and because of their bandwidth-hogging nature. As such, network providers like Comcast had been experiencing increasing pressure from copyright holders in the entertainment industry to do something to protect their proprietary content traveling over the network. At the same time, network providers were watching BitTorrent and similar applications gobble up bandwidth—often accounting for 50 to 90 percent of their network traffic.

Service providers reasonably claimed they had a right to manage such traffic to ensure the majority of their customers received their expected level of service. The problem—and Comcast's big mistake— was that when claims initially surfaced accusing it of blocking Bit-Torrent traffic, it denied the reports. It was not until the Associated Press conducted its own tests in which it attempted to upload a copy of the *King James Bible* over Comcast's network, and was repeatedly blocked from doing so, that Comcast was forced to admit to its actions.

While the company maintained it had the right to manage network traffic, the public outcry was insurmountable. Although the practice of managing the flow of data over networks, or "traffic shaping," was common among most Internet service providers, it usually involved slowing down certain bandwidth-hogging traffic at peak hours and giving others priority. The net effect generally ensures that most consumers enjoy reliable service. However, Comcast's actions were distinguishable in two ways. First, Comcast was targeting—and actually blocking—BitTorrent traffic specifically, instead of slowing down all peer-to-peer traffic. Second, its method involved falsifying information about its network traffic.

It was not a wise move. Unsurprisingly, Free Press and Public Knowledge immediately filed a complaint with the FCC, alleging that Comcast's network-management techniques were "unreasonable and discriminatory." In addition, application developers worried that, if Comcast were allowed to continue, its actions would strike a crippling blow to other file-sharing networks like eDonkey and Gnutella, which were increasingly being used by legitimate media companies to transmit legal video, music, and other bandwidth-demanding files. Still others worried that Comcast and other ISPs would expand their targets to different types of applications like Joost (Internet TV), eBay (an online auction and shopping website), and Skype (a Voice over Internet Protocol service), which would stifle a wide range of "edge" innovation and investment. Consequently, the practice of managing data traffic was denounced as a whole.

The outcry did not fall on deaf ears. Comcast immediately entered into direct talks with BitTorrent, and less than seven months later the two had reached an agreement to address the issues associated with rich media content and network-capacity management. In exchange for Comcast's promise to switch to a protocol using an agnostic and transparent capacity-management technique, BitTorrent acknowledged the need of ISPs to manage traffic congestion. Both companies agreed to work with other ISPs, technology companies, and the Internet Engineering Task Force to develop new, more efficient distribution architecture for the delivery of rich media content.

But the FCC, under Chairman Martin, could not resist the opportunity to use Comcast's faux pas as an example of undesirable industry behavior. It was also a good opportunity to expand FCC jurisdiction in a way that would give them control over the Internet. In August 2008 the agency found that Comcast had disobeyed its Internet Policy Statement. The commission did not issue an injunction or cease-and-desist order against Comcast, since the company had already agreed to discontinue the practices objected to by the agency. Instead, to monitor Comcast's present and future compliance with its policy statement, the FCC required Comcast submit to it, within thirty days: (1) the precise contours of its previous network-management practices; (2) a compliance plan "with interim benchmarks that describe[ed] how it intend[ed] to transition from discriminatory to nondiscriminatory network management practices [by the end of 2008]; and (3) publicly disclose its newly implemented and protocol-agnostic network management practices."[65] The commission warned that failure to

---

65. In the Matters of Formal Complaint of Free Press and Public Knowledge against Comcast Corporation for Secretly Degrading Peer-to-Peer Applications and Broadband Industry Practices Petition of Free Press et al. for Declaratory Ruling That Degrading an Internet Application Violates the FCC's Internet Policy Statement and Does Not Meet an Exception for "Reasonable Network Management," 23 FCC Rcd 13028 (2008) [hereafter

comply with its requirements or failure to implement its transition to protocol-agnostic network management would subject the company to further enforcement actions.

Comcast filed the requested documents with the commission on September 19, 2008, and on January 5, 2009, filed certification that it had fulfilled its promise to switch to protocol-agnostic network-management practices.[66] However, the FCC sent a letter on the 18th of that month, asking Comcast to clarify its treatment of VoIP services, expressing its concern that the company made no distinction between VoIP services in its filing, but appeared to treat its own VoIP differently than those provided by others. The commission also suggested that if Comcast's VoIP is a separate service from its broadband service, it is possible that it should be classified as a "telecommunication service," subject to Title II's more stringent regulations. Thus, the commission asked Comcast to explain why it omitted the effects the company's network-management practices would have on its own VoIP service from its required filings, and why that service should not be treated as a telecommunications service under Title II.[67]

"FCC Comcast Decision"], 19 ¶ 54. *See also* Kathleen Ann Ruane, "The FCC's Authority to Regulate Net Neutrality after Comcast v. FCC," Congressional Research Service, 4, October 27, 2011.

66. Letter from Kathryn A. Zachem, vice president, Regulatory and State Legislative Affairs, Comcast, to Marelene Dortch, secretary, FCC, re: In the Matters of Formal Complaint of Free Press and Public Knowledge against Comcast Corporation for Secretly Degrading Peer-to-Peer Applications; Broadband Industry Practices: Petition of Free Press et al. for Declaratory Ruling That Degrading an Internet Application Violates the FCC's Internet Policy Statement and Does Not Meet an Exception for "Reasonable Network Management," File No. EB-08-IH-1518, WC Docket No. 07-52 (September 19, 2008); Letter from Kathryn A. Zachem, vice president, Regulatory and State Legislative Affairs, Comcast, to Marelene Dortch, secretary, FCC, Re: In the Matters of Formal Complaint of Free Press and Public Knowledge against Comcast Corporation for Secretly Degrading Peer-to-Peer Applications; Broadband Industry Practices: Petition of Free Press et al. for Declaratory Ruling That Degrading an Internet Application Violates the FCC's Internet Policy Statement and Does Not Meet an Exception for "Reasonable Network Management," File No. EB-08-IH-1518, WC Docket No. 07-52 (January 5, 2009).

67. Letter from Dana R. Shaffer, chief, Wireline Competition Bureau, and Matthew Berry, general counsel, FCC, to Katherine A. Zachem, vice president, Regulatory Affairs, Comcast Corporation, Re: In the Matters of Formal Complaint of Free Press

On January 30, 2009, Comcast filed its answer, stating that its VoIP service is in fact a separate service from its broadband service, and therefore was neither subject to the commission's requirements regarding its network-management practices, nor affected by its new regime related to these practices. The company also argued that the question of whether its VoIP service should be treated as a telecommunications service was irrelevant to the topic at hand, but asserted it was not a telecommunications service.[68] As noted by the Congressional Research Services Report, "The Commission has yet to take any action in response to Comcast's letter, though the issues raised by the Commission related to Comcast's VoIP services are more generally addressed in the Commission's Open Internet Order."[69] We will discuss that order shortly.

Although Comcast voluntarily agreed to meet the FCC's requirements, and had already ceased its network-management practices that had formed the basis of the commission's objections, Comcast appealed the agency's decision to the D.C. Circuit Court.[70] As grounds, the company first argued that the FCC's order was unenforceable as a matter of law because the commission had only issued a policy "state-

---

and Public Knowledge against Comcast Corporation for Secretly Degrading Peer-to-Peer Applications; Broadband Industry Practices: Petition of Free Press et al. for Declaratory Ruling That Degrading an Internet Application Violates the FCC's Internet Policy Statement and Does Not Meet an Exception for "Reasonable Network Management," File No. EB-08-IH-1518, WC Docket No. 07-52 (January 19, 2009). *See also* Ruane, *supra* note 65, at 5.

68. Letter from Kathryn A. Zachem, vice president, Regulatory and State Legislative Affairs, Comcast, to Marelene Dortch, secretary, FCC, Re: In the Matters of Formal Complaint of Free Press and Public Knowledge against Comcast Corporation for Secretly Degrading Peer-to-Peer Applications; Broadband Industry Practices: Petition of Free Press et al. for Declaratory Ruling That Degrading an Internet Application Violates the FCC's Internet Policy Statement and Does Not Meet an Exception for "Reasonable Network Management," File No. EB-08-IH-1518, WC Docket No. 07-52 (January 30, 2009).

69. *See* Ruane, *supra* note 65, at 5.

70. Petition for Review, and, in the Alternative, Notice of Appeal, Comcast Corporation v. Federal Communications Commission, 579 F.3d 1 (D.C. Cir. 2009).

ment" regarding network management practices, and thus there was no "law" to enforce:

> For the FCC to conclude that an entity has acted in violation of federal law and to take enforcement action for such a violation, there must have been a 'law' to violate. Because the commission has no constitutional or common law existence or authority, but only those authorities conferred upon it by Congress, the 'law' in an FCC proceeding must be either a statutory provision or an agency rule or precedent properly promulgated pursuant to an underlying statute. Here, no such law existed.[71]

The company also argued that, in attempting to enforce the order, the FCC violated several procedural requirements and constitutional requirements, and perhaps most importantly, the FCC lacked the statutory authority to enforce such rules to begin with because the commission failed to justify its exercise of ancillary authority over broadband Internet service providers.

With regard to Comcast's first argument, that the FCC could not enforce a law that did not exist, the company was right. In fact, the FCC's first foray into Internet regulation was nothing short of preposterous. Regardless of one's opinion of Comcast's initial action, it does not take a legal expert or libertarian to see the lunacy and danger of a federal agency declaring a violation of rules that do not exist and bullying a private company into following them. But the court never weighed in on that argument, instead vacating the FCC's order against Comcast because of the FCC's failure to tie its assertion of ancillary authority to any "statutorily mandated responsibility."[72]

As suggested above, the FCC did not claim to have express authority to regulate cable Internet services, but said that regulation of such

---

71. Comcast Corporation v. Federal Communications Commission, 579 F.3d 1 (D.C. Cir. 2009), Document: 01215971557, Opening Brief for Petitioner Comcast Corporation, 20 (July 27, 2009).

72. Comcast v. Federal Communications Commission, No. 08-1291, 2010 U.S. App. LEXIS 7039 (D.C. Cir. April 6, 2010).

services as "reasonably ancillary to the . . . effective performance of its statutorily mandated responsibilities." In doing so, the commission relied on Section 230(b) of the Communications Act, which states that, "it is the policy of the United States . . . to promote the continued development of the Internet and other interactive computer services [and] to encourage the development of technologies which maximize user control over what information is received by individual families and schools who use the Internet." The commission argued that the combination of this policy statement in the act, in addition to the commission's general rulemaking authority under Title I, were sufficient grounds upon which to assert ancillary jurisdiction over broadband. The court disagreed.

As far back as 1968, the Supreme Court has recognized that the FCC has "ancillary authority" to regulate certain services even though Congress did not expressly grant the commission the authority to regulate them; however, its jurisdiction is not limitless.[73] Instead, as the D.C. Circuit noted in its decision, in the Supreme Court's most recent decision, *American Library Assn. v. FCC*, the Court found the agency had such authority "only if it demonstrates that its action— here barring Comcast from interfering with its customers' use of peer-to-peer networking applications—is 'reasonably ancillary to the . . . effective performance of its statutorily mandated responsibilities.'"[74] Thus, in order to regulate the industry, the agency must demonstrate that two conditions are met: (1) the commission's general jurisdiction grant under Title I covers the regulated subject, and (2) the regulations are reasonably ancillary to the commission's effective performance of its statutorily mandated responsibilities.[75] While the D.C. Circuit found that cable Internet services fall within the FCC's general jurisdiction under Title I, the court also found that the commission

---

73. *See* United States v. Southwestern Cable Co., 392 U.S. 157 (1968); United States v. Midwest Video Corp., 406 U.S. 649 (1972) [hereafter "Midwest Video I"]; FCC v. Midwest Video Corp., 440 U.S. 689 (1979) [hereafter "Midwest Video II"].

74. Comcast v. FCC, 600 F. 3d 642, 644 (D.C. Cir. 2010).

75. *See* Ruane, *supra* note 65, at 5.

had failed to satisfy the second—ancillary—requirement because section 230(b)'s policy statement could not be considered be "statutorily mandated responsibilities" under the Communications Act.[76]

By the time the D.C. Circuit handed down its decision in the Comcast case, Chairman Martin was long gone, replaced by President Obama's Julius Genachowski, a new chairman with his own vision of how to circumvent the law and the courts' pesky decisions in order to institute network neutrality.

Still, to this day, many industry insiders are convinced the FCC's action had everything to do with Martin's disdain for the cable industry and Comcast in particular, and little to do with the agency's attempt to fix a problem, which by that time had already been fixed. In fact, by the time the FCC had issued its ruling, the chairman had amassed a strikingly large and colorful record of hostility toward the cable industry.

Martin's disdain for cable first came to light in 2005, when he disclosed that he had secretly ordered his staff to revise findings of a report on pricing for so-called "à la carte" cable services. Martin wanted to force cable companies to offer consumers the ability to purchase subscriptions to individual channels instead of bundling them together. In spite of the report's initial findings to the contrary, Martin's "revised" study showed that in some hypothetical circumstances, certain consumers could save money purchasing cable channels on an "à la carte" basis. Additionally, Martin made continued attempts to cap Comcast's growth at 30 percent or pay TV subscribers nationally; allowed the $16.9 billion acquisition of Adelphia Communications by Time Warner, Inc. and Comcast to languish for 404 days prior to approval, all the while allowing the bankrupt cable operator to bleed its subscribers (the merger was the longest cable-system transaction in recent history, its review period more than doubling the typical 180-day standard); used undeflated prices to exaggerate cable rate trends; purged data showing declining cable rates; ordered his staff to reject Comcast's

---

76. Comcast v. FCC, 600 F.3d at 653. *See also* Ruane, *supra* note 65, at 5–6.

request for a waiver of rules regarding the installation of set-top boxes without access security built in; and the list goes on.[77]

Martin's campaign against Comcast in particular was waged until his last minutes in office. As one cable insider describes:

> The last day of the Bush Administration, on Martin Luther King Jr. weekend . . . a very historic inauguration was going on, and the Chairman of the FCC ordered people to come to work on Martin Luther King weekend, to issue final orders against [Comcast], in the middle of the night. It was just blatant. Just anything that was loose around there, he just was signing and getting them out, against [Comcast] and against [the cable] industry as well. All of which, by the way, have been overturned by the courts since. There were some people who felt bad that they were sort of forced to order others to do it, but they did it. It was just very weird—those last 18 months were surreal and the abuse of power was pretty bad.

Obama's FCC chairman, Julius Genachowski, would, for different reasons, deal an equally crippling blow to the industry.

---

77. *See generally*, Deception and Distrust: The Federal Communications Commission Under Chairman Kevin J. Martin: A Majority Staff Report Prepared for the Use of the Committee on Energy & Commerce, House of Representatives, 110th Congress, December 2008.

Chapter Five
NETWORK NEUTRALITY AND WHY IT WILL RUIN THE INTERNET

"The hardest thing to predict is the future"—Yogi Berra

The network-neutrality movement gets a new leader: Obama's FCC Chairman, Julius Genachowski.

EVEN BEFORE BARACK OBAMA took office, his presidential campaign had embraced network neutrality to rally its progressive base. And Julius Genachowski, a long-time "edge" man who had spent most of his professional career in Silicon Valley, became Obama's chairman of the Technology, Media, and Telecommunications Policy Working Group. Genachowski was more than ready to champion the cause. Free Press, which early on allied itself with the online grassroots giant Moveon.org, found both its coffers and influence ballooning in symbiosis with Obama's elevation to the presidency.[1] Moreover, the group's list of major contributors looks like a "who's who of left-wing liberal foundations." These groups, like Pew Charitable Trusts, the Joyce Foundation, the John D. and Catherine T. MacArthur Foundation, and George Soros's Open Society Institute, have made sure Free Press,

---

1. John Fund, "The Network Neutrality Coup: The Campaign to Regulate the Internet Was Funded by a Who's-Who of Left-Liberal Foundations," *Wall Street Journal*, December 21, 2010.

with its forty staffers and annual budget of $4 million, is supported in the manner to which it has become accustomed.[2] In addition, when President Obama moved into the White House, Free Pressers were rewarded with plum positions at the FCC. Jennifer Howard, who used to handle the group's media relations, is now Genachowski's press secretary, and Mark Lloyd, who coauthored a major Free Press report calling for the regulation of political talk radio, is now the FCC's chief diversity officer.[3]

And of course, when Obama took office, he personally selected Genachowski, his former classmate, *Law Review*, and basketball buddy, to chair the FCC and carry out his campaign promise to make network neutrality the law. The new president and his old friend spent a great deal of time together as they assumed their new roles. In fact, records show that Genachowski visited the White House forty-seven times between January 31 and August 31, 2009. Treasury Secretary Timothy Geithner came in a distant second, visiting the president only five times during the same period.[4]

Surrounded by Free Pressers, and anxious to appease the party base, the new chairman used his first official speech—ironically given at the Brookings Institution—to announce his plans to codify the network-neutrality principles as rules. The next month Genachowski followed through with a proposed list of network-neutrality rules, enforceable, the FCC alleged, because of its supposed "ancillary authority" to regulate broadband as an information service.[5]

But the courts would not cooperate. In April 2010, the D.C. Circuit vacated former Chairman Martin's attempt to sanction Comcast, ruling that the FCC had failed to demonstrate it had jurisdiction to regulate network management under Title I of the Communications Act. Attorneys for the FCC probably had some notion of what was

---

2. Ibid.

3. Ibid.

4. Peter Suderman, "Internet Cop: President Obama's top man at the Federal Communications Commission tries to regulate the Net." Reason.com, March 2011, http://reason.com/archives/2011/02/08/internet-cop/singlepage; John Fund, *supra* note 1.

5. Peter Suderman, *supra* note 4.

to come after Judge A. Raymond Randolph admonished them during oral arguments by saying, "you have yet to identify a specific statute" that gives the agency jurisdiction to regulate broadband. "You can't get an unbridled, roving commission to go about doing good," he warned. In the court's opinion, Judge Randolph held:

> Policy statements are just that—statements of policy. They are not delegations of regulatory authority. It is true that Congress gave the [commission] broad and adaptable jurisdiction so that it can keep pace with rapidly evolving communications technologies. It is also true that the Internet is such a technology, indeed, arguably the most important innovation in communications in a generation. Yet notwithstanding the difficult regulatory problem of rapid technological change posed by the communications industry, the allowance of wide latitude in the exercise of delegated powers is not the equivalent of untrammeled freedom to regulate activities over which that statute fails to confer the Commission authority.[6]

Unfortunately for Comcast, the court's decision would have little impact on its own network management policies, at least for the next seven years or so. Earlier that same year, Comcast sought approval for a merger with NBC Universal through which it would acquire a 51 percent stake in the entertainment firm. In return for approval of the $13.8 billion deal, the FCC saw that Comcast agreed to a slew of conditions, many unrelated to the merger directly, and including a condition that Comcast would adhere to its now illegal network-neutrality principles.[7] Inside sources suggest, however, that while certain conditions imposed on such a merger involving vertical integration would be

---

6. Comcast v. FCC, 600 F. 3d 642, 661 (D.C. App. Ct. 2010) (internal quotations omitted).

7. *See generally* Josh Wright, "FCC Approves Comcast-NBC Merger with Conditions," Truth on the Market, January 20, 2011, http://truthonthemarket.com/2011/01/20/fcc-approves-comcast-nbc-merger-with-conditions/; *see also* Georg Szalai, "Regulators Approve Comcast-NBC Universal Deal with Conditions," *Hollywood Reporter*, January 18, 2011, http://www.hollywoodreporter.com/news/regulators-approve-comcast-nbc-universal-72809.

expected, the FCC exceeded its authority with regard to the Comcast-NBC Universal transaction. These sources allege that the FCC explicitly ordered Comcast to abide by network-neutrality rules that go beyond its "open-Internet order," and refrain from speaking out against network neutrality as a condition to the approval of the deal. Sources also point to the National Cable & Telecommunications Association (NCTA), the principal trade association of the cable industry, of which Comcast is the largest member, having been curiously silent on the network-neutrality issue since Comcast began merger talks with NBC Universal. If these allegations prove true, the FCC's coercive tactics would constitute governmental action to silence Comcast's speech, in blatant violation of the corporation's First Amendment rights.

Still the D.C. Circuit's decision sent FCC efforts to codify network-neutrality rules for the rest of the industry into a tizzy. The court had found that the FCC failed to demonstrate statutory authority to regulate the Internet, guaranteeing a legal challenge if the agency did try to codify the principles, and Congress had not given the FCC a clear mandate to do so. Genachowski quickly weighed his options.

The chairman's next move was to propose reclassifying broadband Internet access service as a common-carrier service under Title II, setting it squarely within the cross hairs of FCC regulatory authority. His proposal, however, raised a host of legal problems, not the least of which was that the FCC, as an executive agency, did not have the power to define its own governing statutes, and thus could not reclassify broadband access providers as telecommunication services itself; that was Congress's job.[8] Genachowski next tried what he called the "Third Way: A Narrowly Tailored Broadband Framework." Under this new plan, the FCC would attempt to regulate access providers as utilities under Title II, but would not subject them to the full force of its regulatory muscle. Instead, the commission would waive some of the requirements similar utilities would otherwise be subjected to

8. *See* Suderman, *supra* note 4.

in a process known as "forbearance."[9] But the uproar was swift and unequivocal from within the industry, from 275 members of Congress on both sides of the aisle, from the White House, and even from some network-neutrality proponents like Public Knowledge, all of whom recognized that the "Third Way" was really a third rail not even true believers dare touch.

While Genachowski was licking his wounds, Free Press was mounting a full-court press. They wanted Title II reclassification in no uncertain terms, and it did not matter that the White House, in the midst of an economic crisis, was worried that the uncertainty associated with such a move would drive investment from one of the few thriving industries. Nor were they bothered by the public's having apparently abandoned the network-neutrality ship, as suggested by every single one of the ninety-five congressional candidates who had signed a petition supporting network neutrality losing in the 2010 elections.[10] There were also increasing signs that the longstanding tradition of self-governance within the industry would itself prevail. For example, two companies on opposite sides of the issue, Google and Verizon, proposed a joint policy framework that would impose some minimal restrictions on wireline providers but leave the new frontier of wireless data networks alone. Genachowski waited. At first it seemed that the FCC would indeed defer to Congress. Agency members began working with the House Energy and Commerce Committee chairman, Henry Waxman, on a bill that would impose network-neutrality rules on broadband providers but was anchored in Title I. The bill failed to garner serious congressional support.

Still, Genachowski seemed undeterred. In the fall of 2010, just as Congress got ready to enter its lame-duck session, the chairman hurriedly assembled a small group of industry insiders who would be forced to choose between two regulatory options: the bad option was a set of rules closely mirroring those already struck down by the D.C. Circuit,

---

9. *See* Suderman, *supra* note 4.

10. Ibid.

and a worse option that would submit access providers to archaic phone-monopoly style regulations under Title II.[11] The entire "process" was unprecedented, and according to several industry sources, illegal. These sources claim that many of the official negotiations conducted by the FCC chief of staff, Edward Lazarus, were held in secret, closed-door sessions, in clear violation of the Administrative Procedure Act's *ex parte* communications requirements, which mandate that all such meetings be recorded and available to the public.[12]

Genachowski managed to conjure up qualified support for the bad option. As one congressional insider commented, "What essentially some of us believe happened is that the [other broadband carriers] were coerced. They were told, 'All right, we know you don't want Title II. Sign up for this middle ground, or we're going to reclassify.' And it was that threat that got them to sort of say, 'All right, we won't appeal. We won't fight it up on the Hill, and we won't appeal it.' Verizon ultimately did not sign onto this, but everybody else did." So, on December 1, Genachowski announced that the FCC would vote on the final rules within weeks, allowing for a substantially shortened public-comment period than granted for the initial rule and Notice of Inquiry. Moreover, on the night of Friday, December 10, just two business days before the public-comment period expired, the commission dumped almost two thousand documents into the record.[13] It did the same with an additional thousand documents less than twenty-four hours before the end of the public-comment period. And Genachowski sucked any last morsel of marrow from the process when he mandated that the text of the proposed rules be kept secret from the public until after they were passed by the agency.[14]

---

11. Robert M. McDowell, "The FCC's Threat to Internet Freedom," *Wall Street Journal*, December 19, 2010, http://online.wsj.com/article/SB10001424052748703395204576023 452250748540.html.

12. Administrative Procedure Act, 5 U.S.C. § 557.

13. *See* Suderman, *supra* note 4.

14. Larry Downes, "Chairman Genachowski and His Howling Commissioners: Reading the Network Neutrality Order (Part 1)," *Technology Liberation Front*, December 30,

On December 21, 2010, the FCC passed its network-neutrality rules 3 to 2 over the dissents of its two Republican commissioners. Under the guise of preserving the Internet "as an open platform for innovation, investment, job creation, economic growth, competition and free expression," the FCC adopted three rules:

1. **Transparency.** Fixed and mobile broadband providers must disclose the network-management practices, performance characteristics, and terms and conditions of their broadband services.
2. **No blocking.** Fixed broadband providers may not block lawful content, applications, services, or non-harmful devices; mobile broadband providers may not block lawful websites, or block applications that compete with their voice or video telephony services.
3. **No unreasonable discrimination.** Fixed broadband providers may not unreasonably discriminate in transmitting lawful network traffic.[15]

If the rules seem vague or extremely general, it is because they are. The FCC intends to enforce them through adjudication, on a case-by-case basis, making it exceedingly unclear which actions by broadband service providers the agency will deem a violation. Whether this uncertainty will be used to constrain providers or not, it is clear is that the FCC has given itself incredibly wide latitude to enforce the rules.

While the commission states that there is only "one Internet," it concedes that there are different network structures and capabilities, particularly between the technical capabilities of wireline broadband access providers and wireless providers. Wireless networks, according to the commission, are still in the development stages without the large capacities that wireline networks have, thus the rules with regard

---

2010, http://techliberation.com/2010/12/30/chairman-genachowski-and-his-howling-commissioners-reading-the-net-neutrality-order-part-i/.

15. Preserving the Open Internet, 76 FR 59192-01 (2011) [hereafter "Open Internet Order"].

to wireless providers are stated in narrower terms.[16] The rules only apply to "broadband Internet access service" providers defined as:

> A mass market retail service by wire or radio that provides the capability to transmit data and receive data from all or substantially all Internet endpoints, including any capabilities that are incidental to and enable the operation of the communications service, but excluding dial-up Internet access service. This term also encompasses any service that the Commission finds to be providing a functional equivalent of the service described in the previous sentence, or that is used to evade the protections set forth in the Part.[17]

Thus, the rules apply to *all* broadband access providers (with the exception of those services offered to large-scale enterprise customers), including cable, fiber, wireless, or any other access method that offers its services to retail customers.

Despite their wide latitude, the rules do *not* apply to "edge-service" providers, including application and content providers. This is interesting because the FCC asserts the Communications Act grants it jurisdiction over "the utilization of networks and spectrum to provide communication by wire and radio." In excluding edge providers from the rules, one might conclude that the commission does not believe this grant of jurisdiction extends to regulation of the content of the communications traveling over those networks and spectrum. However, as one Congressional Research Service study noted, the commission has asserted jurisdiction over the contents of communication in the past, through, for example, its Fairness Doctrine, and its indecency regulations on broadcast content. Given its history of regulating communication content, the study aptly surmised, ". . . the Commission may believe that it does have jurisdiction over edge services and may merely

---

16. *See* Kathleen Ann Ruane, "The FCC's Authority to Regulate Net Neutrality after Comcast v. FCC," Congressional Research Service, CRS Report for Congress, October 27, 2011.

17. *See* Open Internet Order, *supra* note 15, at 59193.

be refraining from exercising its jurisdiction at this time."[18] There is certainly no doubt in our minds.

The first rule, regarding transparency, is also the least controversial of the three. In fact, many network-neutrality opponents agree that transparency with regard to ISP practices is a desirable goal and even necessary for a well-functioning market. And many service providers have already taken concrete and considerable steps toward explaining their services and network-management practices to consumers.

With regard to wireline services, the rule requires broadband service providers to supply to customers, both on their websites and at the time of sale, disclosure regarding its network-management practices.[19] While the rule is intended to allow providers to use their discretion with regard to determining exactly what information to disclose to customers, the commission identified three primary topics such disclosures should cover: network practices, performance characteristics, and commercial terms.[20] The rule applies to wireless providers in a similar fashion. While mobile broadband providers are not required to allow all third-party devices to attach to their network, they must disclose their certification procedures for such devices and applications.[21]

The second two rules are considerably more controversial, and inherently damaging to the industry. Despite the fact that all major broadband providers currently claim they do not block the transmission of lawful content over their networks, the FCC maintains the no-blocking rule is necessary to ensure openness and competition among the services. The rule covers all lawful communication over the Internet, and in addition to forbidding blocking, forbids "impairing or degrading" lawful content so as to render it unusable. However, the provision is subject to reasonable network management. A network-management practice is reasonable, according to the order, "if it is

---

18. *See* Ruane, *supra* note 65 in Chapter 4, at 9.

19. Ruane, *supra* note 65 in Chapter 4, at 9.

20. *See* Open Internet Order, *supra* note 15, at 59192 ¶ 56.

21. Ibid., 59192 ¶ 97; Ruane, *supra* note 65 in Chapter 4, at 9.

appropriate and tailored to achieving a legitimate network management purpose, taking into account the particular network architecture and technology of the broadband Internet access service."[22]

Because slowing down the speed at which video is delivered may make it unwatchable, or otherwise disrupt the experience, intentionally doing so would violate the open-Internet rules. But, because the rule is subject to reasonable network management, during times of high traffic, a broadband provider may find it necessary to slow the delivery of streaming video, for example, to allow all of its customers to have Internet access in a particular area. Slowing down traffic in this context, as a management tool, would likely not be considered a violation of the rule.[23] You can anticipate the difficulties in investigating an alleged violation.

The no-blocking rule is narrower with regard to wireless services because it only prevents the blocking of lawful websites, rather than forbidding the blocking of all lawful content. It also forbids the blocking of Internet services, which might compete with a wireless provider's voice and telephony services, implying that such providers cannot block programs like Skype from operating over their networks.[24]

Finally, the unreasonable discrimination rule recognizes that many fixed broadband access providers are also Internet content providers. In addition, many have affiliations with certain other content providers. As such, the agency reasons, they have both the capacity and the incentive to favor transmission of their own content and the content of their affiliates. Thus, the rule forbids unreasonable discrimination in transmitting lawful network traffic over a consumer's broadband Internet access service, but reasonable network management does not constitute discrimination.[25] The more transparent an access provider is about its traffic-management policies, the more likely those poli-

---

22. Ibid., 59192 ¶ 82; Ruane, *supra* note 65 in Chapter 4, at 11.

23. *See* Ruane, *supra* note 65 in Chapter 4, at 11.

24. Ibid., 12–13. *See also* Open Internet Order, *supra* note 15, at 59192 ¶ 99, ¶¶ 101–102; Ruane, *supra* note 65 in Chapter 4, at 11.

25. *See* Open Internet Order, *supra* note 15, at 59192 ¶68; Ruane, *supra* note 65 in Chapter 4, at 12.

cies will be considered reasonable.[26] While the rule does not prevent wireline broadband providers from developing tiered levels of service, allowing heavy users to pay more for faster speeds, and lighter users to pay less, the commission did express concern for "pay for priority" arrangements, whereby a broadband provider and a third party could agree to favor some traffic over other traffic. Such arrangements could violate the unreasonable-discrimination rule, although, as the Congressional Research Service report noted, "It is unclear what the difference between tiered services and pay for priority services might be. Presumably, the Commission will flesh out this distinction and many others as cases come before the Commission."[27] The commission did not apply the unreasonable discrimination rule to wireless providers.

The rule is at once so vague and potentially sweeping, it is easy to see how it could cripple network providers' abilities to manage their networks, and stifle innovation as providers become unwilling to experiment with new traffic-management tools or even fully implement those already in their repertoires for fear that they may be deemed "unreasonable."

Verizon immediately appealed the order but was told by the D.C. Circuit Court that it had nothing to appeal, since at that time the FCC had yet to officially publish its rules, formally enacting them as law.

The Illusion of Network Neutrality

The FCC's Open Internet Order is the agency's answer to the long campaign by network-neutrality supporters for government regulation to ensure broadband providers do not attempt to control access to the Internet and the breadth of content on the Internet. But the order gives the FCC regulatory jurisdiction that is so broad, and the rules themselves are so vague, they have left both network-neutrality

---

26. Ibid., 59192 ¶ 70; Ruane, *supra* note 65 in Chapter 4, at 12.

27. Open Internet Order, *supra* note 15, at 59192 ¶¶ 70, 72, and 76; Ruane, *supra* note 65 in Chapter 4, at 12.

proponents and opponents scratching their heads. On the one hand the rules give the FCC the sweeping authority:

> 1) To regulate how fixed and mobile broadband carriers disclose their network management practices, performance characteristics and terms of service; 2) to regulate how fixed and mobile broadband carriers provide access to content, applications, services and devices; 3) to determine whether the way fixed broadband providers carry network traffic is unreasonably discriminatory; 4) to regulate how fixed and mobile broadband carriers charge for carriage of traffic; and 5) to determine whether fixed and mobile providers' network management techniques are reasonable.[28]

On the other hand, the rules are so replete of specifics defining would-be violations or detailing methodologies for investigating alleged transgressions, they are either an endless landscape of loopholes or minefields, depending on your point of view. Either way, the uncertainty threatens to stifle growth of the entire industry as both sides wait to see how the agency attempts to both clearly define and enforce its rules. What is certain is that the process will not be quick or easy, and litigation will further slow the process due to an anticipated backlog of complaints.

More importantly, the rules are doomed to fail to accomplish their objective because their objective is untenable: network neutrality is an illusion, a fallacy. In order to understand why, we must first address the concerns raised by proponents. In Chapter 1 we broke down those concerns into seven separate but related categories.

In a nutshell, network-neutrality proponents claim that without regulation, broadband providers will have the unfettered ability to (1) block or degrade non-favored content and applications in order to prioritize favored content and applications, splitting data transmis-

---

28. House Report, Disapproving the Rule Submitted by the Federal Communications Commission with Respect to Regulating the Internet and Broadband Industry Practices. 112th Congress, 1st Session. Report 112-51, 6; *see also,* In re Broadband Industry Practices WC Docket No. 07-52, Report and Order, FCC 10-201 (rel. Dec. 23, 2010).

sion into slow and fast lanes. Because of the profitability of the fast lanes, proponents claim, providers will have little incentive to invest in improving or maintaining the slow lanes. (2) As a result, network providers will be able to force content and application providers to pay heavy fees for access to these fast lanes, which in turn will (3) stifle competition and innovation at the "edges" of the networks as smaller and start-up companies find themselves unable to afford access to the Net. This will result in (4) a diminution of political and other expression on the Internet, since there will be fewer and fewer who are able to have their voices heard. All the while, left unchecked, (5) the powerful network providers will increasingly integrate vertically into content and application markets. (6) And the combination of this vertical integration, along with special relationships between network providers and the surviving content and application providers, will create a network of walled gardens, where consumers are force-fed service agreements that limit their freedom to access the content and use the applications of their choice. (7) The totality of circumstances will result in legal and regulatory uncertainty in the area of Internet access, which will further decrease investment into developing content and application innovations.[29]

But these seven "concerns" can be further distilled into three main categories: (1) The broadband access market is essentially a duopoly dominated by cable and telephone companies that will abuse their market power through vertical leveraging and other anticompetitive behavior that will result in market failure and consumer harm. (2) Even without full-fledged market failure, broadband access providers will create a two-tiered Internet where only content and application providers with the deepest pockets will be able to afford fast-lane transmission across the networks. This in turn will have a "chilling effect" on innovation by guy-in-his-garage and small mom-and-pop edge providers. Regulation is thus needed to level the playing field. (3) Because access providers have the potential to discriminate with

---

29. *See generally*, FTC Staff Report.

regard to access to their networks, regulation is needed to preserve free speech and expression on the Internet.[30]

We argue that attempting to address the latter two concerns through regulation is unwarranted, unwise, and unprecedented. Addressing the first concern with additional regulation would be redundant to an already well-established and well-equipped body of law designed specifically to handle market failure: antitrust.

Let's dispel with the "free speech" concern first. The notion that regulation is needed to preserve free speech and expression on the Net is not only misguided, but arguably a thinly veiled attempt by liberals to impose the Fairness Doctrine on the Internet.[31] The Fairness Doctrine, as discussed earlier, was an FCC policy instituted in 1949 that threatened broadcasters with fines if they failed to "afford reasonable opportunity for the discussion of conflicting views" on controversial issues of public importance. Suffice it to say, network neutrality is the Fairness Doctrine on steroids—or, perhaps more aptly put, Fairness Doctrine 2.0.

Remember, it was just a few years ago that liberals like Rep. Nancy Pelosi (D-CA), Sen. Tom Harkin (D-IA), and Sen. Debbie Stabenow (D-MI) launched a reinvigorated campaign to reinstate the doctrine in response to conservative dominance of talk radio. Although their efforts, at least with regard to broadcast, were stymied in Congress, network neutrality has the potential to cast a much bigger net. It is simply no surprise that the same people who have long favored government control of media and communications are the same people who advocated for the Fairness Doctrine, and are also front and center in the network-neutrality campaign. Network neutrality would require Internet access providers to treat all bits of online traffic and communications the same,

---

30. *See* Neuchterlein, "Antitrust," *supra* note 95 in Chapter 3, at 34–37.

31. *See* Adam Thierer, "Net Neutrality: A Fairness Doctrine for the Internet," October 2007, http://www.pff.org/issues-pubs/ps/2007/ps3.11fairnessdoctrineinternet.html; *see also* Neuchterlein, *supra* note 95 in Chapter 3, at 37–38.

but there is no reason to believe that the end result would be any less chilling on speech than the Fairness Doctrine before it.

We will address concerns (1) and (2) together. First, the premise that neutrality is something that ever existed on the Net and thus something to preserve is simply false. Network neutrality itself is a fallacy with regard to the Internet environment as a whole, and certainly with respect to the network architecture at the core of the Internet.

To review, Tim Wu, Jonathan Lessig, and others describe network neutrality as a design architecture, where data is transmitted via the "best efforts" principle, meaning the transmitting device keeps sending data packets until the receiving device signals that it has received them—data is transmitted blindly, without regard to its individual characteristics. Where the network's intelligence is built into the equipment at either end of the connection—the edge of the network, thus adhering to the "end-to-end" principle. The pipes over which the data travels are "dumb" or indifferent to the nature of the applications the packets will run within their destination computers. But the network-neutrality proponents go even further: they elevate the principles that describe the physical architecture of the Internet to a kind of populist philosophy that they claim always has driven and defined the Internet environment, and should continue to do so.

The first problem, as we discussed in Chapter 3 and will describe in further detail below, is that the architecture of the Internet, in large part, no longer adheres to this model. In some ways, it never did. Moreover, non-neutrality is ubiquitous to the Internet environment. Additionally, since the Internet was privatized in 1996, its growth and essence have been driven by and responsive to trade in the market rather than its design or architecture.

As policy analyst Steven Titch remarks, the only time it is conceivable to argue that the Net was neutral was in the earliest years when the ARPANET, and subsequent NSFNET networks, were used solely by universities, and all communication and commands were text-based. "That changed when the first browsers were introduced—graphical user interfaces brought an end to nominal Internet neutrality because they allowed information to be presented in a whole new way."[32] As described in Chapter 4, browsers (beginning with Mosaic and Netscape), with their graphical interfaces, began to make the Internet a user-friendly environment.[33] Suddenly the Internet was accessible to almost anyone, and as such represented a new, virtually limitless platform for entrepreneurs and businesses of all types to reach consumers. But that did not mean the Internet had become some sort of "massive leveler of economic inequality."[34] Quite the opposite. It had become a new commercial frontier, and browsers provided the first tools for businesses to begin to distinguish themselves from one another, and ultimately to seek advantage over others in delivering and presenting end users with products and information. This transition for the Internet, from a private, research-fueled network of networks, to one open to all, for both scholarly and commercial purposes, obliterated any claim to neutrality on the Net.[35]

Indeed, as Hazlett and Wright point out, the Internet market is far more complicated and nuanced than the FCC recognizes, and since the Net was privatized, the terms of trade have not been "open end-to-end." Instead, they are economic, "the standard building blocks of markets: property and contracts, layered upon a general legal regime enabling ownership, production and trade." So, it is not the network design that dictates the terms of trade; trade must dictate network design. And it has.[36]

---

32. Steven Titch, "The Internet Is Not Neutral (and No Law Can Make It So)," Reason Foundation, May 1, 2009, http://heartland.org/sites/all/modules/custom/heartland _migration/files/pdfs/28419.pdf.

33. *See* Christopher S. Yoo, "Free Speech and the Myth of the Internet as an Unintermediated Experience," *George Washington Law Review* 78 (2010): 701 (browsers are the new competitors online and consumers care more about what is searchable than what is actually online. It follows that the abundance of content is no longer the priority—the quality of service is).

34. *See* Neuchterlein, *supra* note 95 in Chapter 3, at 35.

35. Ibid.

36. Thomas W. Hazlett and Joshua D. Wright, "The Law and Economics of Network Neutrality," George Mason University Law and Economics Research Paper, August 15,

Today, content providers, application providers, and virtually all Internet business and information sources, compete to capture consumers. Websites consistently upgrade their interfaces with graphics, links, and the latest video players to make them user-friendly and inviting. Social networking sites like Facebook similarly cater to end users. Look at how many times the site has updated its interface or changed its algorithms, ostensibly—albeit not always successfully—to improve the social networking experience for its users. These modifications are borne by competition, and competition is not neutral; there are winners and losers. After all, only ninety-year-olds have Yahoo e-mail accounts or continue to use the AOL browser.

And non-neutrality is purposely built in to the algorithms of search engines like Google.[37] First, any search engine is inherently subjective. After all, search engines prioritize results, placing links to some websites at the top of the page, while relegating others to the bottom, or even several pages back. But while Google has helped lead the charge for network neutrality, its search engine is about as non-neutral as they get. Google may argue that its phenomenal success is due to its search algorithm's ability to cypher through the seemingly endless possible websites in cyberspace and return search results that correlate the usefulness of the results to the end user's search, but it is just not that simple.[38] In fact, Google's ultra-secret search algorithm reportedly has over a thousand variables or discrimination biases that decide which content gets priority in its search results, and Google-owned content gets moved to the front of the pack. If you don't buy it, try it.[39] You will notice that Google-owned YouTube, Google Maps, and Google Earth typically show up at the top of search results. As Scott Cleland, author of the book *Search & Destroy: Why You Can't Trust Google Inc.*

2011, 13–14, http://www.law.gmu.edu/assets/files/publications/working_papers/1136Law&EconomicsofNetworkNeutrality.pdf.

37. *See* Yoo, "Free Speech," *supra* note 33, at 701.

38. *See* Scott Cleland, "Why Google Is Not Neutral," The Precursor Blog, http://precursorblog.com/content/why-google-is-not-neutral.

39. Ibid.

points out, "Google also provides itself specialized ad formats that are better than non-Google advertisers get. To drive home how obvious it is that Google's search engine is not neutral as claimed, there is actually a search engine called 'Google Minus Google' that removed the Google-favored content to make the results more neutral." Cleland points to a whole slew of additional ways Google is not neutral: the fact that Google "improved" its international search results by "demoting non-country search results," its organizational bias against the existing domain addressing system of the World Wide Web—and the list goes on.[40] Our point is that Google is, by design, non-neutral, and while it has done a magnificent PR job creating the illusion of neutrality, it is all smoke and mirrors.

The fact is, Google is a gatekeeper, as much, if not more than, any network provider. Moreover, consumers need Internet gatekeepers in order to organize, prioritize, and filter the nearly limitless array of Internet content to make it possible for us to find relevant content. Treating all content equally would mean giving independent blogs with a few followers the same credence as CNN.com. As Time Warner pointed out in a 2010 FCC filing,

'Google has led the charge to adopt regulation to ensure Internet openness, yet it has the ability and incentive to engage in a range of decidedly non-neutral conduct due to its control over so many aspects of the Internet experience,' said one representative filing. 'Google's core search application relies on a pay-for-priority scheme that is squarely at odds with its proposed neutrality requirements for broadband-internet-access service providers.'[41]

Content and application providers like Google, YouTube, and Yahoo have painted the battle as one between David and Goliath, where they—multibillion-dollar corporations—are the Davids facing off

---

40. Scott Cleland, "Why Google Is Not Neutral"; *see also* Scott Cleland, *Search & Destroy: Why You Can't Trust Google Inc.* (Saint Louis, MO: Telescope Books, 2011).

41. *See* Nate Anderson, "Regulating Google's Results? Law Prof Calls 'Search Neutrality' Incoherent," ars.technica.com (January 19, 2011).

against the Goliath network providers; yet where nothing could be farther from the truth. Not only do such companies have as much ability and incentive to discriminate against certain users or other—smaller—content and application providers, they, as demonstrated above, implore business models that are as potentially discriminatory and non-neutral as the practices they so vehemently beg the FCC to protect them from.

Another example of the Net's non-neutrality is the ever-increasing use of CDNs by content and application providers alike. CDNs help content providers circumvent congestion on the Net by being strategically placed to deliver content to end users through the quickest and most efficient route.[42] But CDNs are not free. You either have to be a mega-corporation like Google, able to afford the multibillion-dollar investments needed to build the overlay networks, or you have to pay commercial CDNs like Akamai, Limelight, and Level 3, which maintain a network of caches across the Internet, for their services.[43] Either way, CDNs are designed to, and do, enable privileged content and application providers to out-compete their rivals. They are thus decidedly non-neutral. Still, the FCC was clear (in a long footnote to its Open Internet Order) that network-neutrality rules do not apply to CDNs.[44] The FCC's justification? CDNs, unlike ISPs, do not control the last-mile connections to end users and thus do not have the ability to harm third-party traffic not being delivered by the CDN.

Interestingly, Internet Service Providers have recently been deploying CDNs. The ISP can store proprietary content in its CDN and strategically place its proprietary CDN so as to transmit proprietary content faster, more efficiently, and at a higher quality. For example, "content companies and CDNs can be topologically right on the Comcast network . . . [so] the delivery of that content [can] be up to twice as fast."[45] Comcast owns CDNs, which it can use to deliver selected con-

---

42. Greg Goth, "New Internet Economics Might Not Make It to the Edge," *News and Trends,* IEEE Computer Society, January/February 2010.

43. *See generally* Titch, "Google," *supra* note 8 in Chapter 4.

44. FCC Open Internet Report and Order, footnote 235, 44.

45. *See* Goth, "New Internet Economics," *supra* note 41.

tent more efficiently. Whether or not this violates network-neutrality principles is unclear. It is possible that the proprietary CDNs would constitute private networks that are unaffected by network-neutrality regulations. As a result, such practices could become a general means of skirting network-neutrality regulation and ensuring that proprietary content, or vertically integrated content providers, are transmitted more efficiently. Indeed, network-neutrality regulation may force ISPs to use this mechanism of ensuring efficient delivery of some content as a means of overcoming the challenges posed by congestion, burstiness, or other effects of network inefficiency.

Network neutrality is also a fallacy with respect to the architecture of the Internet, in that the architecture is not neutral.

A favorite analogy of network-neutrality proponents is to compare the architecture of the Internet to an electric power grid. Says Lessig:

> The Internet isn't the only network to follow an end-to-end design, though it is the first large-scale computer network to choose that principle at its birth. The electricity grid is an end-to-end grid; as long as my equipment complied with the rules for the grid, I get to plug in.[46]

Lessig and other network-neutrality proponents argue that maintaining this end-to-end design—mandating it, in fact, with network-neutrality rules—is the only way to ensure continued innovation, in that applications make the Internet useful. Quoting Tim Berners-Lee, Lessig continues:

> 'There's a freedom about the Internet: as long as we accept the rules of sending packets around, we can send packets containing anything anywhere.' New applications 'can be brought to the Internet without the need for any changes to the underlying network.' The 'architecture' of the network is designed to be 'neutral with respect to applications and content.' By placing

---

46. Lawrence Lessig, *The Future of Ideas: The Fate of the Commons in a Connected World* (New York: Random House, 2001), 39.

intelligence in the ends, the network has no intelligence to tell which functions or content are permitted or not.[47]

According to Lessig and other network-neutrality proponents, if network providers are not forced to adhere to the end-to-end and best-efforts principles, they will attempt to control the data traversing their networks to the detriment of content and application providers and especially end users. After all, as the argument goes, most Americans get their broadband from their cable providers and you do not have to look much further than cable television business models—where the cable company retains control of which channels it will provide and how those channels will be packaged—to get a glimpse of the future of the Internet.

And characterizing network neutrality as a mechanism of escaping the ominous threat of private corporate control of how individuals use the Internet has been an effective rhetorical tool for harnessing public support. Proponents have convinced large segments of the general population that the failure to implement network-neutrality regulation will result in an anticonsumer environment, where access to content is based on how cozy content providers are with the particular broadband providers, not on the personal proclivities of end users.[48]

We disagree. The non-neutrality of the Net is a good thing for consumers, for network providers, and for content and application developers alike. Moreover, the overwhelming scholarly and historical research demonstrates that it is many of the Internet's non-neutral

---

47. Ibid.

48. *See* "Net Neutrality—Should Businesses Care?," *IBM Systems Magazine*, October 2007, http://www.ibmsystemsmag.com/ibmi/trends/whatsnew/Net-Neutralitya%E2%82%AC%E2%80%9DShould-Businesses-Care-/. *See also* Davina Sashkin, "Failure of Imagination: Why Inaction on Net Neutrality Regulation Will Result in a De Facto Legal Regime Promoting Discrimination and Consumer Harm," *CommLaw Conspectus* 15 (2006): 263 (analogizing a non-neutral Internet to privately owned streets and highways where SUVs are potentially the only cars allowed because their manufacturer is a vertically integrated subsidiary of the company that owns the roads).

characteristics, along with the deregulatory policies of the last twenty years, which have allowed the Internet to continue to evolve to meet consumer needs and innovators' demands. There is simply no problem that requires fixing. And when isolated problems have arisen, like the Comcast debacle, backlash has been almost instantaneous and unequivocal. In fact, a key oversight of the push for network neutrality has been the weight of consumer power on the market. Consumer might is shored up with an ample body of antitrust law, specifically designed to combat anticompetitive and ultimately anticonsumer behavior by corporations. Finally, handing the FCC the reigns of Internet oversight is a mistake. The agency has time and again demonstrated itself to be an inherently political body, more like a mini-congress than an expert agency.

In spite of network-neutrality proponents' arguments to the contrary, the Internet is not akin to an electric grid. It follows that network providers are not and should not be treated as common carriers, or otherwise mandated to treat the data that flows over their networks neutrally, since doing so will prevent the maximization of efficient transmission of certain applications and content. As Christopher Yoo points out, the faults in the grid analogy begin at the most basic level. For starters, the Internet involves far more sources and termination points for network flow than an electric power grid. Next, data traffic is not like electricity traffic; it is bursty or subject to sudden, brief periods of high-volume traffic that disrupts the network flow. The combination of these two characteristics makes coordinating data traffic over the Internet far more difficult than coordinating traffic through an electric power grid. Moreover, traffic coordination is two-sided—upstream and downstream—so there are more dimensions to measure. Additionally, the "burstiness" is especially disruptive because it would confuse prices based on volume, and, unlike the one-way network traffic in an electric grid, the Internet is a multi-way network, which obscures traffic issues beyond repair.[49]

---

49. *See* Daniel F. Spulber and Christopher S. Yoo, "Rethinking Broadband Internet Access," *Harvard Journal of Law & Technology* 22 (2008): 54.

But even more importantly, as Stephen Titch points out, where electricity competition *has* been privatized, differentiation is usually based on price—in other words, prices are "tiered" according to user consumption. It follows that "no competitor has made electricity 'better' in that it lengthens the life of light bulbs, or can produce the same cooling or heating output for less k W consumption." On the contrary, consumers depend on the energy efficiency of the equipment they connect to the network to derive more value for their energy dollars. So, it is the better air conditioners, or florescent versus incandescent lighting, that save you money, not the quality of the electricity coming out of your sockets.[50]

Data, on the other hand, while consisting of binary electronic or optical pulses of 1s and 0s, actually "have independent value that derives from the content or application that all those ones and zeros represent when processed by the right equipment or software. Routers, PCs, and other information appliances in the home or workplace are designed to take specific data and covert it into something of value that transcends its base digital format."[51] So thinking of the Internet as just a transport network for raw, generic data is inaccurate. Instead, it is a transport media for content and applications, which are both diverse and dynamic. "This is the grand irony of network neutrality," Titch maintains. "By insisting that all data be treated the same way as it crosses the network, it fails to recognize the value of the content and application contained in the bitstream."[52] It follows that different kinds of content and applications may warrant different treatment by network providers to maximize their own utility to end users, especially at times of peak demand, when there is additional strain on the network. This is particularly true since the transmission capacity of a network is finite. And the pressure on networks is ever increasing—particularly at the last mile—as the number of users burgeons, and as certain content and applications become increasingly bandwidth intensive.

---

50. *See* Titch, *supra* note 32, at 9.
51. Ibid., 10.
52. Ibid.

The idea that network providers can add intelligence to their networks to improve the general flow of content and applications over those networks is not a novel idea. Since the Internet was conceived, the goal of computer scientists, inventors, and entrepreneurs has been to develop the most robust and dynamic network architecture possible. And while the design was modeled on end-to-end and best-efforts principles, the networks have never been completely "dumb." Network providers and their associated ISPs almost always offer standard filtering applications that protect consumers from spam, viruses, and other unwanted content and applications. Technically, such features violate the end-to-end principle, since they discriminate against and actually block packets traversing the networks on the basis of their "cargo."[53] You would be hard-pressed to find anyone, including the most vehement network-neutrality supporter, who does not encourage this kind of data discrimination. With finite transmission capacity and an uptick in bandwidth-intensive applications such as gaming, video streaming, video teleconferencing, streaming multimedia, VoIP, and remote surgery applications that require a fixed bit rate or are delay sensitive, the network's ability to guarantee a certain level of performance to data flow becomes more necessary.

The term adopted by the computer network industry is Quality of Service (QoS), and refers to the network's ability to "provide different priority to different applications, user, or data flows, or to guarantee a certain level of performance to data flow."[54] Interestingly, QoS itself is not exactly a novel idea, but one that was contemplated by the earliest innovators. In fact, calling TCP/IP, the Internet's communication protocol, a "dumb pipe" is simply technically inaccurate. Instead, even in the original Request for Comments (a best-practices document developed as part of the standards-making process of the Internet Engineering Task Force), a so-called Type of Service (TOS) field was reserved in every packet, or data envelope that carries content

---

53. *See* "Digital Crossroads," *supra* note 3 in Chapter 3, at 175.
54. *See* Spulber and Yoo, *supra* note 48, at 356.

in the IP packets (which can be thought of as data envelopes that carry data or content across the networks).[55] That TOS contained mechanisms that identify how network devices should process those packets. Even the developers of the original TCP/IP standards developed for DARPA incorporated mechanisms that treated high-precedence traffic differently than other traffic, and informational flags for the prioritization of different packets traveling on the networks. They recognized the fact that QoS and packet prioritization would be essential and inevitable components of a growing Internet. The TCP component of the protocol suite has its own network-congestion algorithm, which reduces the throughput rate of a process when a dropped packet is detected, indicating network congestion on a wireline network.[56]

A significant shift toward building intelligence into the core of the networks began nearly twenty years ago, as businesses began to use the Internet for their own internal enterprise networking. Soon, such businesses demanded greater encryption, quality control, and prioritization in their own national and global communications networks. This required the phone companies, which provided the networks, to accommodate the businesses by extending such controls from the edges of the portion of the networks owned by the phone companies at their cores.[57] As a result, Stephen Titch explains:

> [A] new alphabet soup of protocols and formats such as the Multiprotocol Label Switching (MPLS), the Session Initiation Protocol (SIP), and the Simple Object Access Protocol (SOAP), emerged in the mid-to-late 1990s and the early part of this decade, specifically designed to give service providers tools to improve quality, reliability, and management of IP data as it crossed the Internet. These quality of services were in turn sold to enterprise customers in the form of 'Good, Better, Best' quality tiers.[58]

55. Kai Zhu, "Bringing Neutrality to Network Neutrality," Boalt Hall School of Law, White Paper Competition, 2007, 5, http://step.berkeley.edu/White_Paper/Zhu.pdf.

56. For a detailed discussion, *see* Kai Zhu, "Bringing Neutrality to Network Neutrality."

57. *See* "Digital Crossroads," *supra* note 3 in Chapter 3, at 175.

58. *See* Titch, *supra* note 32, at 7.

A best-effort network does not support QoS, so a network that offers QoS in its transmission is no longer a best-effort network.

Still, the Internet is not a single-owner network; it is a series of exchange points interconnecting private networks. Thus, the true core of the Internet is not managed by a single entity, but by a number of different network service providers. As such, no standard QoS mechanism has yet been deployed across the entire Internet landscape. But the Internet Engineering Task Force (IETF) has focused on two approaches to Internet-deployable QoS. The first is an architecture called Integrated Services (IntServ), which relies on the application to trigger QoS by using the Resource Reservation Protocol (RSVP) to request and reserve resources. The second architecture is called differentiated services (DiffServ), which marks data packets according to the type of service they require. In response, routers and switches use various queuing strategies to tailor packet performance to expectations.[59] While neither QoS architecture is satisfactory to deploy over the entire Internet, and while network providers may not be able to guarantee a promised level of QoS delivery throughout the rest of the Internet's many networks, prioritization can and does allow service providers to offer different levels of QoS within the last-mile ISP's network. Still, irrespective of the extent to which a network is able to guarantee QoS, the fact is, the prioritization of data is a central and mandatory component of traffic management over the Internet's networks, and data prioritization is not neutral. It follows that it is the consumer who ultimately pays the highest price when the network provider is limited in its ability to manage traffic over its own network, since the transmission of data requested by the consumer might be slowed or otherwise degraded due to congestion or the network's inability to support his or her desired applications.

Still, the debate over what kinds of prioritization should be permitted, and to what extent, has been an explosive focal point of the

---

59. For a detailed technical discussion of each QoS architecture, *see* "Internetworking Technology Handbook," Cisco, http://www.cisco.com/web/about/ac123/ac147/ac174/ac197/about_cisco_ipj_archive_article09186a00800c8314.html.

network-neutrality debate. There are several types of data prioritization. The first is uniform application-based prioritization, called "differential pricing" or more commonly "access tiering," by network-neutrality proponents. Differential pricing uses algorithms to place all applications of a certain type, like video, P2P, or VoIP, into a specific access tier that receives equal priority in delivery. It could also be used to deprioritize certain traffic at peak times. While application-based prioritization for traffic management purposes has not been particularly controversial, the idea that network providers might charge content and application providers for this priority *has* drawn a firestorm of controversy. In fact, a single quote from AT&T's chief executive officer, Ed Whitacre, on the topic may have done as much or more to fuel the network-neutrality debate as the entire Comcast controversy. Explaining a plan in which AT&T would charge for optimizing applications, Whitacre famously told *Bloomberg Businessweek* in 2005, "They use my lines for free—and that's bull. For Google or a Yahoo or a Vonage or anybody to expect to use these pipes for free is nuts!"[60] Not even a year later, Verizon senior vice president John Thorne voiced similar sentiments when he said, "The network builders are spending a fortune constructing and maintaining the networks that Google intends to ride on with nothing but cheap servers. It is enjoying a free lunch that should, by any rational account, be the lunch of the facilities providers."[61]

Network-neutrality proponents immediately fired back. Tim Wu called the idea of tiered access for a fee "the Tony Soprano business model." And in a June 8, 2006, *Washington Post* column, Lawrence Lessig and Robert McChesney claimed such plans would allow companies like AT&T and Verizon to "sell access to the express lane to deep-pocketed corporations and relegate everyone else to the digital

---

60. Patricia O'Connell, ed., "At SBC, It's All about 'Scale and Scope,'" *Bloomberg Businessweek,* November 6, 2005, http://www.businessweek.com/magazine/content/05_45/b3958092.htm.

61. Arshad Modammed, "Verizon Executive Call for End to Google Free Lunch," *Washington Post*, February 7, 2006, http://www.washingtonpost.com/wp-dyn/content/article/2006/02/06/AR2006020601624.html.

equivalent of a winding dirt road. Worse still, these gatekeepers would determine who gets premium treatment and who doesn't."[62]

Yet, there are major faults with Lessig and McChesney's argument. First, technically speaking, creating fast lanes or priority lanes for certain customers does not necessarily mean that everyone else is relegated to a slow lane where services are actually degraded. In fact, say Litan and Singer, "the analogy of unaffiliated content providers being relegated to the 'digital equivalent of a winding dirt road' is hyperbole."[63] This position, they point out, "could be correct only to the extent that overall broadband network capacities are constant and no content application ever tries to absorb more than its fair share of capacity. . . ."[64] But neither is true; instead, networks have been consistently expanding their capacities, and a growing number of popular applications, like P2P and Skype, automatically seek to absorb as much available bandwidth as possible. Even good-old reliable TCP additively increases its throughput rate toward infinity until it detects congestion. Litan and Singer maintain that offering enhanced QoS and prioritization is analogous to painting a stripe down the middle of a road to create two lanes. Instead of creating a fast and a slow lane, the change is likely to speed up all traffic by preventing any single driver from hogging both lanes by driving down the middle of the road.[65] Moreover, even with revenues from priority customers, the bulk of a network provider's revenue will still come from regular users. Thus, network providers have a strong incentive to maintain high-speed mass transport lanes in order to keep, and continue to expand, its main customer base.[66]

---

62. Lawrence Lessig and Robert W. McChesney, "No Tolls on the Internet," *Washington Post*, June 8, 2006, http://www.washingtonpost.com/wp-dyn/content/article/2006/06/07/AR2006060702108.html.

63. Ibid.

64. Ibid.

65. Robert Litan and Hal Singer, "Unintended Consequences of Net Neutrality Regulation," *Journal on Telecommunications and High Technology Law* 5 (2007): 8.

66. *See* ibid.

Second, Lessig and McChesney seem to forget that network and content and application providers are mutually dependent. So, if the network provider is limited in its ability to procure revenues, whether through prioritization, vertical integration (as discussed below), or other methods, it also limits its ability to improve the networks upon which the edge providers depend. And network providers have invested billions of dollars building out their own networks and are likely to invest billions more to build next-generation networks to serve mass-market customers. Moreover—going back to the electric-grid analogy—unlike the government agencies or regulated monopolists who built the original grids in return for a guarantee to earn reasonable rates of return for their services, broadband providers were given no such guarantees. There are no government programs to underwrite the broadband build-out, with the exception of its assessing special fees on telecommunications providers to help subsidize broadband connections for schools and libraries.[67]

Adding to the pressure on access providers is the fact that in 2009, Congress directed the FCC to develop a national broadband plan, meant to spur broadband investment and deployment in underserved regions.[68] By its own estimates, the FCC puts the cost of this plan at $350 billion, the bulk of which is presumed to come from private investment within the industry. Charging for application-based prioritization provides a revenue stream to the network provider to both support its services and continue to invest in its network.

By favoring application, service, and content providers to the detriment of network-access providers, the Open Internet Order not only ultimately harms all parties, it also decreases social welfare. In testimony before the Committee on Energy and Commerce Subcommittee on Communications and Technology, investment analyst and visiting scholar at Georgetown University Anna-Maria Kovacs explains:

---

67. See "Digital Crossroads," *supra* note 3 in Chapter 3, at 176.

68. "National Broadband Plan: Connecting America," Broadband.gov, *http://www* .broadband.gov/plan/.

The Order appears to be premised on a view of the Internet ecosystem that assumes that the edge is embryonic and innovative and the core is mature and static. Application providers, including content and service providers, are free to transform their business plans at will. One of their key inputs—transport—is provided to them gratis over the networks of broadband Internet access providers, carriers with whom they may compete at the application level. Conversely, the Order restricts the carriers' flexibility in designing their business plans, limits their sources of revenue, dictates that they spend capital to expand their networks at the edge-providers' will, and forces them to subsidize competitors who cannibalize their customer base.[69]

So, broadband providers are forced to invest billions of dollars in their networks, but under the rules, their avenues for recovering their costs are narrowed. This in turn jeopardizes the very infrastructure upon which the Internet is built.

In short, the FCC's Open Internet Order picks winners and losers. As Kovacs notes:

Over time, the order represents a direct transfer of wealth from broadband access providers to those whose content rides over the network. That means that it provides those who ride the network with a strategically vital financial weapon to use against [broadband providers] who in many cases are their competitors. To put it another way, it takes all the bargaining power away from the [broadband provider]—who is making a very large investment for low returns—and giving it to the content provider who is making relatively little or no investment to enable it to access end-users and in some cases is already getting very high returns.[70]

---

69. H.J. Res 37, "Disapproving the rule submitted by the Federal Communications Commission": Hearing before the House Committee on Energy and Commerce Subcommittee on Communications and Technology, 112th Congress (2011) (testimony of Anna-Maria Kovacs) [hereafter "Testimony"].

70. Anna-Maria Kovacs, "FCC's Open Internet Order—A Financial Translation," December 31, 2010, 7.

The problem is that businesses at the core and at the edges of the network are inextricably intertwined, so characterizing the order as a transfer of wealth from network providers to application providers does not begin to describe the resulting harm to both. As Kovacs explains, "to protect the edge, it is vital to protect the core. Far more devastating to Google, Skype, or Netflix than being charged for transport on the Internet is an Internet whose evolution and capacity are flash-frozen for lack of investment." Kovacs continues, "consumers are attracted to the Internet for its applications but those applications can only reach consumers over the network. Internet applications may as well not exist at all without the networks that are at the core of the Internet, and innovative applications can only follow a step behind the networks' upgrades in capacity and quality. The fastest, highest quality, most creative edge content is at the mercy of the slowest link in its path from provider to consumer."[71]

Moreover, competition is fierce in the market for content provision. This intense competition encourages innovation, dynamic business forms, and lower prices. On the other hand, the market for Internet service provision is duopolistic in most major markets. This leads to stagnation, conscious parallelism, and inflated prices. Non-neutrality (sometimes referred to as Net diversity) does shift revenue from content providers to ISPs, and that is exactly what we want. When market participants realize surplus revenue, it is an enticing invitation for new entry. With the new entry promoted by net diversity, we can expect competition and innovation in the ISP market to intensify dramatically. The absolute best thing that we could do for the Internet is to introduce robust competition to the ISP market. Furthermore, by deregulating the peering point, we can discover which parties truly have bargaining power. Allowing firms to discover who holds the hammer through arms-length negotiation is not only fair, it also gives rise to the most efficient form the Internet market can take.[72]

---

71. *See* Testimony, *supra* note 68.
72. Ibid.

Investment is fueled by a competitive market in which companies continually strive to outperform their rivals, with the goal of winning customers and increasing profits. But in order to compete with each other, companies must be able to distinguish their services from one another. In the network-provider market, lack of competition means providers lose incentive to continue to invest in improving their networks, and suddenly investment and innovation on the edges of the networks are stymied because the networks can no longer provide the speed or quality of transmission that the latest applications and services require.

Verizon, for one, has been making capital investments of more than $17 billion per year for several years now; AT&T has made similar levels of investment. As one Verizon executive put it, "We wouldn't be making the investment if we didn't think that we had competition, if we were sitting fat and happy." But in order to keep the market competitive, and to keep the investment capital pouring in, these companies need flexibility. They need to be able to adjust their business plans to changing market conditions. Preventing such companies from distinguishing themselves by charging for prioritization, or limiting their ability to vertically integrate into the content and application markets, severely limits their flexibility and thus undercuts their potential revenue sources.[73]

Differential pricing also increases social welfare by encouraging content providers to take advantage of superior QoS to tailor their applications to the demands of end users. As a result, "content providers will purchase superior service from ISPs when it improves their ability to market their services to Internet subscribers."[74] Although some content providers, unable to pay for enhanced service, will suffer, as Dennis Weisman and Robert Kulick explain:

---

73. *See* "Testimony," *supra* note 68.

74. Dennis L. Weisman and Robert Kulick, "Price Discrimination, Two-Sided Markets and Network Neutrality Regulation," *Tulane Journal of Technology & Intellectual Property* 13 (2010): 81.

This is the hallmark of the competitive process and, as such, economic theory indicates that total economic welfare will likely increase when content providers as a whole are better able to serve Internet subscribers. Conversely, protecting less efficient content providers by prohibiting access tiering would harm society by impeding more efficient content providers and limiting the choices available to the Internet subscribers they serve. Indeed, this outcome would actually represent a form of truly pernicious discrimination since it would involve an arbitrary transfer of economic wealth to less-efficient content providers to the detriment of society.[75]

Two inherent characteristics of the broadband market further illuminate why network-neutrality regulations will be detrimental to social welfare. First, the broadband market is not just any market, it is a distribution market and, as in many competitive markets, non-neutral or discriminatory business models are common in distribution markets. Furthermore, as discussed above, the broadband market is a capital-intensive market, with steep upfront costs and low marginal costs of serving additional customers. As Thomas M. Lenard, president of the Progress & Freedom Foundation, points out, "In these situations, the economically efficient way of covering costs is through some form of price discrimination."[76] Such discrimination may come in the form of paid prioritization, or QoS discrimination, and the bundling of distribution services.

Lenard analogizes the broadband business to another distribution business, the supermarket. Such a business typically does not have market power; even so, it routinely engages in practices that, from a regulatory perspective, might be characterized as discriminatory or non-neutral. As Lenard explains:

For example, supermarkets typically charge manufacturers for shelf space, in fees commonly called 'slotting allowances.' Supermarkets also receive various

---

75. Ibid.
76. Ibid.

forms of incentives for special displays in prominent locations (e.g., end-aisle and checkout areas). Other sorts of deals and promotional allowances influence the allocation of shelf space. Of course, another important determinant of shelf placement is how much a product will sell and the profit derived from the sale. These practices are part of the system by which a competitive marketplace allocates scarcity—e.g., shelf space and the consumer's attention span.[77]

Lenard points out that we see analogous competitive practices in Internet commerce, like websites that pay for first-on-screen placement and pop-ups. Like payments for shelf space, placement, or special displays, such payments are fueled by competition for access to potential customers.

And indeed, the social-welfare benefits of differential pricing have long been recognized and implemented as policy, even in telecommunications. For example, common-carrier telephone companies are permitted to offer customers differential service options for long-distance and local service. Additionally, as Weisman and Kulick point out, "extended area service, local measured service, flat-rate service and flat-rate calling plans are all examples in which regulators have permitted customers to choose between difference price-quality combinations for their telecommunications services."[78] Similar schemes have been permitted in electricity service.

While we reserve the majority of our discussion on antitrust for Chapter 7, it is at least noteworthy here that preventing network providers and contract providers from contracting with each other for enhanced QoS would actually institutionalize a type of economic harm in the broadband market that antitrust law is designed to prevent. As Weisman and Kulick explain:

---

77. Thomas M. Lenard, "Comments to the Federal Communications Commission Regarding Broadband Industry Practices," Technology Policy Institute, June 14, 2007, 4, http://www.techpolicyinstitute.org/files/4.pdf.

78. *See* Weisman and Kulick, *supra* note 73, at 18.

[I]n the antitrust sphere, prohibiting a firm from contracting over the most efficient distribution channel is recognized as a form of 'raising rivals' costs' that firms may use to anti-competitively hobble their rivals. Because content providers' demand for superior QoS is derived from subscriber's demand for higher access speeds, agreements between content providers and ISPs for superior service would only occur under circumstances where it is more efficient for content providers to negotiate enhanced QoS than it is for subscribers.[79]

In addition to being a distribution market, broadband is a two-sided market. As such, access providers provide a platform, or meeting place, for two distinct groups (end users and content, application, and service providers), which provide each other with network benefits. It follows that the platform provider—the broadband access provider in this case—must facilitate the participation of its customers on both sides of the market, since the participation of end users on one side is directly related to the participation of the content, application, and service providers on the other, and vice versa. The access provider must therefore set prices that will bring both sides together.[80] It follows that

... because each transaction on the network creates value for network participants who are not part of the transaction and because users on one side of the market may be more sensitive to prices than users on the other side, the value of the network depends on both the total price level and how the total price is allocated between the two sides of the market.[81]

Optimal pricing in a two-sided market, therefore, requires attention to, and the balancing of, these factors on each side of the platform. Another principle inherent to the two-sided market is the seesaw principle, which suggests that lowering prices on one side of the market tends to raise prices on the other. It follows that network-neutrality

---

79. Ibid.
80. Ibid.
81. Ibid., 11.

rules that foreclose differential pricing for content, application, and service providers on one side of the market will force up prices for end users on the other side of the market.[82]

In doing so, network-neutrality regulations will cause social harm because a large contingent of end users who would be able to afford broadband access at lower prices, or who are unwilling to pay for access at such high prices, will be foreclosed from purchasing Internet access at all. This result is ironically contrary to the inclusiveness that is supposedly at the heart of the network-neutrality campaign, and telecommunications policy itself.[83]

You do not have to be an economist to understand the potential harm in preventing broadband businesses from continuing to experiment with business models. The market for broadband is still a new and rapidly changing market, and simple logic dictates that it would be unwise to enforce the FCC's Open Internet Order or any other regulatory regime that purports, or attempts, to improve the functionality of such a dynamic market. The regulatory environment affects the incentives of all market participants—from broadband providers to content providers to application services—to take risks in the market.[84] None of these companies know what the broadband market is going to look like in five or ten years; they are constantly making very expensive bets as to which products and business models will be the next "big thing." Therefore, imposing a network-neutrality regime that would limit potential business models, and particularly one as ambiguous as the Open Internet Order, where it is almost impossible to predict which models will pass regulatory muster, will undoubtedly inhibit investment in broadband, deter entry by new competitors, and limit the content and applications available to consumers.[85]

---

82. Ibid., 13.

83. J. Gregory Sidak, "A Consumer Welfare Approach to Network Neutrality Regulation on the Internet," *Journal of Comparative Law and Economics*, 2 (2006): 351–52, http://www.criterioneconomics.com/pdfs/gsidak_pdfs/A_Consumer_Welfare_Approach_to_Network_Neutrality_Regulation_of_the_Internet-2.pdf.

84. Ibid.

85. *See* Lenard, *supra* note 75, at 3.

While the FCC does not fully ignore the network providers' dependency on revenues—it does, after all, permit providers to charge individual end users (us) for access, and has even indicated a willingness to permit tiered end-user pricing plans—these revenues are not nearly enough to sustain the industry. Consider that the networks that today provide broadband access developed it as an incremental service on their networks originally designed for other purposes—wireline and wireless networks were originally designed to carry voice, and cable was originally designed to carry video. "In order to build a subscriber base," Kovacs explains, "broadband was priced as incremental to the revenues generated by the original services, and it comes nowhere near paying for any of those networks' full costs. As long as the original revenues are there to fund the network, there is no problem. But when the original voice and video sources dry up, broadband will have to carry the full cost of its network."[86] This will mean broadband providers will be forced to charge subscribers substantially higher access costs, and may also cut capital investment. So why would this happen? Well, part of it is just attributable to competition-fueled advances in technology: the revenues of one facilities-based provider—say a wireline provider—may shrink if another facilities-based competitor—say a wireless provider—is able to provide a technology that is more desirable (due to quality, cost, and so forth). It is certainly not that far-fetched to imagine a day when no one uses a traditional landline anymore. And while such losses are unfortunate for the wireline provider, that is the way the system works: the better technology wins. What it does mean is that now that same broadband provider is forced to cover all of its costs through its broadband access services.

Now, if that broadband provider is also losing customers to over-the-top voice providers like Skype, Vonage, or Google Voice, and the FCC forbids that provider from charging such services for the utilization of its enormously expensive network, that is—to use Kovac's own words—"regulatory arbitrage of the most destructive sort." In such circumstances, "the wireline carrier is forced to either lose its

---

86. See "Testimony," *supra* note 68.

voice customers altogether, or give away its voice service free to its retail customers as well as to the wholesale VoIP providers. Either way, the carrier will have to make its broadband service cross-subsidize its own services, just as it subsidizes Skype's."[87] Inevitably, individual subscribers will see their subscription prices spike. Possibly less noticeably to the subscriber at first, investment in the network will also stall as more subscribers are unable to afford the cost of services, and revenues shrink even more.

Conversely, because the broadband market is "two-sided"—that is, both end users and content and application providers derive value from the sale of broadband access—network providers' ability to charge content and application providers could not only support additional broadband penetration, but enable providers to subsidize access prices for low income end users.[88]

There is another important negative consequence of preventing network providers from charging edge providers for access to their networks: the prohibition is likely to harm new entrants (such as start-up edge providers) from entering into business arrangements that might help them compete against incumbents, which can afford to make deals for capacity with CDNs.[89]

Thus, restricting the ability of network providers from distinguishing themselves from their competitors, either through charging edge providers for paid prioritization or, as we argue below, through vertical integration with other services, not only hampers the network providers' ability to earn profitable returns on their substantial investments in infrastructure, but also threatens to stifle the ability of edge newcomers to enter the market. This in turn freezes in time the status

---

87. Ibid.

88. *See* "Broadband Connectivity Competition Policy," Federal Trade Commission, June 2007, 90, http://www.ftc.gov/reports/broadband/v070000report.pdf [hereafter "FTC Broadband Report"] (citing Joseph Farrell and Philip Weiser, "Modularity, Vertical Integration, and Open Access Policies: Towards a Convergence of Antitrust and Regulation in the Internet Age," *Harvard Journal of Law & Technology* 17 (2003): 87).

89. *See* "Testimony," *supra* note 68, at 6.

quo, particularly when it comes to multibillion-dollar edge companies like Google, Amazon, or eBay. "You know, we've had this debate with Google sitting at this table, lots of hours spent with Google," remarked a top Verizon executive,

> and Google says, 'We're really looking out for the little guy, the guy in the garage who comes up with the next idea. We want to make sure they get access to your network.' And I say, 'Give me a break.' What you want to do is protect your position, because you now have built a system of servers all across the country. You are able to provide better service to customers across the country because you have built the infrastructure. How does anybody compete with you Google? The only way someone can compete with you is to partner with us, because we have an infrastructure that is nationwide. We have the ability to deliver, take their new gismo or whatever, their new service, and actually deliver it to customers across the nation in a very efficient way, and compete with you Google. . . . And from our perspective, what incentive do we have to stop the guy in the garage from using our network, providing better services to our customers, allowing us to win that Comcast customer over to us? . . . [S]o our perspective is that the net-neutrality argument, which in its worst form is a bit is a bit is a bit, prevents differentiation prevents us from managing the network so you use it efficiently, and runs the risk of stopping the new innovator from coming into the marketplace and being able to compete effectively with established players.

Network executives note that although Google has maintained a pro-network-neutrality position from the inception of the movement, the underlying rationale for its support has shifted rather dramatically over time. One Comcast executive remarked, "I think years ago when this started, they viewed us, potentially correctly so, as a potential bottleneck to their access to end use. And I understand that. I think over time, what they were able to do, was to really leverage the status quo for as long as possible. . . . The government cannot stop the evolution, but what the Order does is rule against the network providers, in favor of the edge providers; the edge providers of today, not necessarily those of the future, even though it talks a lot about the guy in the garage developing the next applications."

Vertical Integration and the Walled Garden

Putting aside the irony of Google's position on network neutrality, and the inherent unfairness of a regulatory regime that imposes heavy-handed regulations on one segment of an industry while letting the other off scot-free, the following is a fact: the more flexibility network providers have in adjusting their business models to demands, the more likely we are to see the Internet environment as a whole continue to flourish. This flexibility should encompass the ability of network providers to integrate vertically into content and application markets, by developing their own products and services or by entering into exclusive deal arrangements with specific content and application providers.

However, network-neutrality supporters have vociferously opposed the vertical integration of network access providers into the content and application markets. And they have spent a lot of time ruminating about the various evils that will befall us all, should network providers be permitted to integrate. At the outset, it is vital to note that the arguments for or against vertical integration and data prioritization are inherently linked and often overlapping because the relevant concerns are interrelated. Without regulation, network-neutrality proponents claim, broadband providers will block or severely restrict access to non-favored sites and services. A site or service would be non-favored if it refused, for example, to pay for use of the provider's network. However, it might also be non-favored if the network provider was permitted to vertically integrate into that market and either develop its own competitive proprietary service or strike a deal with an outside company to provide its service exclusively over its network. For example, as already noted, in 2011 Comcast purchased NBC Universal. So, let's say Comcast now decides that all of its customers will have access to unlimited real-time downloads of all NBC shows for an extra

$5 per month. Network-neutrality proponents warn that not only does Comcast have the ability to make such an offer, but it could also, for example, block or degrade access to non-NBC sites, or force such sites to pay hefty fees for access to Comcast customers. This would not only limit the market for such non-favored content, it could also force Comcast customers to pay the extra money each month for NBC, since gaining access to other sites would be slow if not impossible.

Thus far, the FCC has bought the vertical integration fear-mongering completely. The Open Internet Order warns:

> Broadband providers may have economic incentives to block or otherwise disadvantage specific edge providers or classes of edge providers, for example by controlling the transmission of network traffic over a broadband connection, including the price and quality of access to end users. A broadband provider might use this power to benefit its own or affiliated offerings at the expense of unaffiliated offerings.[90]

In addition, the order goes on, "Today, broadband providers have incentives to interfere with the operation of third-party Internet-based services that compete with the providers' revenue-generating telephony and/or pay-television services." We would go on, but you get the idea.

Ultimately, the FCC and network-neutrality proponents warn, the result of broadband providers' unchecked actions will be a balkanized Internet, no longer open, but instead a maze of walled gardens, where end users are simply no longer able to access certain content and applications through certain access providers. End users will suffer because their choices will be limited, and investment at the edge of the networks will dry up because there will no longer be a guaranteed market for new products.

However, like data prioritization, vertical integration not only has the potential to benefit broadband providers, consumers, and

---

90. *See* Open Internet Order, *supra* note 15, at 21.

would-be market entrants alike, it may be economically necessary to support continued development and innovation in the broadband market. In the very least, it is efficient in a market where there are high switching costs.

Returning to Lenard's supermarket analogy, he explains vertical integration is not an unexpected business model in the broadband market:

> Consumer goods are primarily purchased from retailers. When consumers purchase products from retailers, they are purchasing the products and the distribution services bundled together. Since most consumer goods are bundled with distribution, we would expect that at least some viable Internet business model may entail a bundled product offering that is sufficiently attractive for consumers to become subscribers at prices that support the large infrastructure of investments that are required. The bundled product offering is going to have to be put together and sold by the broadband provider.[91]

Such arrangements are analogous to supermarkets that sell their own store brands alongside name brands, and will involve vertical integration of some sort, whether through the development of proprietary content and services by broadband providers, contractual arrangements with outside companies, or—most likely—a combination of both.

The most obvious benefit of vertical integration—to broadband providers at least—is the potential to earn additional profits from selling its new products—whether they be content, services, applications, or all of the above. It also generates the possibility of enticing new customers with new products. In addition, there may be technical or information efficiencies for an entity to be vertically integrated.[92] But such integration is also likely to benefit consumers. The logic goes: if more customers are attracted to a provider's network because of the

---

91. *See* Lenard, *supra* note 75, at 4.
92. *See* "FTC Broadband Report," *supra* note 87.

number or the quality of vertically integrated services it is able to provide, the more incentive the company will have not only to build out and improve its network, but to continue to invest in new technology that will increase the types of content and services it can offer.

An example would be if Comcast starts marketing its own VoIP service that is competitive with Skype and others already in existence. But let's say it starts getting really great reviews, and suddenly it is the VoIP that everyone is clamoring to have. The only way to get it is to switch over to Comcast for broadband. Now, because of the increased interest in Comcast's services, maybe Comcast can offer you an attractive access price, and maybe your monthly rate is even more affordable if you bundle your broadband, VoIP, and other services. As more and more customers sign up, Comcast's revenues increase and the company has increased incentives to continue to improve its services, develop new ones, and build out its network.

Now, Comcast could then turn around and start blocking or degrading access to a competitor's service like Skype, but why would it? The company has an interest in keeping Skype customers. If such customers get frustrated and leave for other broadband providers, Comcast loses their business.

Despite fear mongering by network-neutrality proponents, broadband providers simply lack the incentive to discriminate against non-favored content, applications, and services. Internet consumers demand broad access to the Internet. As Lenard puts it succinctly, "Competitors' content can increase subscribership at a very low (or zero) marginal cost. So it is unlikely to be in a broadband provider's interest to block content that consumers want."[93]

Put simply, network value increases proportionately with the number of users. Thus, a broadband provider has a huge financial incentive to give customers the access and services they want. If a broadband provider decides to severely limit its consumers' access to certain content and applications, it risks losing those customers and will also

---

93. *See* Lenard, *supra* note 75.

only attract customers who are interested in the particular content and applications permitted on that network. But if you do not believe us, just ask AOL.

America Online emerged in the 1980s and 1990 as one of the first, and most successful, closed online service providers of proprietary content. It was a "closed" service provider, meaning consumers using AOL (as it was later rebranded) could only access its own proprietary content and use its proprietary applications. America Online successfully marketed itself as the online service provider for non-techies, people unfamiliar with computers, most notably contrasting itself with CompuServe, a provider that had long served the technical community.

When considering potential future incentives for broadband providers to impose the walled-garden model, it is important to note that walled gardens served both consumers and the markets well at a certain point in Internet history. As Hazlett and Wright point out, "The market turned to 'walled gardens' during an important time, and the model succeeded because consumers were well served (and therefore had a higher demand for the ISP subscriptions) by the proprietary content that the 'gardens' grew. This enabled a critical extension of e-commerce into the mass-market, both by encouraging AOL's 'carpet bombing' of America with millions of easy-to-use dial-up sign-up disks, a marketing investment of considerable scale, and then by driving an enormously positive response to the campaign by consumers."[94]

AOL played a pivotal role in popularizing the Web by bringing it into the homes of millions and millions of Americans. In 2000, AOL merged with Time Warner—one of the world's largest media companies—and many observers believed the new entity would become the most dominant and powerful vertically integrated media company. After all, AOL gave Time Warner direct access to millions of American homes to which it could deliver its movies, books, magazines, and music, while Time Warner provided the cable lines that could ensure the high-speed delivery of all of this content.

---

94. *See* Hazlett and Wright, *supra* note 35, at 16.

For a short while it seemed those observers' predictions would come to fruition. By 2002, AOL boasted 34 million paid subscribers.[95] However, that was its peak. Shortly thereafter, the growth and profitability of the AOL division stalled. For starters, the merger happened just as the dot-com bubble burst, and just before the country slid into a post-9/11 economic recession. But arguably more importantly, at least from AOL's perspective, was the fact that AOL's integrated Internet service model became markedly less appealing to consumers as the non-AOL content market flourished.[96] Almost as quickly as they had flocked to AOL because of its ease and prominence, consumers—many of whom now had several years of Internet know-how under their belts—departed for less restrictive services, where they could explore anything and everything the Internet had to offer. Although AOL attempted to retain customers by altering and thus opening its business model, it was too little too late. By 2006, its customer base had decreased to 18 million, by 2007 that number slid to 10.1 million, and by 2010 its subscriber based dropped to 4.4 million.[97] By May 2009, Time Warner announced it was ending its eight-year relationship with AOL and spun off the company into a separate public company.

The demise of AOL's popularity illustrates the disadvantages of the "walled garden" model in a broadband market, where, as noted above, the winners are the network providers with the most customers. It is, therefore, in the best interests of network providers to make sure their networks continue to provide a great degree of "openness" in order to retain their current customers and expand their networks.[98] This is particularly true in the broadband market, where networks exhibit strong network externalities and "bandwagon effects." As Thierer puts

---

95. Ibid.

96. Ibid.

97. *See* Linda Rosencrance, "AOL Revenue, Subscribers Plummet," Computer World, November 8, 2007, http://www.computerworld.com/s/article/9046103/AOL_revenue_subscribers_plummet_?intsrc=news_ts_head; see also "Form 10-Q," U.S. Securities and Exchange Commission, http://www.sec.gov/answers/form10q.htm.

98. *See* Thierer, *supra* note 33 in Chapter 3, at 293.

it, "Because the value of a network tends to grow in proportion to the number of individuals using that network, the more users the better since greater interconnectedness generates substantial benefits for all users of network and the network provider."[99]

But, as noted above, walled gardens, both as economic and engineering models, have served important purposes in the past and may continue to do so—at different times and to varying extents—in the future. We do not know what the optimal configuration of high-speed networks will look like down the road, but as Hazlett and Wright explain, "markets reflect efficiencies"; that is, markets, and thus the companies comprising those markets, will seek to conform their business models to those that return the most profits.

The layered model of the Internet is one such model; although revolutionary in its own right, it would be short-sighted to assume there will not be equally revolutionary innovations in the future.[100] While, at this time at least, this means that it is highly unlikely that a broadband provider would compromise its customer base by erecting a walled garden, it is equally true that "The marketplace reveals efficiencies by continually testing new options and discovering what innovations might improve upon extant operations." Thus, this continuous experimentation or evolution means that there is not a given structure or business model that is the "correct" model to freeze in place by law, as the FCC intends to do. Instead, companies must have the flexibility to experiment with various business models, to increase their profitability and keep their customers happy.

In addition to incentivizing incumbents, like Comcast, to expand their own businesses, vertical integration may provide opportunities for new entrants to gain traction in the market that they would not otherwise have.

Most importantly, broadband providers do not have incentive to block competitor content, services, or applications because the broadband market is largely competitive, and where it is not, competition

99. Ibid.
100. Ibid., 292.

is increasing. Today, consumers demand broad access to the Internet, and a provider who denies access to certain content, applications, or services that are valued by consumers will lose customers to competitors. Now, you often hear the argument from network-neutrality supporters that the difficulties and sometimes costs associated with switching providers disincentivizes consumers from taking such actions. This may be true to a certain extent, but one must remember that every day the Internet access landscape is growing more competitive, and consumers have more options, and many have Internet access not only through their broadband provider, but via their mobile device (like smartphones or tablets). So, let's say your broadband provider decides to block your access to Facebook, for example (oh, the humanity!). Not only in many markets do you have the option of switching to one or more other providers, in smaller markets, you might abandon your broadband provider and simply use your mobile device to access the Internet. It is also possible that you just do not have another option today. As long as the broadband landscape remains competitive, which requires rejecting the FCC's attempts to mandate network neutrality, you will have more options . . . soon. The surest way to guarantee that you do not is to permit the FCC to implement a regulatory regime that pits one segment of the industry against the other and stifles investment and innovation in both.

There Is Simply No Problem That Needs Fixing: No Market Failure

There is no denying that the Internet has blossomed and continues to grow at a phenomenal pace, thanks to the deregulatory policies that have allowed it to do so for four decades. The markets are healthy and competitive, and yet the FCC and network-neutrality proponents insist that major government oversight is necessary to keep it so. The argument is illogical. As Thomas W. Hazlett and Joshua D. Wright put it:

> The FCC's net neutrality policy perches on irony: if the new rules are needed
> to preserve the salubrious structure of the Internet, why has the asserted

threat failed—by the FCC's own analysis—to yet undermine the 'open platform'? Why have broadband ISPs resisted the easy profits available from foreclosing competition among applications, squeezing their subscribers, and profiting from the very actions feared?[101]

There is no evidence warranting a need for the FCC's network-neutrality rules, and the abandonment of nearly two decades of a hands-off approach to government regulation of the Net. While proponents argue the FCC's rules are necessary to keep the Internet open and innovative, both network-neutrality proponents and the FCC itself have completely failed to demonstrate any semblance of market failure or provide an economic analysis that could possibly justify this massive government intervention into the Internet.

In fact, the FCC mentions—almost in passing in footnote 49 of its order—that it has not, nor intends to conduct, any market power analysis of the broadband market.[102] We argue that in order to justify the kind of government interference in the broadband market the FCC's Open Internet Order signifies, the agency must have not only strong evidence of a significant market failure, but proof that the benefits of regulation outweigh the costs.

It does not. Instead, in its Open Internet Order, the FCC relies on exactly two concrete examples of network providers actually blocking specific traffic over their networks. The first example is Comcast's action blocking BitTorrent traffic. But, as previously discussed, Comcast and BitTorrent resolved the issue independently, long before the D.C. Circuit rejected the FCC's enforcement. And they did so collaboratively, with their engineers working together to develop alternative solutions to traffic management that benefited both parties involved. The market therefore provided its own efficient, collaborative solution, without network-neutrality mandates and FCC interference.

---

101. *See* Hazlett and Wright, *supra* note 35, at 12.
102. *See* In re Broadband Industry Practices, *supra* note 28, at n. 49.

The second example of an Internet provider blocking specific applications occurred in 2004, when Madison River Communications (a rural telephone company) admitted to blocking the VoIP service of Vonage over its DSL connections. The move prompted the FCC to open an investigation. While the company provided several network-management justifications for blocking content, the FCC found none of them acceptable. Still, the case was closed, before any formal fact finding or legal finding, when Madison River agreed to a settlement, agreeing to stop discriminating against VoIP traffic and make a voluntary payment of $15,000 to the U.S. Treasury in exchange for the FCC dropping its inquiry.[103]

While the FCC lists a number of other so-called examples of actions by broadband providers to "limit openness," every other example listed is either an unsubstantiated allegation or speculation of supposed future harm.[104] It is rather perplexing that two instances of discriminatory practices by network providers could possibly justify the end of a regulatory-free Net.

Simply put, there is no evidence to justify the FCC's massive regulatory overhaul of the broadband market. And other federal agencies agree.

In fact, two other government agencies with substantial expertise in and historical oversight of the telecommunications markets have warned the FCC to exercise restraint. Specifically, the Federal Trade Commission found there are two aspects of the broadband Internet-access industry that heighten the concerns raised by regulation: (1) its nascence, and that there are indications that the industry is moving in the direction of more—not less—competition; and (2) there is no evidence of "any significant market failure or demonstrated consumer harm from conduct of broadband providers." The agency fur-

---

103. Dirk Grunwald and Douglas Sicker, "Measuring the Network—Service Level Agreements, Service Level Monitoring, Network Architecture and Network Neutrality," *International Journal of Communication* 1 (2007): 552.

104. The Internet and Broadband Industry Practices: Hearing Before the House Committee on Energy and Commerce, 112th Congress, 112–51 (2011).

ther warns that "policy makers should be wary of enacting regulation solely to prevent prospective harm to consumer welfare, particularly given the indeterminate effects on such welfare of potential conduct by broadband providers and the law enforcement structures that already exist."[105] The Department of Justice agrees and found that there is no evidence of broadband monopolies in most regions. While the agency found that certain localities in which there is only one broadband provider should continue to be monitored, it warned against the temptation to interfere in areas where there is robust duopoly:

> Between the ongoing deployment of wireline broadband networks, the geographic expansion of wireless broadband services (hopefully spurred by the availability of additional spectrum to broadband wireless services), and increased transparency, the Department is hopeful that the vast majority of American households will benefit from significant competition in their local broadband markets. Put differently, most regions of the United States do not appear to be natural monopolies for broadband service. Nonetheless, some locales may well have only one terrestrial provider able to offer broadband services, especially to consumers who seek to use the most bandwidth-intensive applications, e.g., video teleconferencing. The Department recommends that the Commission monitor carefully those areas in which only a single provider offers—or even two providers offer—broadband service. Although enacting some form of regulation to prevent certain providers from exercising monopoly power may be tempting with regard to such areas, care must be taken to avoid stifling the infrastructure investments needed to expand broadband access.[106]

The Federal Trade Commission also warns of the "the almost certainty" of unintended consequences of a broad regulatory scheme, with respect to both consumer welfare and invocation, that may not be known until far into the future:

---

105. *See* "FTC Broadband Report," *supra* note 87, at 160.
106. *See* In re Broadband Industry Practices, *supra* note 28 (ex-parte submission).

Industry-wide regulatory schemes—particularly those imposing general, one-size-fits-all restraints on business conduct—may well have adverse effects on consumer welfare, despite the good intentions of their proponents. Even if regulation does not have adverse effects on consumer welfare in the short term, it may nonetheless be welfare-reducing in the long term, particularly in terms of product and service innovation. For example, prohibitions of certain business conduct, such as vertical integration into content and applications or the offering of prioritization services by broadband providers, may not have immediate effects on consumer welfare, but could result in a long-term decline in investment and innovation in broadband networks. Broadband providers that cannot differentiate their products or gain new revenue streams may have reduced incentives to upgrade their infrastructure.

Further, broadband regulatory schemes almost certainly will have unintended consequences, some of which may not be known until far into the future. After all, even the most carefully considered legislation is likely to have unforeseen effects. In the broadband Internet context, regulation that nominally seeks to protect innovation in content and applications by prohibiting broadband providers from charging for prioritized delivery over their networks actually could erect barriers to new content and applications that require higher-quality data transmission. A new entrant in the streaming video market, for example, might prefer to purchase a certain quality of service from broadband providers, rather than investing in the server capacity and other resources necessary to provide that level of service on its own. Once a regulatory regime is in place, moreover, it may be difficult or impossible to undo its effects.[107]

As both the DOJ and the FTC recognize, imposing a heavy-handed, industry-wide regulatory scheme on an industry that is currently thriving is almost guaranteed to damage the industry. So too is a scheme that imposes network-neutrality rules on one unlucky sector of a decidedly non-neutral industry. Moreover, the latter is blatantly unfair. Ultimately, though, it is the consumer whose welfare will suffer

---

107. *See* "FTC Broadband Report," *supra* note 87, at 160.

the most as the consequences—both foreseen and unforeseen—of the FCC's ill-conceived order begin to emerge.

As we will show next, the unintended consequences will be felt equally, if not more severely, in the wireless realm. Moreover, as we will demonstrate in Chapter 7, there is already a well-established body of law ready to deal with anticonsumer or anticompetitive behavior by broadband access providers. It is called antitrust.

Chapter Six
SPECTRUM REFORM

AS NOTED IN CHAPTER 5, the Open Internet Order's restrictions on the ways that Internet service providers administer their networks are more relaxed for wireless carriers because wireless telephony is a nascent industry. Still, even as the industry takes form, wireless communication has become a major competitor to and potential replacement for wireline. In short, wireless innovation—certainly as much as, if not more than, wireline—is too important to be bound by network-neutrality restrictions.

In Chapter 2 we discussed the regulatory blunders that have defined FCC oversight of the television broadcast industry (one flavor of wireless communication), and argued that this history is a great predictor of how the FCC will handle regulatory oversight of the Internet.

In this chapter, we argue that the inherent characteristics of wireless communication provide an even more fundamental reason for rejecting network-neutrality rules. Specifically, our concern about overregulation of the wireless industry stems from the scarcity of the medium through which wireless signals are transmitted: spectrum. Ironically, spectrum scarcity is the same concern that was historically used to justify industry regulation. This justification continues to be espoused by network-neutrality proponents today. Spectrum scarcity is problematic because it gives rise to interference between wireless signals and to congestion of data packets as usage of wireless frequencies increases toward the maximum channel capacity. Handing over control of the Internet to government regulators, however, may cripple the ability of the average American to access content on wireless networks. There are far more optimal methods of resolving scarcity and spectrum interference than regulation. The typical, non-regulatory solution to this problem is to create well-defined property rights and causes of action to remedy violations.[1]

This chapter argues in favor of a net diversity (or non-neutrality) regime over a network-neutrality scheme by dispelling the myths of neutrality and by illuminating how the complex world of spectrum better lends itself to net diversity. After an explanation of the workings of spectrum, interference and congestion, eight wireless-specific arguments will demonstrate the flaws of net neutrality.

First, the fixed-price regime promoted by network neutrality is unsustainable given the scarcity of spectrum. Second, one price for all users creates an unjust cross-subsidy between low-intensity and high-intensity Internet users. Third, tiered pricing improves network management by making assumptions about network congestion more predictable. Fourth, critical network congestion is imminent and net diversity holds promise to solve this problem. Fifth, the problems of network congestion and spectrum interference do not necessitate regulation. Rather, more efficient solutions are available in the private sector. Sixth, because companies are profit maximizing, fears that ISPs will block consumer-preferred content are unfounded. Seventh, transparency mandated by network neutrality is paramount for strong markets and effective regulation, but advocating for the entire network-neutrality suite for the sake of transparency is an unnecessary oversimplification. Finally, shifting incentives and resources to innovate from content providers to network administrators invites new entrants into the ISP market, which, in turn, incentivizes necessary spectrum reforms.

Spectrum is a precious and finite resource, which makes broadband, telephone, and other communications possible without cumbersome and expensive wirelines. To regulate flat-rate access to the Internet would put a strain on spectrum too strong for the Internet to

---

1. Ronald Coase, "The Problem of Social Cost," *Journal of Law & Economics* 3 (1960): 1.

survive. The smarter, more efficient, and more creative solution lies in a net-diversity regime that allows private parties to negotiate, compete, and innovate to both fix the problems plaguing the current spectrum scarcity crisis and offer reasonable costs and access to consumers.

Spectrum

James Maxwell, a British mathematician and physicist, created a revolutionary theory of electromagnetism that unified areas of scientific inquiry previously considered unrelated.[2] Magnetism, optics, and electricity were respected areas of study in the latter half of the nineteenth century, but Maxwell knit them together for the first time with electromagnetic theory.[3] He posited that there were waves of energy in the air around us, all the time, although we could not see them. These electromagnetic waves could not only pass through the air, but some could pass through walls and other physical objects, too. This was all just theory until 1887.

In that year, Heinrich Hertz made a receiver from a coil of wire, an antenna from an odd stick of metal, and set out to prove conclusively that electromagnetic waves did indeed exist, traveling through the "aether."[4] Hertz was a true scientist, interested in discovery for discovery's sake. So, when asked about what, if any, implications there were to his grand discovery, Heinrich replied, "Nothing, I guess."[5]

His humility would quickly come to bear through the further invention of another European scientist, Guglielmo Marconi. In 1894, Marconi made history by sending information through the air for the first time.[6] He accomplished this feat using electromagnetic waves, collectively known today as spectrum, that oscillate at different

2. James Clerk Maxwell, "On Physical Lines of Force," *Philosophical Magazine*, 1861.

3. Ibid.

4. D. E. Hughes, "Research in Wireless Telegraphy," *Electrician* 43, 1899.

5. Institute of Chemistry, Hebrew University of Jerusalem, Hertz biography, digitized photographs, chem.ch.huji.ac.il/history/hertz.htm.

6. Prebir K. Bondyopadhyay, "Guglielmo Marconi—The Father of Long Distance Radio Communication—An Engineer's Tribute," 25th European Microwave Conference, 879, 1995.

frequencies to convey binary information. Since 1887, the frequency of these vibrations had come to be measured in hertz (Hz), or cycles per second.[7]

Marconi's fame and fortune, however, were not yet established. The Italians first shunned his invention, so Marconi then traveled to England to present his findings. They honored his invention there and granted him a patent to start the Wireless Telegraph and Signal Company.[8] Radio was the first and most important innovation to use spectrum-based communications. Radio spectrum (like that of television and telephony) is measured in megahertz (MHz), which describes one million cycles per second.

Radio caught on quickly as a revolutionary way for ships to communicate in case of emergency. Prior to the invention of radio, the crew aboard a sinking ship was limited to only the forty or so words per minute that a proficient Morse Code typist could type. This may have been sufficient for standard communications like "S.O.S.," but in case you needed to discover whether an approaching ship belonged to an enemy or an ally, radio was a lifesaver. Later, in 1906, sailors learned that radio had moved beyond Morse Code, when suddenly they heard new sounds coming over their radios. First, it was just the sound of violins, then a wish to "Have a merry Christmas," then the result of the presidential election contest between James Cox and Warren Harding. This was just the beginning of the spectrum evolution.

Interference

In 1912, the United States enacted the Radio Communications Act, the first piece of legislation specifically granting federal power to regulate spectrum.[9] It required radio operators to have a license, but licensure

---

7. "IEC History," International Electrotechnical Commission, http://www.iec.ch /about/history/overview/.

8. John W. Klooster, *Icons of Invention: The Makers of the Modern World from Gutenberg to Gates* (Santa Barbara, CA: Greenwood Press, 2009).

9. "An act to regulate radio communication," August 13, 1912, http://earlyradiohistory .us/1912act.htm.

standards were easy to fulfill.[10] In 1926 the attorney general stripped the secretary of commerce of the power to regulate time and power usage, so multiplexing was no longer an option.[11] The secretary abandoned his efforts and left the industry to self-regulate.[12] Chaos ensued.[13] No one could use the valuable spectrum resource because, ironically, too many broadcasters were using it.

This proverbial "shouting match at a cocktail party" was an acceptable solution until the propagation of radio technology during the First World War. People began broadcasting right on top of one another, upping their power output to try to out-shout competitors. The secretary of commerce tried to find room for everyone with a degree of time-multiplexing, but demand still far outstripped supply. To make matters worse, the secretary lacked the power to deny licenses to private parties on the grounds of interference.[14] Also, a station could now use frequency that had not been assigned to it, which previously was a violation.[15]

When self-governance in the private sector failed, Congress finally adopted the Radio Act of 1927, which created the Federal Radio Commission with wide licensing and regulatory powers.[16] The commission had the power not just to regulate traffic, but also to determine what kind of traffic there would be. "Regulation of radio was therefore as vital to its development as traffic control was to the development of the automobile."[17] Because spectrum is a scarce resource and in high

---

10. Ibid.

11. Yochai Benkler, "Overcoming Agoraphobia: Building the Commons of the Digitally Networked Environment," *Harvard Journal of Law & Technology* 11 (1997): 1297.

12. Ibid.

13. Ibid.

14. *See* Hoover v. Intercity Radio, Co., 52 App.D.C. 339 (1923). "The duty of issuing licenses to persons or corporations coming within the classification designated in the act reposes no discretion whatever in the Secretary of Commerce. The duty is mandatory; hence the courts will not hesitate to require its performance."

15. Zenith Radio Corp. v. U.S., 437 U.S. 443 (1978).

16. *See* Benkler, *supra* note 11.

17. National Broadcasting Co. v. U.S., 319 U.S. 190 (1943).

demand, the common thought back then resulted in regulation as a means of avoiding a tragedy of the commons.

Today, spectrum is used for all wireless communication. Whether the rock-and-roll radio that you blast in your car, the web app that you use to identify it, the phone call that you make to tell your friend, or the TV she turns on to check out the music video, all of this information is communicated using channels in the electromagnetic spectrum.[18] A whole school of science has developed around this transfer of information, called "information theory."[19] Its central tenet is Shannon's Law, which shows that the theoretical maximum error-free capacity for signal transfer over a channel is determined by the ratio of signal strength to noise.[20] "Noise" is defined as any and all electromagnetic activity detected by the receiver that is not the sender's intended message.[21] This law of physics proves an understanding of broadcast communications that is, in fact, quite intuitive. The stronger a sender's signal and the less background noise, the greater the signal capacity of the channel. Three important lessons follow from this: One is that the weaker the signal, the more vulnerable it will be to interference. The second is that each signal is perceived as noise by the broadcasters of signals in other signal bands. And the third lesson is that no technological innovation can alter the nature of this theoretical maximum.

Noise occurs because electromagnetic waves interfere with each other. Interference is a definitive problem for spectrum broadcast. When two transmitters broadcast waves on the same channel, a receiver will interpret the crossed signal as noise. This is called co-channel interference. When waves meet, some peculiar results can be produced. When the peak or nadir of one wave coincides with the peak or nadir of another, the signal amplitude can be magnified or nullified. These

---

18. Alternatively known as bands or frequencies.

19. Robert G. Gallagher, *Information Theory and Reliable Communication* (New York: John Wiley and Sons, 1968).

20. C. E. Shannon, "A Mathematical Theory of Communication," *Bell Systems Technology Journal* 27 (1948): 379.

21. Ibid.

"multipath problems" are an inevitable consequence of broadcasting two signals on the same channel. The effects are exacerbated by changing terrain, city skyscrapers, and even solar flares. These obstacles cause the waves to refract, reflect, and arrive at the receiver later than expected. Then they are perceived as noise rather than as part of the signal. Given all these obstacles, how does one overcome interference?

Thankfully, there are a variety of methods for doing so, all couched in the term "multiplexing."[22] One kind of multiplexing that can overcome the problem of co-channel interference is to geographically separate spectrum users.[23] This method takes advantage of the fact that the broadcast power of a signal dissipates over distance so that multiple users can broadcast on the same frequency.[24] However, this is an imperfect solution. Imagine these waves propagating outwards from single sources, like circular ripples in a pond. If these sources are too far apart, the signal, rippling out from the source, will completely dissipate before it reaches the signal ripples from the adjacent source. This leads to coverage gaps that are problematic for wireless providers. On the other hand, if you move the sources of the waves closer together until there is no still surface of the pond, the concentric circles from one source will necessarily overlap with one another. Hence, in order to achieve complete coverage of an area, some geographic interference is necessary.

The upshot of co-channel interference caused by geographic proximity (relative to other kinds of interference) is that it is easy to identify the source of interference.[25] Thus, it is possible to negotiate a settlement with the cause of that interference in order to remediate the

22. Curt White, *Data Communications and Computer Networks: A Business User's Approach* (Independence, KY: Course Technology PTR, 2007), 140–43.

23. "Digital Modulations in Communications Systems," Hewlett Packard, http://www.scribd.com/doc/37284968/37/Multiplexing-geography.

24. Ibid.

25. Paulo Cardieri and Theodore Rappaport, "Statistical Analysis of Co-Channel Interference in Wireless Communications Systems," *Wireless Computing and Mobile Computing* 1 (2001): 111.

situation. This type of interference, however, is not always the case. On the contrary, spectrum broadcast often generates wild and unpredictable interferences. "Skip" interference is one such unpredictable consequence of spectrum broadcast that occurs when waves heading towards outer space bounce off of the ionosphere at night, allowing the signal to traverse hundreds of miles beyond the intended range.[26] If you have ever experienced driving in your car, for example, in Pennsylvania, while picking up a Maryland radio station on your AM dial, you are familiar with the quirky way that spectrum propagates.

Another more complex variety of interference is harmonic resonance.[27] Every wavelength generates other wavelengths beyond its intended frequency, called "subharmonies."[28] Those subharmonies in turn produce their own subharmonies such that the broadcast on one frequency can also cause interference on a distant, distinct channel.[29] In the same way that skip interference can jump long distances and frustrate efforts to reduce interference through geographic separation, subharmonic interference can jump from one frequency to a distant, seemingly unrelated channel.[30] This phenomenon is useful in some aspects of our lives. Those who study music, for example, will recognize this as the same phenomenon responsible for chords fitting into octaves, fifths, and so on. In the world of radio transmission, however, interference can be disastrous, causing signals to become garbled or lost entirely.[31]

---

26. J. D. Laster, "Interference Rejection in Digital Wireless Communications," *Signal Processing Magazine* 14 (1997): 3.

27. Andrea Frova and Mariapiera Marenzana, *Thus Spoke Galileo: The Great Scientist's Ideas and Their Relevance to the Present Day*, trans. Jim McManus (New York: Oxford University Press, 2006), 133–37.

28. Ibid.

29. Ibid.

30. Ibid.

31. Yet another kind of interference is caused by intermodulation, when two frequencies that would otherwise not cause interference with a third frequency interfere with it nevertheless when the sum of difference between the amplitude of the two otherwise noninterfering signals equals the amplitude of the third.

Geographic separation is not the only way to combat interference. The FCC divides the available spectrum into frequency bands and distributes them among various licensees.[32] However, it can be difficult to constrain broadcast strictly within one particular band because every signal transmitted within a certain band bleeds slightly into the adjacent bands, where it can cause interference. This kind of interference, therefore, is named "adjacent channel" interference.[33]

Certain amounts of interference can be overcome by simply adding more power to the broadcast, effectively yelling over the top of other transmissions.[34] However, this solution has limited utility from a network standpoint because as more and more radio providers yell louder and louder trying to be heard, in the end, no one is intelligible and the signals become scrambled.[35]

Congestion

Congestion is a similar problem in many ways to interference. The broadcast of too many signals can cause interference that makes a receiver unable to pull a coherent message out of many competing signals. Likewise, the input of too much data into a router (a device that receives and forwards network traffic) can cause congestion, slowing the movement of data or losing data entirely. There are several definitions of congestion to be discussed.

Broadly speaking, congestion refers to network overload, but there are more precise definitions. Queuing Theory defines congestion as when the arrival rate of data at a node (a place on the network where spectrum channels intersect or branch) is greater than the service rate, which is the speed at which the router forwards data.[36] Imagine a group of people trying to enter an amusement park through a turnstile.

---

32. This is known as Frequency Division Multiple Access (FDMA).

33. Shannon, *supra* note 20.

34. Ibid.

35. Ibid.

36. J. E. Flood, "Telecommunications Traffic," in *Telecommunications Switching, Traffic and Networks* (New York: Prentice Hall, 1998).

When a queue develops at the turnstile because people are arriving at a faster rate than the turnstile will let them through, Queuing Theory describes the turnstile as being congested.[37] All of the people in line will eventually get through the turnstile; some will just have to wait.

The networking textbook definition of congestion, on the other hand, defines a network as being congested only when the router runs out of buffer space, which otherwise secures against losing any data waiting in the queue, and drops bundles of data, or "packets."[38] There are only a limited number of packets that can be queued in the memory buffer of a router at one time. When that number is exceeded, packets begin to be dropped. In our previous metaphor, this is the equivalent of the point at which the line to get into the amusement park is so long that people are dissuaded from waiting and decide to return another day.

Finally, the economic definition of congestion states that congestion occurs only when a marginal increase in traffic by one user imposes a cost on existing users.[39] While exacting in theory, this concept is difficult to measure. The economic definition of congestion would consider that the turnstile can offer admittance to patrons at a given rate with no additional delay. Entrance to the amusement park is congested specifically by the one person who causes a delay that exceeds the base rate of admission allowed by the turnstile.

It is necessary to understand these various definitions of congestion before coming to a conclusion about the efficiency of tiered-pricing models. This is because *the best model is the one that allows everyone use of the Internet that is as free from limits on data usage as possible.* Some limits or constraints are necessary due to the scarcity of the

---

37. The congestion intensity is calculated under the Queuing Theory by dividing the arrival rate by the service rate.

38. Sally Floyd, "On the Evolution of End-to-End Congestion Control in the Internet: An Idiosyncratic View," IMA Workshop on Scaling Phenomena in Communication Networks, October 1999.

39. Christopher Yoo, "Network Neutrality and the Economics of Congestion," *Georgetown Law Journal* 94 (2005): 1847.

underlying spectrum resource. The consequences of those constraints may include dropped packets, slow connections, or variable pricing based on usage. Regardless, understanding the nature of the network resource is paramount.

The major analytical difference between congestion and interference is that interference is often caused by unknown parties, sometimes even by natural phenomena. On the other hand, congestion can be traced back to particular individuals because every packet has a source, IP address, and port number built into it, describing where the packet came from and where it is going.

Real congestion problems started, ironically, with the move from narrowband to broadband.[40] Text messaging, e-mail, and basic web content require perfect data integrity, which may encumber some network resources. Bandwidth-intensive applications, like streaming video, gaming, and VoIP, however, require steady flow more than perfect data integrity, which places an entirely new kind of burden unbounded by restrictions on service rate. The Internet was not made perfectly. It has had to continually evolve in order to stay ahead of the curve of evolving technologies. Additionally, regardless of how much spectrum is dedicated to Internet data, the amount of data forwarded through the network will always expand to fit capacity.

Among the strategies network operators may employ to control network congestion are price discrimination, volume caps, deep packet inspection, quality-of-service guarantees, and rate limiting for some customers' use of high-demand classes of traffic.

Net diversity in both wireless and wireline uses a price-discrimination model that charges different users different prices for Internet access based on their Internet needs and their willingness to pay. Top-tier clients who pay a premium receive unlimited access to Internet content accompanied by quality-of-service guarantees. Quality-of-service guarantees ensure that the Internet user will be able to enjoy a certain minimum throughput rate, instead of just advertising the maximum

---

40. Ibid.

rate as most ISPs currently do regardless of whether the user will be able to use that maximum rate. Users who pay less are subject to volume caps that limit the amount of monthly data that they are allowed to upload or download from the network. This helps network administrators to manage their networks by providing them with accurate prognoses of what the maximum amount of traffic on their network could look like. Another promising solution, albeit one that violates the end-to-end principle discussed in Chapters 3 and 5, is deep packet inspection (DPI, used to prioritize certain traffic). This solution manages congestion from the relatively omniscient perspective of being able to see all network traffic, and thus network administrators may allocate flows based on the kind of data in the datagrams. Deep packet inspection has received some negative publicity because of the privacy concerns it implies (some people are less than comfortable with an Internet arbiter being able to see what is in their data packets). Yet, all of these options within the scope of net diversity provide consumers with choices, and network administrators with solutions to congestion. Contrarily, a network-neutrality scheme limits options for both consumers and administrators. We are not suggesting deep packet inspection for any and all purposes should be condoned or encouraged. We simply point out that it is a necessity in combating spam, blocking the spread of computer viruses, and alleviating congestion. We also note that it has been used for years by web and software-based service providers for behavioral advertising, security protections, and content filtering. It is an option that must be kept on the table. It is also likely that transparency in network-management practices will help to create a balance between consumer privacy concerns and reasonable utilization of DPI for the benefit of those consumers.

Net Neutrality and Spectrum Reform

Licenses to use spectrum are sold to Internet Service Providers (ISPs) like Verizon and AT&T through an auction held by the FCC. Since spectrum is scarce, it becomes particularly important that the most efficient users own it. However, it is impossible to tell who the most efficient user will be before the auction takes place. Our auction system uses ability-to-pay as a proxy for efficiency because liquid capital markets enable efficient users to gain the funding necessary to invest in their networks. Hence, the winning bidder is often the most efficient provider of Internet services. Network-neutrality restrictions institutionalized by the Open Internet Order make it difficult for valuable spectrum resources to end up in the hands of the most efficient users. These restrictions on the property rights contained in the license held by the winning bidder artificially depress the value of spectrum by placing restrictions on the administration of a network that uses that spectrum.

As we have described with regard to wireline, it is important for a network administrator to have discretion in how to control traffic on its network for the same reason that it is important that the Transportation Authority has discretion in how to control traffic on its roads. In its role as a network administrator, your cell phone company uses its own allocation of spectrum in a vast network of turnpikes that lead your information to your desired recipient. Network neutrality mandates that all traffic be treated equally, but as any driver knows, not all traffic behaves in the same way.

We discussed in Chapter 3 how different communications protocols send their data through the network in different ways. There are responsible Volvo drivers, like TCP, that value, above all, arriving at the destination intact. Then there is that Mack truck bearing down on you, honking its horn as if it has no brakes. That is UDP. We also discussed in Chapter 3 how data traffic is "bursty." It would make matters simpler if it were bursty in the way that freeway traffic is bursty during rush hours. However, while network traffic follows a fractal pattern (a detailed self-similar pattern that repeats itself) its volume at any given point in time is unpredictable.

On the road, we treat traffic differently based on how congested it is, the way that a driver is driving, or the time of day. Network neutrality means that network providers do not have this luxury. That makes networks governed by network neutrality less valuable. This was shown in the FCC Spectrum Auction of 2008, when a block of valuable 700 MHz spectrum, known as the C-Block, was sold for 40 percent of the price of similarly situated blocks.[41] When this happens, taxpayers lose.

The advent of new technologies is serving both to increase demand for spectrum and to increase the efficiency with which we use it. This has led some commentators to speculate that we can build out our spectrum use infinitely because new technological innovation will always be there to accommodate increased use.[42] It is easy to blithely cast aside concerns that interference and congestion will cripple the network because innovation will always be there to save us. But network-neutrality restrictions reduce incentives to innovate and build out network capacity by prioritizing unlimited access and content innovation rather than spectrum reform. Contrarily, a network-diversity scheme shifts the incentives from content innovation to network innovation by increasing network competition, thus ensuring that more resources will inevitably be put toward investing in research and development of efficient spectrum usage. In order to ensure that network capacity remains greater than network usage, a network administrator needs to make an upfront investment in spectrum and in the machinery of spectrum broadcast that *exceeds* predicted usage. To fall short would mean a disastrous network collapse. Spectrum is auctioned in blocks of predetermined size, so it is impossible to buy exactly the amount you need.

Since undershooting demand would be disastrous, it is necessary to have more on hand than expected usage.[43] This necessity perpetuates the illusion that spectrum is abundant because it seems as if there is always more of it than we need. That is because ISPs generate the revenue necessary to continue to invest in network build-out.

---

41. Susan P. Crawford, "The Radio and the Internet," *Berkeley Technology Law Journal* (forthcoming), Cardozo Legal Studies Research Paper No. 197, http://ssrn.com /abstract=1088204.

42. *See generally* Kevin Werbach, "Supercommons: Toward a Unified Theory of Spectrum Commons," *Texas Law Review* 82 (2004): 863; *see also* Benkler, *supra* note 11.

43. *See* Yoo, *supra* note 39.

There are costs to operating this network, and consumers are charged accordingly. These costs, however, are much lower for wireless carriers, which do not have to spend as much to build out and upkeep facilities. Consequently, wireless consumers should theoretically pay less. Network-neutrality restrictions limit the ways in which mobile broadband providers can control traffic within its network, because such a scheme mandates consumers' full, unlimited access to every "lane" of Internet traffic. That produces inefficient outcomes that cause the ISP to pay more. They then pass those costs onto the consumers.

As we described in the last chapter, this is particularly egregious because the Open Internet Order demands that the network costs created by heavy users be borne by lighter users. They are forced to pay a higher rate than the burden that they place on the network in order to compensate other users' excessive enjoyment of the Internet. It also places a potentially heavy user at risk of moral hazard because society places no restrictions on heavy usage under a network-neutrality regime. Every user of the Internet has incentives to increase his or her usage toward infinity. Each user reaps the full benefit of increased usage, and the harm that his usage causes is distributed among all network users. Pricing Internet access in a way that creates accountability for network usage makes the Internet a more sustainable resource and enables network administrators to invest in spectrum build-out.

Given Spectrum Scarcity, the Current Fixed-Price Paradigm Is Simply Unsustainable

Combining a limited and precious resource with unlimited worldwide access to that resource is problematic. Treating the Internet as if it were an infinite fountain of information is certain to limit its utility to everyone in the long run, if it does not render it completely useless. There needs to be some kind of control placed on the use of this resource in order to preserve its utility.

As consumers, we need to take responsibility for our use of the Internet in order to make sure that it can continue to help us move ahead as a human community. In a network-neutrality scheme, light

Internet users subsidize heavy Internet users. It does not hold people accountable for their use of scarce spectrum. Flat-rate pricing results in excessive consumption of resources like the Internet. This excessive use arises because congestion costs represent a negative externality that individuals who use the Internet heavily and are responsible for causing congestion are not forced to bear.[44] What is necessary is a mechanism to hold people accountable for how they use—and how much they use—this finite resource. Network diversity internalizes the congestion cost of usage. The promise of net diversity is the ability to charge light users less for Internet and heavy users more, therefore encouraging responsible spectrum usage.

Where network neutrality mandates that everyone be charged the same amount of money regardless of use, net diversity allows network administrators to charge consumers based on their choices. Net diversity allows network administrators to use price in order to adjust Internet usage to a sustainable level. This represents our best chance to wield control of the Internet, rather than allowing it to escape us and destroy itself.

One Price for All Network Users Cross-Subsidizes the Heavy Users for the ISP's Expense of Purchasing Spectrum

While the Open Internet Order does not ban tiering regimes, network-neutrality buffs regard them suspiciously since such regimes threaten to raise the cost of the unlimited Internet that they currently enjoy. They do not want the policy landscape to change in a way that prevents individuals from taking advantage of the commons. While these concerns are valid, the costs of banning tiered regimes are overriding.

A regime under which all Internet users pay the same price regardless of their usage is fundamentally inequitable. Under such a regime, those who burden the network by pirating full albums while streaming video and Skyping with their friends pay the same as the intermit-

---

44. See, for example, Eitan Berglas, "On the Theory of Clubs," *American Economic Review: Papers & Procedures* 66 (1976): 119.

tent Internet user just learning how to use Gmail. As we discussed in Chapter 3, however, different usage patterns place different burdens on the network. In the long run, these burdens can be meliorated only through the purchase of greater spectrum resources at FCC auction. The development of new technologies can provide us with greater efficiency, but can never provide us with more capacity than the theoretical maximum that Shannon's Law dictates. Using one price for all network users cross-subsidizes heavy users, so that they effectively get a free ride. As with wireline, tiered access represents an escape from the injustice of the cross-subsidy.

Tiered Pricing Improves Network Management

As we have discussed, it is important for network administrators to be able to make assumptions about prospective usage of their network so that they can ensure that the resources they keep on hand are sufficient to exceed demand. When consumers place themselves in different groups because of their willingness to pay for increased usage, it will, for the first time, give ISPs a way to predict maximum usage levels of their service. It seems intuitive that network administrators could look at past usage to determine future usage, but that is untrue for two reasons. First, network technologies are developing at an astonishing rate. The popularization of streaming video placed a large, unexpected burden on networks. Then the transition to cloud computing added a new stress to the network. The largest disturbances tend to be the most unpredictable. Second, data about how people interacted with the Internet under an antiquated architecture would say little about how they will act with the new incentives and limitations provided by the tiered-pricing model.

When network administrators can look at their subscribers and know the exact maximum strain that each will place on the network, the administrators will be able to craft more accurate predictions than ever before about expected network usage. This means more financial savings for consumers and for ISPs, as well as a more secure Internet architecture for everyone.

Critical Network Congestion Is an Imminent Problem

The Internet is a shared resource, and the substrate used to access it is scarce, so that almost by definition, congestion will occur. Empirical analyses have shown that congestion has always been a problem for the Internet.[45] New technologies that both contribute to and work to resolve congestion are being invented at an accelerating rate over time.[46] Furthermore, TCP and BitTorrent are greedy, profit-maximizing protocols. Because TCP increases its through-put rate until a packet is dropped (usually caused by congestion), any available bandwidth built out by an ISP will be quickly filled up by the millions of users whose TCP protocols are hungry to eat up all available bandwidth. BitTorrent is even more aggressive, as it searches out the two or three nodes on the network with the highest throughput rate and opens multiple connections with each of them. Critical network congestion is an imminent problem for both network administrators and consumers. Usage caps, tiered-service models, and limitations on content are necessary tools for an ISP to regulate access to its resources so that everyone can have an equal opportunity to enjoy the Internet.

Even network-neutrality proponents agree that sometimes network administrators need to treat different network traffic differently.[47] That is why the Open Internet Order contains this idea of openness subject to "reasonable network management."[48] What is the balance that is struck by reasonable network management? As we pointed out in the last chapter, it turns out that no one is really sure.

---

45. *See* Yoo, *supra* note 39.

46. Ray Kurzweil, *The Singularity Is Near: When Humans Transcend Biology* (New York: Penguin Books, 2005).

47. *See* Lawrence Lessig, *The Future of Ideas: The Fate of the Commons in a Connected World* (New York: Random House, 2002), 156–58. *See also* Tim Wu, "Network Neutrality, Broadband Discrimination," *Journal on Telecommunications & High Technology Law* 2 (2003): 158–62, 173–74.

48. *See* Open Internet Order, *supra* note 15 in Chapter 5. "We believe these rules, applied with the complementary principle of reasonable network management, will empower and protect consumers and innovators while helping ensure that the Internet continues to flourish, with robust private investment and rapid innovation at both the core and the edge of the network."

The question pertains to what, if any, assumptions ISPs can make about the kind of traffic that their network should anticipate. It is necessary to make some assumptions about network usage, and to charge customers accordingly. Otherwise, charging each user a flat rate for Internet access incentivizes increased usage of the Internet toward infinity; consumers would not have to pay anything for their additional downloads, streaming, or phone calls. Under a flat-rate regime, all usage beyond what is encapsulated within the flat rate is not only free, it reduces the per-data byte cost of overall usage. It is clear that if everyone continues to increase his or her usage toward infinity, this will lead to disaster because spectrum is scarce.

Proponents of network neutrality propose that capacity is predictable enough to protect against such disaster. It is true that if everyone were using the same application all day on the network, then it would be easy to define an Erlang formula that predicts network capacity.[49] People, however, use a wide variety of applications in unpredictable ways. The primary finding of the literature on the economics of congestion is that competitive markets will reach an efficient equilibrium if each user is charged a usage-sensitive price, which is set equal to their marginal contribution to congestion.[50] Ideally, a network administrator would be able to charge each user the exact cost that his or her usage imposes on the network. This way, the cost to the user and the cost to the administrator would remain in constant equilibrium. However, the transaction costs entailed in charging such a finely tuned rate makes such a practice prohibitively expensive.

So, how many assumptions can the network administrator make about prospective use in designing a pricing scheme that takes into account the cost that usage imposes on the network? This is the question that courts face in evaluating the network-neutrality challenges interpreting the "reasonable network management" exception to the Open Internet Order. The growing consensus among network-diversity

---

49. The Erlang is a dimensionless unit used in telephony to measure carried load on service-providing elements.

50. *See* Benkler, *supra* note 11.

advocates is that this exception may be found to be so inclusive as to swallow the rule against tiered pricing, and render the prohibition on wireless providers unnecessary. In any case, network administrators, not courts, are the best individuals to make these decisions. A good way to view the injury that network neutrality causes to our Internet experience is the shift in responsibility for making this decision from network specialists to lawyers and judges who are not experts in the field. Network congestion is a critical problem that will lead to a potential shutdown, unless experts in the field are the ones given the discretion and deference to innovate and make these decisions.

Although Interference May Necessitate Regulation, Congestion Does Not

Interference and congestion are conceptually similar in that they disrupt communication, but they stem from different causes and, thus, could be treated differently by the government. While the government should have a completely hands-off approach to congestion problems, there may be a limited role for government to resolve disputes over interference.

Government regulation of spectrum distribution is inefficient. In order to avoid adjacent-channel interference, the government builds buffer zones between licensed channels. The spectrum used for these buffer zones is incredibly valuable, and yet in the hands of the government, its only purpose is to not be used. In the hands of private parties this could be different. The entirety of the spectrum could be licensed to private parties without the necessity of buffer zones. If interference solely from an adjacent channel became a problem, licensees of those channels could negotiate with each other to accommodate the need and eliminate interference. For example, some low-power, high-value uses may require a larger buffer to accommodate their sensitivity to interference, which can be bought from whichever private company owns the adjacent band of spectrum.[51] However, not all interference problems are so simple.

---

51. Coasian analysis leads us to understand that transaction costs will be relatively low in this situation with few, easily identifiable parties. The party with the higher-value usage

Unlike the government's ideal role in solving congestion issues, the government may serve an important role in resolving interference disputes. These two issues should be kept separate because congestion issues can always be traced back to an individual source, while the causes of interference are varied and harder to identify. Attributing all interference on a channel to adjacent-channel interference over-simplifies what is always a complex relation of interfering signals. This complicating factor should not be minimized. Conceding that transaction costs will be high in a privately ordered regime in some cases, we can cede control of those situations to government regulators with a measure of "interference temperature," an idea suggested by the FCC's spectrum policy task force.[52] However, like congestion, interference may sometimes be traceable to easily identifiable parties. In those cases, there should be a mechanism for the private resolution of disputes.

It is always possible to identify the sources of Internet congestion. Each packet comes equipped with both a destination address and a source address. Since all parties are identifiable, there is no need for government to regulate congestion with highly restrictive net-neutrality rules. Rather, the proper solution is well-defined property rights and ceding regulation of congestion to private ordering.

Companies Are Profit Maximizing, So the Threat That They Will Exclude Consumer-Preferred Content Is Minimal

As discussed in Chapter 5, proponents of network neutrality argue that a "no blocking" requirement is necessary because ISPs have the ability and incentive to reduce openness by blocking competitive services. Such detractors imagine a situation in which an ISP like Comcast

---

would be able to offer a profit to the party with a lower-value use. Because they are profit maximizing, we can rely on private arms-length negotiation to accomplish the same result as government regulation, but with fewer transaction costs. Of course, other kinds of interference will always complicate the issue.

52. See Federal Communications Commission Spectrum Policy Task Force, "Report of the Interference Protection Working Group," November 15, 2002, http://transition.fcc .gov/sptf/files/IPWGFinalReport.pdf.

would establish an agreement with a content provider like CNN whereby, in order to benefit CNN, Comcast would block access for its customers to another competing content provider like the *New York Times* or *Huffington Post*.

This concern, however, is illusory. As we will see in the next chapter, the entire body of antitrust law embodied in the Sherman Antitrust Act is designed to prevent collusion in restraint of trade. Such a collusively organized boycott would be illegal under the rule of reason decided in *FTC v. Indiana Federation of Dentists* in 1986.[53] Also, in order to accomplish this deal between profit-maximizing firms, the content provider would have to offer a sum to the ISP that was at least equal to the amount of revenue that the ISP would lose by restricting its customers from full Internet access. This is problematic not only because that loss is difficult to quantify, but also because, in the market's current state of duopoly, competition is as much for the market as it is for market dominance. A profit-maximizing firm would not contract itself out of existence.

Transparency Is Paramount, But It Does Not Justify the Restrictions Placed on Network Management by the Open Internet Order

The transparency requirement of the Open Internet Order is one element critical for ISPs to adopt, although most did so without government mandate. Transparency ensures that fixed and mobile broadband providers share with consumers all of the information necessary for them to make an educated decision about which provider to use. Importantly, this disclosure must include information about how the provider manages its network. This includes information on congestion management, application-specific behavior, device attachment, and security practices. It must include information on each of the provider's specialized services, and commercial terms like privacy policies and customer service inquiries.

---

53. *See* FTC v. Indiana Fed'n of Dentists, 476 U.S. 447 (1986).

Transparency in wireless and wireline is imperative because it improves competition. It provides consumers and regulators with the information necessary to encourage a competitive market. When consumers have adequate information, they are able to make informed choices about which service provider best fits their needs. Regulators are able to better monitor the telecommunications market and detect anticompetitive behaviors before they become abusive. After all we have discussed about Internet users being accountable for their usage, transparency requires network administrators to be accountable for their product as well.

We must maintain constant vigilance in maintaining our precious and scarce spectrum resources. Congestion threatens to cripple our communication networks. It is undoubtedly admirable to pass legislation aimed at preserving unlimited access to the Internet for everyone. But at the heart of this worthy aspiration is a misunderstanding of the basic principles underlying network communication. Although information is a public good that can freely be replicated in unlimited quantities, and theoretically can be shared with the world at a negligible cost, the Internet is more than just information. There also needs to be a way to access that information over wireless channels in order to meet consumers' information needs. That requires scarce spectrum. Just because spectrum is scarce, however, does not necessitate government regulation. Well-defined private-property rights will be sufficient in situations where transaction costs are low to promote an efficient allocation of network resources. Any market failure that might prevent such free exchange is mitigated by the presence of competition. Net diversity will shift resources to the ISP market, which will attract new entrants and provide fierce competition in that space. In any case, it is unjust for companies to continue to cross-subsidize heavy users on the backs of those who use the Internet sparingly. The fairest regime is one in which *everyone is accountable* for his or her own use.

Chapter Seven
ANTITRUST

AS WE HAVE SHOWN, the idea that the Internet should be a populist utopia ushered in by network-neutrality regulation is based on a misapprehension of how the Internet works technologically and how it *has* been characterized historically. The Net is not neutral, and no amount of government regulation can make it so.

There is, additionally, no basis for network-neutrality proponents' claim that cable and telephone companies have formed a broadband "duopoly" in which they have unfettered control of the broadband access market that they will abuse by harming competition in the adjacent content and applications markets, and ultimately consumers. But even if there was a basis for the concern—and there may be in the future—there is already a body of law specifically developed to deal with such problems, and not one but two government agencies exceptionally well positioned to deal with anticompetitive disputes when they arise. The body of law is called antitrust, and the agencies are none other than the Federal Trade Commission (FTC) and the Department of Justice (DOJ).

In this chapter we will provide a brief history of antitrust law, its purpose, and the delegation of duties between the agencies that implement it. We will then discuss why the FTC and DOJ are better suited than the FCC to regulate—if and when necessary—the Internet-access market. We will also discuss how antitrust law should be applied to the market.

Antitrust law is competition law. That is, in the United States, it is the body of law that seeks to promote competition by regulating anticompetitive conduct and unfair business practices. It is based on the principle that competition protects consumer welfare, and competition is "that state of affairs in which output is maximized, price is minimized, and consumers are entitled to make their own choices."[1] Antitrust law forbids practices that hurt businesses, consumers, or both, or that unreasonably restrain competition. It does so through prohibiting agreements or practices that threaten free trade, banning anticompetitive practices such as predatory pricing, tying, price gouging, and refusal to deal, and by supervising mergers and acquisitions.

The Sherman Act was the first antitrust law. It was enacted in 1890 and remains the foundation for most federal antitrust regulation. Its namesake, Sen. John Sherman (R-OH), presented the law to Congress as a means of preventing corporations from restraining trade, production, and consumer welfare. He explained, "Firms and corporations . . . are organized to prevent competition and to advance prices and profits" and there "is no object of greater importance to the people . . . as to prevent and destroy them."[2] "If we will not endure a king as a political power we should not endure a king over the production, transportation, and sale of any of the necessaries of life." Sherman's sentiments were drawn from the fears during the late 1800s that monopolies in railroads, oil, steel, sugar, and mining were dominating whole sections of America's free-market economy. He was also responding to the rise of nefarious business practices, such as conspiracies, cartels, restraint of trade, rank discrimination, and more. Many of these practices were initially exposed by investigative journalists such as Ida Tarbell in her monumental, multivolume *History of the Standard Oil Company* and the "fictional" account of conditions in

---

1. Herbert Hovenkamp, *Federal Antitrust Policy: The Law of Competition and Its Practice*, 3d ed. (Hornboock Series, 2005), 358 §5.6b (citing *FTC v. Ind. Fed'n of Dentists*, 540 U.S. 447 (1986)).

2. John Sherman, *John Sherman's Recollections of Forty Years in the House, Senate, and Cabinet: An Autobiography*, vol. 2 (Chicago: Werner Company, 1895), 1076.

the meat-packing industry called *The Jungle*, by Upton Sinclair. These works generated a massive public backlash against the industries they exposed and sparked demands for reform. Teddy Roosevelt branded this new species of journalists as "muckrakers," an appellation they wore with pride and that lives on to this day as the highest compliment one can pay a journalist.

Their initial targets were the late-nineteenth-century monopolies called "trusts," which took their name from the legal device of business incorporation called trusteeship. These trusts were partly the product of cumbersome state procedures for forming corporate structures.[3] To circumvent the expensive and time-consuming process of forming a corporation, individuals created trusts to capitalize joint business ventures.

Trusts proliferated especially fast as a result of rapid industrialization following the Civil War. While markets expanded and productivity grew, output often exceeded demand and competition intensified. At first, many businesses sought to form cartels—formal organizations of competing businesses that agreed to fix prices and control output in order to increase profits and business security. But eventually, many of these competing businesses consolidated as trusts through mergers and acquisitions by a few of the nation's most powerful people. Soon, corporate giants such as John D. Rockefeller and J. P. Morgan controlled huge chunks of the U.S. oil and steel industries.[4] These trusts could then fix prices and run would-be competitors out of business by selling their own goods at a loss until the pesky newcomer was driven out of the market. By 1890 the Sherman Antitrust Act, which sought to prevent further conglomeration of money, power, and anticonsumer tactics, was inevitable and Congress approved it almost unanimously.

---

3. *See generally* "West's Encyclopedia of American Law, Antitrust Law," http://iris.nyit.edu/~shartman/mba0101/trust.htm.

4. "FTC Guide to Antitrust Law," Federal Trade Commission, http://www.google.com/url?sa=t&rct=j&q=&esrc=s&source=web&cd=1&ved=0CGsQFjAA&url=http%3A%2F%2Fftc.gov%2Fbc%2Fantitrust%2Ffactsheets%2Fantitrustlawsguide.pdf&ei=6fASULe_L4fl0QHfu4DgCA&usg=AFQjCNHnweBYG4x16sfzIbxDLmKlFcspjQ.

The act is composed of three sections: Section 1 delineates and prohibits specific kinds of anticompetitive conduct. For example, it outlaws "every contract, combination or conspiracy in restraint of trade." Section 2 bans individuals from "monopolization, attempted monopolization, or conspiracy or combination to monopolize." Section 3 of the act simply extends the provisions of section 1 to the U.S. territories and the District of Columbia. Sections 1 and 2 were intended by Congress to supplement each other to prevent businesses from violating the spirit of the act, while technically remaining within the law.[5] Violations of either section were initially punishable by a maximum fine of $50,000 and up to one year in jail. This fine grew over time and is currently set at $500,000 per violation.

It was not immediately apparent that the act would have the teeth necessary to tear apart the powerful trusts. For starters, the Supreme Court undermined the law's authority in the seminal case *United States v. E.C. Knight Co.*, in which the Court held that manufacturing was not interstate commerce and thus not within Congress's regulatory domain. In so doing, the Court severely narrowed the scope of industry activities that were subject to the federal antitrust law. Consequently, conglomerates merely had to constrain their violating activities to a single state to avoid fines, injunctions, or criminal prosecution.[6]

However, in 1902 President Theodore Roosevelt made headlines as a "trust buster" when he went after the Northern Securities Company, a railroad holding company organized by the financial titan J. P. Morgan, and empire builder James J. Hill. The railroad company had threatened to monopolize transportation in the Northwest. In 1904, the case went to the Supreme Court and, this time, the Court held for the plaintiffs and ordered Northern Securities Company be dissolved. While the trust-buster nickname stuck to Roosevelt, who eventually initiated more than forty antitrust cases against giant monopolies, the nickname

---

5. "Antitrust: An Overview," Legal Information Institute, http://www.law.cornell.edu/wex/antitrust.

6. United States v. E.C. Knight Co., 156 U.S. 1, 15 (1895).

may be even better suited for his successor, President William Howard Taft, who abolished ninety trusts in a single term in office.

Possibly the most well-known antitrust case of that era was *Standard Oil Co. of New Jersey v. United States*.[7] The administration alleged that Standard Oil Co., owned by J. D. Rockefeller, had used economic threats against competitors and secret rebate deals in the 1870s and 1880s to build a massive monopoly in the oil industry. In 1911, the Supreme Court agreed that the company had committed multiple violations of the Sherman Act and ordered dissolution of the monopoly. The company was broken into three-dozen separate—competing—companies. Many of their names should be familiar, including Standard Oil of New Jersey (later known as Exxon and then ExxonMobil), Standard Oil of Indiana (Amoco), Standard Oil Company of New York (Mobil, which later merged with Exxon to become ExxonMobil), and Standard Oil of California (Chevron).

Though the case was a triumph for antitrust proponents, the decision still attempted to constrain the reach of the federal statute. In writing the opinion for the Court, Chief Justice Edward White limited the act's language prohibiting "restraint of trade" to those contracts that restrained trade "unduly," which, the Court held, occurred only if the contract resulted in one of three consequences of monopoly identified by the Court: higher prices, reduced output, or reduced quality. Broader interpretation of the language, the Court reasoned, could violate one's freedom of contract by potentially banning everyday contracts.[8] In its holding, the Court also adopted the "rule of reason" first enunciated by William Howard Taft in *Addyston Pipe and Steel Company v. United States*, when Taft served as the chief judge of the United States Court of Appeals for the Sixth Circuit. According to the rule, not all big companies, and not even all monopolies, are evil and thus subject to dissolution. Instead, a monopoly had to "unreasonably restrain" competition to violate antitrust law. The courts and

7. 221 U.S. 1 (1911).

8. Standard Oil Co. of New Jersey v. United States, 221 U.S. 1 (1911).

not the executive branch determined whether or not a restraint on trade was unreasonable.[9] As Judge Learned Hand later concurred:

> What engendered these compunctions is reasonably plain; persons may unwittingly find themselves in possession of a monopoly, automatically so to say: that is, without having intended either to put an end to existing competition, or to prevent competition from arising when none had existed; they may become monopolists by force of accident. Since the Act makes 'monopolizing' a crime, as well as a civil wrong, it would be not only unfair, but presumably contrary to the intent of Congress, to include such instances. A market may, for example, be so limited that it is impossible to produce at all and meet the cost of production except by a plant large enough to supply the whole demand. Or there may be changes in taste or in cost which drive out all but one purveyor. A single producer may be the survivor out of a group of active competitors, merely by virtue of his superior skill, foresight and industry. In such cases a strong argument can be made that, although the result may expose the public to the evils of monopoly, the Act does not mean to condemn the resultant of those very forces which it is its prime object to foster: finis opus coronat.

"The successful competitor, having been urged to compete," he warned, "must not be turned upon when he wins."[10]

Congress passed the Clayton Antitrust Act of 1914 after courts found certain activities fell outside the ambit of the Sherman Act. Specifically, the Clayton Act added the following to the list or prohibited practices: price discrimination between different purchasers when such practices tend to create a monopoly; exclusive dealing arrangements; tying arrangements; and mergers and acquisitions that substantially reduce market competition. In 1936, the Robinson-Patman Act amended the Clayton Act to outlaw certain practices in which manufacturers discriminated in price between equally situated dis-

---

9. Addyston Pipe and Steel Company v. United States, 85 F. 271 (6th Cir. 1898).
10. United States v. Aluminum Co. of America, 148 F.2d 416, 429-30 (2nd Cir. 1945).

tributors. The amendment was an effort to support competition by small local stores against larger chain distributors. The most recent amendment to the Clayton Act was the Hart-Scott-Rodino Antitrust Improvements Act of 1976, which requires companies to notify the government when they are planning major mergers.

In addition to the Sherman Act and its progeny, the Federal Trade Commission Act of 1914 instructs the FTC (also formed under the act) to foil "unfair or deceptive acts or practices" and "unfair methods of competition," as well as to "prevent fraud upon the purchasing public."[11] The act also gives the agency the administrative authority to expand upon existing antitrust laws or close any gaps by regulating new anticompetitive practices that might not have existed at the time of the act's initial enactment.[12] While the FTC enforces the spirit of the Sherman Act through its enabling statute, the Fair Trade Commission Act, it is limited in terms of the specific practices that it may outlaw. For instance, the FTC may not outlaw a practice unless it "causes or is likely to cause substantial injury to consumers."[13] Some practices that have failed to pass this test include suits claiming emotional harm or offense from an enterprise's commercial activity; commercial practices that only cause trivial consumer injury or that are sufficiently outweighed by other, constructive practices; and unilateral actions by various actors in the industry to avoid business with some subsidiary or provider.[14] In addition, the FTC may not take action against an enterprise if the enterprise's practices have not *actually* reduced or harmed competition.[15] Consequently, even if a corporation violates antitrust law, neither a private party nor the FTC can take

---

11. Federal Trade Commission Act, 15 U.S.C. § 45 (2006).

12. *See* Elizabeth Killingsworth, "Antitrust: U.S. Laws and Regulations," Association of Corporate Counsel, http://www.acc.com/legalresources/quickcounsel/auslar.cfm.

13. 48 A.L.R. Fed.2d 421 (2010).

14. Debra J. Pearlstein, *Antitrust Law Developments* (Chicago: American Bar Association, 5th ed. 2002), 362–79.

15. F.B. Leopold Co., Inc. v. Roberts Filter Mfg. Co., Inc., 882 F. Supp. 433 (W.D. Pa. 1995) *aff'd*, 119 F.3d 15 (Fed. Cir. 1997).

action unless the corporation's violation was harmful to consumers or to competition within the relevant market. In addition, while both the Antitrust Division of the Department of Justice and the FTC can bring civil lawsuits to enforce antitrust laws, only the DOJ may bring criminal antitrust suits under the federal laws.

Antitrust law is the proper body of law to handle the network-neutrality debate because the concerns raised by network-neutrality proponents are fundamentally grounded in antitrust concepts: market and monopoly power, market failure, and vertical leveraging. It follows that the competitive issues involved in this debate are not new to antitrust law, and its vast body of jurisprudence is well-equipped to provide the analytical framework for evaluating potentially anticompetitive conduct and business arrangements within the broadband access market. Under an antitrust analysis, the ultimate issue would be whether broadband access providers engage in single or multi-firm conduct—whether through vertical integration, blocking or degrading competitors' content, price-gauging, and so on—that is either intended to, or is likely to, harm competition and consumers in the relevant market.[16]

Antitrust oversight offers some major advantages over regulatory oversight of the broadband access industry by the FCC. First, as we discussed earlier, imposing any regulatory regime on an industry, and particularly a young and rapidly evolving industry like the broadband access market, is bound to have unintended consequences, such as stifling investment and competition, and limiting diversity of business models to name a few, for years or even decades to come. So why risk imposing a prophylactic regulatory regime when antitrust's *ex post* remedies offer a more precise mechanism for targeting the most damaging behavior? Moreover, antitrust law itself provides safeguards to overregulation since antitrust plaintiffs must demonstrate that the anticompetitive behavior of a corporation resulted in *actual harm* to a

---

16. *See* FTC Broadband Report, *supra* note 18 in Chapter 3, at 120; *see also* Jonathan E. Nuechterlein, "Antitrust Oversight of and Antitrust Dispute: An Institutional Perspective on the Net Neutrality Debate," *Journal on Telecommunications and High Technology Law* 7 (2009): 58.

relevant *market* to prevail. The standard antitrust approach to nascent industries is the wait-and-see approach, withholding regulation until the industry matures; this approach would well serve the wireline and burgeoning wireless industry as well.

Conversely, the FCC failed to perform any semblance of a market analysis prior to imposing its clumsy regulatory regime to the industry. (In fact, the commission has consistently declared the Internet-access market to be vibrant and competitive.) Instead, the agency imposed sweeping regulations that purport to remedy a cacophony of predicted *future* evils based on one or two concrete examples of singular corporate missteps. There is not one iota of evidence that broadband network providers have acted in any way to harm relevant markets, and therefore, under antitrust law, no basis for interfering in the industry. It is easy to understand then why both federal antitrust agencies were so vehement in their warnings to the FCC that the risks of its *ex ante* regulatory scheme far outweigh any tangible benefits.

That the FCC is attempting to overregulate an industry it is charged with overseeing is not surprising. As Jonathan E. Nuechterlein explains, "The FCC's narrow focus on a single industry creates incentives for the agency to keep itself relevant by erring on the side of market intervention in close cases."[17] It also means that the agency "must answer permanently and exclusively to a relatively narrow cast of market actors and their congressional allies."[18] Moreover, the FCC is bound by loose statutory standards like its obligation to "serve the public interest" and the "public convenience and necessity."[19] When combined, these features make the FCC the least-ideal agency to be charged with regulatory oversight of the broadband access market. As Nuechterlein points out:

> Today's net neutrality debate is a study in rhetorical ugliness. What it badly needs, if it is to be solved properly, is a referee inclined towards calm and objectivity and rigorous adherence to economic principle. In other words, it

---

17. Nuechterlein, "Antitrust Oversight," *supra* note 16, at 58.

18. Ibid., 57–58.

19. Ibid., 58 (citing 47 U.S.C. §§ 201(b), 214(c), 309(a), 310(d)(2000)).

needs analytical perspective, a greater detachment from political forces, and an expertise in addressing the type of complex antitrust issues presented [in this debate].[20]

The FCC is not the agency for the job. Unlike both the FTC and DOJ, which ultimately oversee the entire American economy, the FCC is an area-specific regulator, responsible for a single economic sector—telecommunications—and therefore is inherently susceptible to political pressures from the special interest groups within that sector. As a result, Nuechterlein points out, when approached with a dispute, such as network neutrality, the FCC focuses heavily on the political question: "How can we reach a compromise that will expose us to the least political damage?"[21] In contrast, an antitrust enforcer asks: "What type of competition dispute is presented here, and how does antitrust law frame the analysis for such disputes?"[22] When viewed in this light, it is not surprising that neither side of the network-neutrality debate is happy with the FCC's answer to the network-neutrality dispute: the Open Internet Order. The order's vague but seemingly vast language is an attempt to appease all relevant interest groups, lacking—if you are a network-neutrality proponent—the teeth to force broadband providers into submission, or—if you are such a provider—an infinite minefield of regulatory IEDs.

Indeed, the idea that the government is a better arbiter of price, usage, and resource allocation than private industry did not begin with the computer age. But it has never worked, and it never will. We provide two brief examples to illustrate our point.

More than a hundred years ago, the government was persuaded by a fervent constituency to regulate the railroad industry, which had played a mammoth role in America's post-Civil War surge to the West. Charges of price gauging, favoritism, and a general disposition toward bullying rather than bargaining in the settlement of disputes were

---

20. Ibid., 57.
21. Ibid.
22. Ibid., 57.

rampant—so rampant that they threatened the political order. When William Jennings Bryan raised passions with his "cross of gold" peroration, his list of grievances in fact ran far beyond the demand for free silver and relief from high interest rates. Transportation was always a problem, a problem that residents of the western states grappled with throughout their working lives.

The government addressed the problem in two ways. The first was to put in place a bureaucracy with a mandate to take the railroad industry and, later, the trucking industry, in tow. The agency was called the Interstate Commerce Commission (ICC). Second, the ICC was charged with encouraging competition in the railroad industry by removing barriers to entry. In time, the regulation of motor carriers became emblematic of the limitations on what could be achieved by substituting the expertise of the federal bureaucrat for that of the entrepreneur and the investor.

The system worked basically by trying to find a regulatory "sweet spot" that made it easy enough for newcomers to fight for a share of the market, but tough enough to prevent the market from being flooded with competitors whose presence would drive down prices. To prevent the latter situation from harming existing carriers, the commission mandated that newcomers must seek root authority from the ICC following a hearing at which the applicant and shippers allied with him would seek to prove to a commission hearing examiner that the new service would serve the "public interest and necessity." To do so, the applicant and those shippers testifying in his support would seek to establish the inadequacy of existing service, while existing motor carriers and their supporting shippers would argue that the market is already sated and that additional participants would simply produce economic glut. Sometimes the proceedings seemed so ridiculous that they became subjects of investigative reporting by programs such as *60 Minutes*.

What turned a bad bureaucratic situation into a national laughingstock was the introduction of "gateways" into the procedure, adjudicating the quest for new authority. In order to serve the public while not materially disadvantaging existing shippers, the commission would often approve an application by a carrier seeking authority to haul commodities between, say, New York and Baltimore, but would add the proviso that the route he elected had to go through Cleveland, rather than in the obvious north-south direction. A plethora of reports highlighting the "gateway" practice proved more than the commission could bear. Within a few years, the entire commission—which also regulated the train industry—was out of business, with transportation decisions left as they should be to the individual most affected by them.

A similar process was also underway with respect to civil aviation. Obviously laissez faire is an incomplete government policy with respect to airlines. Compared to trucks the government must worry about hijacking, terrorism, flight paths, and air safety, all of which are unique and potentially catastrophic problems where no sane individual would demand a hands-off government policy. But once those problems are addressed, there is no reason why a family choosing to live in a remote part of the country is entitled to the convenience of air travel offered at the same price as the one living three or four miles from a major airport. But that is exactly what the Civil Aeronautics Board attempted to do: building inefficiencies into the system instead of permitting carriers to make their own arrangements for hauling passengers and cargo in the most cost-effective way. The result was good politics as farmers, cattlemen, and others turned the Grange into an effective special interest; but it was bad economics, as recognized by most liberals and conservatives alike. It is equally true that there is no valid argument for requiring expensive trunk-line service—again, assuming it is uneconomical. The same is true here: while network-neutrality rules might appease certain constituent groups, they are uneconomical. As a result, the industry as a whole, and the consumers it serves, will pay a steep price.

As this book makes plain, the computer is a breathtakingly novel instrument of commerce, if under certain circumstances it can be used as an instrument of fraud and embezzlement. But in a larger sense, it is little different from the technologies and applications of yesterday and the day before. Buyers and sellers should be left to determine their own terms of trade. Those whose habits or proclivities drive them toward one type of system as opposed to another, or encourage them to take risks that others may pass over, they should be left to the market as the primary arbiter of commercial transactions. The world does not need a recitation of philosophical battles that were settled a half-century ago.

It is only when the market fails that the government should step in. And that is precisely the kind of restraint antitrust demands: regulation of *unreasonable* market behavior. Moreover, unlike the specialized FCC, the agencies charged with antitrust oversight and enforcement, the FTC and the DOJ, are responsible for regulating the *entire economy*, not a single economic sector. Their status as generalists provides for a more "dispassionate analysis" of individual markets and "diminishes the significance of lobbyists for particular interest groups."[23] In enforcing antitrust laws, the FTC and the DOJ are also bound by more exacting statutory standards interpreted through a vast body of judgments made precedent. Those laws are far less malleable than any guiding the FCC. And, from the early 1980s until 1996, antitrust law, enforced by the DOJ, *did* dominate enforcement of telecommunications competition policy in this country—most famously by forcing the break-up of AT&T in 1984.

The DOJ's involvement in the break-up of AT&T was a direct result of the FCC's failure to control AT&T's anticompetitive behavior as the corporation unabashedly used vertical integration to capture potentially competitive markets in the telecommunications sector. "Hold on," you might be thinking to yourself, "I thought you just finished arguing that vertical integration is *not* necessarily problematic, and that all these network-neutrality proponents are in a huff about nothing? So then, is it not contradictory to now note, almost in passing, that vertical integration by AT&T *was* legal action worthy?" The simple answer is: no. AT&T, as we noted earlier, was deemed a "natural monopoly" by the FCC after the turn of the twentieth century and nurtured as such at least with regard to its telephone service.

---

23. *See* Nuechterlein, *supra* note 16, at 57.

But that protection created a sort of "regulatory distortion" that created on the one hand the "incentive to expand the scope of the firm vertically into the sale of unregulated products," but on the other the "concomitant incentive to exclude competitors from such markets."[24] By the early 1970s, the FCC suspected that AT&T was generating excess profits on equipment sales from its vertically integrated subsidiary, Western Electric, and using those monopoly profits to subsidize the cost of its network.[25] Consequently, it was necessary to crack down on the once-tolerated monopoly.

The DOJ's antitrust case introduced testimonial evidence by two former chiefs of the FCC's Common Carrier Bureau, that the commission was not, and never had been, capable of effective enforcement of laws to govern AT&T's behavior. The chiefs blamed the commission's ineffectiveness on structural, budgetary, and financial deficiencies within the agency, as well as its difficulty in eliciting the information it needed from the company, especially with regard to its costs. Judge Harold Greene, who took over the case on his first day on the bench, agreed. "Whatever the true cause," he observed, "it seems clear that the problems of supervision by a relatively poorly financed, poorly staffed government agency over a gigantic corporation with almost unlimited resources in funds and gifted personnel, are no more likely to be overcome in the future than they were in the past."[26]

The suit was eventually settled in 1984. AT&T and the DOJ came to an agreement (known as the Modified Final Judgment, or MFJ), whereby the company would divest its local-exchange service operating companies in order to avoid fines, keep its stronghold over

24. Bruce M. Owen, "The Network Neutrality Debate: Twenty Five Years after United States v. AT&T and 120 Years after the Act to Regulate Commerce," Stanford Institute for Economic Policy Research, February 2007, http://www-siepr.stanford.edu/papers /pdf/06-15.pdf, 10.

25. William Yurick, "Judge Harold H. Greene: A Pivotal Judicial Figure in Tele-communications Policy and His Legacy," http://www.ieeeghn.org/wiki/images/1/1d /Yurcik.pdf.

26. U.S. v. AT&T, 552 F.Supp 131, 168 (Dist. Ct. D.C. 1982).

long-distance, and expand into the computer and data-processing businesses.[27] Importantly, the deal meant that local-exchange services provided by AT&T, which were long regarded as monopolistic, were broken off and isolated from competitive services such as long-distance transmission services, information (computer) services, and equipment supply.[28] These provisions were codified "the bottleneck theory," which supposed that structural separation of monopolistic aspects of a conglomerate from its competitive sectors would yield greater competition in the competitive sectors.[29] Judge Greene expressly identified the theory behind the decision:

> But the overriding fact is that the principal means by which AT&T has maintained monopoly power in telecommunications has been its control of the Operating Companies with their strategic bottleneck position. . . . With the removal of these barriers to competition, AT&T should be unable to engage in monopoly pricing in any market.[30]

In 1984, AT&T's local operations were split into seven independent regional "Baby Bells."[31] The result was not without controversy. In fact, Judge Greene rejected the initial platonic settlement in favor of a settlement with judicial oversight that put himself in charge of administering its terms for twelve years in accordance to what he deemed the "public interest." Scholarly criticism has been primarily

---

27. United States v. Am. Tel. & Tel. Co., 552 F. Supp. 131 (D.D.C. 1982) *aff'd sub nom.* Maryland v. United States, 460 U.S. 1001, 103 S. Ct. 1240, 75 L. Ed. 2d 472 (1983) and *modified sub nom.* United States v. W. Elec. Co., Inc., 890 F. Supp. 1 (D.D.C. 1995) *vacated,* 84 F.3d 1452 (D.C. Cir. 1996) and *amended sub nom.* United States v. W. Elec. Co., Inc., 714 F. Supp. 1 (D.D.C. 1988) *aff'd in part, rev'd in part sub nom.* United States v. W. Elec. Co., 900 F.2d 283 (D.C. Cir. 1990).

28. Glen O. Robinson, "The Titanic Remembered: AT&T and the Changing World of Telecommunications," *Yale Journal on Regulations* 5 (1988): 531.

29. See United States v. Am. Tel. & Tel. Co., 552 F. Supp., 171.

30. Ibid., 171–72.

31. Milton Mueller, *Universal Service, Interconnection and Monopoly* (Washington, D.C.: American Enterprise Institute Press, 1997), 98.

directed at the cumbersome and unnecessarily broad aspects of the MFJ. While imperfect, the MFJ lacked the sweeping regulatory gusto of its successor: the 1996 Telecommunications Act, which once again marginalized the DOJ's role (and consequently the role of antitrust in the telecommunications industry) while giving the FCC a "sweeping new mandate to oversee competitive conditions in telecommunications markets."[32]

Two Supreme Court decisions, *Trinko* and its 2007 decision in *Credit Suisse*, further suggest that when Congress has created a specific regulatory agency—like the FCC—to remedy anticompetitive behavior in a specific industry, antitrust law and its enforcement agencies must yield to the specialized regulatory body. For the reasons already outlined, we disagree. It was a mistake to supplant antitrust's targeted oversight of the telecommunications industry with the FCC's brutish club. In fact, history provides little evidence that traditional regulation—particularly as conceived of and implemented by specialized commissions—*ever* achieved its objective of making nondiscriminatory service available to all at cost-based prices.[33]

Moreover, as we have demonstrated, network neutrality, though disguised in provocative slogans, introduces no new ideas or arguments that antitrust is not already well-equipped to handle.

---

32. *See* Nuechterlein, *supra* note 16, at 43.
33. *See* Owen, *supra* note 24, at 10.

CONCLUSION

THE COMMERCIAL INTERNET has been in existence for more than six-teen years and the basic technology behind it has been around much longer. Many techies might argue that sixteen years in the digital age is equivalent to sixteen centuries in the real world, and that the Internet is therefore not a nascent technology or industry at all. But if the future unfurls itself at even half the rate and dynamism of the past, it will exceed anything that the most brilliant computer scientists and entrepreneurs could have predicted a generation ago. If the Internet is to fulfill its self-perpetuating destiny, it must be allowed to progress, unencumbered by the weight and uneven-handedness of the FCC. The agency has time and again demonstrated its incapacity to coher-ently regulate the industries it is charged with overseeing. It continues to demonstrate its ineptitude with regard to the Internet and threatens to stifle competition and growth for the foreseeable future. What is more, the agency is the perfect catalyst for regulatory creep, fed by its own narcissism and subservient need to appease its political and industry "frenemies."

Most importantly, the agency's network-neutrality rules, as detailed in its Open Internet Order, are simply bad policy founded on a faulty premise: that somehow the Net is neutral and must be preserved as such. As we have shown, the Net is no more neutral than it is a static singular technology. It is a constantly evolving, highly complex network of networks, composed of businesses, industries, academic institutions, and individual users, which since its inception has been limited only by the imaginations and technological inventiveness of those who continue to reimagine its potential. Network neutrality would, for the first time, confine the future development of the Net to a single, false, and untenable ideal, while simultaneously submitting it to the FCC's top-down regulatory regime. Network neutrality must fail.

As of this writing, the next move lies with the Court of Appeals for the D.C. Circuit. You will remember that in January 2011, shortly after the FCC announced its Open Internet Order, Verizon filed a notice of appeal with the D.C. Circuit. However, the court dismissed the notice as premature because the commission had not yet published the order in the *Federal Register*. But in November 2011, the FCC did just that, and Verizon immediately re-filed its complaint. The company alleges the FCC overstepped its jurisdiction in imposing the rules. "Verizon is fully committed to an open Internet," Michael E. Glover, Verizon senior vice president and deputy general counsel, said in a written statement. "We are deeply concerned by the FCC's assertion of broad authority to impose potentially sweeping and unneeded regulations on broadband networks and services and on the Internet itself." The D.C. Circuit has shown some ambiguity about its position regarding the FCC's claim to have ancillary authority to regulate broadband. The court has written, "The general and generous phrasing of § 706 [of the Communications Act] means that the FCC possesses significant, albeit not unfettered, authority and discretion to settle on the best regulatory or deregulatory approach to broadband."[1] Yet, in the same opinion, the court vacated the FCC's "Comcast Order" on the grounds that it stepped outside of the FCC's statutory authority.[2] Although the court's ultimate judgment remains difficult to predict,

---

1. Ad Hoc Telecomms. Users Comm. v. FCC, 572 F.3d 903, 906–07 (D.C. Cir. 2009).

2. Michael C. Sloan, "Net Neutrality at the FCC: A Critique of the Legal Reasoning of Its Net Neutrality Order," Davis Wright Tremaine LLP, 2011, http://www.dwt.com /advisories/Net_Neutrality_at_the_FCC_A_Critique_of_the_Legal_Reasoning_of_its _Net_Neutrality_Order_01_10_2011/.

we are hopeful that the courts or Congress will intervene to block enforcement of the FCC's regulatory scheme.

Still, it is not surprising that this new technology has provoked a battle for ownership and control between private industry and government regulators. After all, similar battles have been fought over every new technological breakthrough in telecommunications since the first radio transmissions of human speech were conducted on Christmas Eve of 1906 between Brant Rock, Massachusetts, and ships in the Atlantic Ocean.[3]

And to a certain extent, many of the arguments lodged by proponents of network neutrality are philosophically identical to those typically advanced by advocates of excessive government regulation: private industry cannot be trusted, entrepreneurs will walk away with too much money, their products will be developed and measured in terms of exalting private selfish interests rather than the public good, and power will be concentrated in the hands of too few. It is a mantra repeated with an intensity matched only by its record of failure.

But as we have said before, the debate over network neutrality is not, and should not be, dismissed as simply one between conservative and liberal ideologies. The debate is unique in many aspects, as unique as the Internet itself. Sure, the Net was originally developed for government purposes, but it quickly became a tool of researchers and later the public, where platforms were purposely left open so that they could be improved and built upon. As such, virtually nothing was patented, and technologies that were patented (remember Gopher?) quickly fell by the wayside. Would we even use the Internet today if World Wide Web inventor Sir Tim Berners Lee (he was knighted by Queen Elizabeth II in 2004) had not made the Web and its Hypertext Transfer Protocol (HTTP) standards based on royalty-free technology, so that they could be easily adopted by anyone? We very likely would not. And in the least, it is unlikely that without the Internet's openness, it would be as vast and dynamic as it is today. This is precisely

---

3. *See* Huber, *supra* note 25 in Chapter 1, at 27.

what so many of the network-neutrality proponents are terrified of: that mega-corporations will dominate the Net, at once patenting their new technologies, and vertically integrating into all of its layers, like a parasite worming its way through the entrails of its host fattening itself on its nutrients as the host itself starves. It is the warning in Jonathan Zittrain's *The Future of the Internet and How to Stop It*. We share these concerns and write this book not in defense of big business, and not as a partisan attack on liberal ideologies (although we have allowed ourselves a few jabs here and there); instead, this book is a defense of what we consider the greatest *independent, unregulated* technological marvel of all time, and we vehemently believe it should remain that way. The Internet sprung to life and flourished *independently*, relying on self-governance in furtherance of the common good. There is simply no reason it cannot continue to do so under the watchful but hesitant eyes of antitrust authorities. The Internet is a fixture in the everyday lives of billions around the world, it is a catalyst for political and social change, and its value as such is not unrecognized. It is only because we can now begin to glimpse, or wrap our brains around, the Internet's potential that many are scared. But we steadfastly maintain that for precisely these reasons, handing the Internet's reins over to the FCC now or ever is absolutely the wrong thing to do, not to mention the most surefire way of sucking the life out of this extraordinary achievement.

ABOUT THE AUTHORS

BOB ZELNICK is the professor of national and international affairs at the Boston University College of Communications. Prior to coming to Boston University, Mr. Zelnick spent 21 years as a correspondent for ABC News during which time he covered the former Soviet Union, Israel, the Pentagon, and Capitol Hill. Before joining ABC, Zelnick covered the Supreme Court for National Public Radio and the *Christian Science Monitor*. He also served as the executive editor of the Frost/Nixon Interviews.

Mr. Zelnick has been a research fellow with the Hoover Institution since 1999. He has written several books on affirmative action, the Arab-Israeli conflict, and politics, including a profile of Al Gore and an account of the 2000 Florida recount.

EVA ZELNICK is a former television news producer for Fox News Channel in Washington, D.C., and New England Cable News in Boston, Massachusetts. Ms. Zelnick is a graduate of the University of Virginia and the Boston University School of Law. She currently serves as an assistant district attorney in Massachusetts and teaches legal research and writing at the Boston University School of Law.

INDEX